"Far from scandalous and dan
true God' is the most influential and in
Thong's fascinating study of this belie
wider discussion that is crucial for our

~ **Dr. Os Guinness,**
Author of *The Call* and *Unspeakable: Facing up to the Challenge of Evil*

"*Finding God in Ancient China* is a remarkable achievement, a profound examination of China's cultural origins and history as a reflection of a continuous Chinese cultural sense of a connection with the divine. Chan Kei Thong reveals a persistent thread of Chinese theistic longing that parallels in a remarkable way the search of ancient Israel for a covenant with the true God. He also demonstrates that Chinese classical literature is entirely consistent with Christian revelation. This book is already having a profound impact in China in a Chinese version."

~ **Dr. David Aikman,**
Author of *Jesus in Beijing: How Christianity is Transforming China and Changing the Global Balance of Power;*
Former Beijing bureau chief for *TIME* magazine

"In this book, Chan Kei Thong skillfully marshals the evidence concerning early Chinese worship, showing how for thousands of years Chinese worshiped and offered sacrifices to Shang Di, a Supreme Being with characteristics similar to those of the God of the Bible."

~ **Marvin Olasky,**
Editor-in-chief, *World* magazine; professor, University of Texas;
Senior fellow, Acton Institute for the Study of Religion and Liberty

"*Finding God in Ancient China* confirms that China once had an age of faith, and that age was China's first golden age. The God whom the emperor-sages Yao, Shun, and Yu believed in was the same God as the Hebrew God. This answers one of the two great questions in my heart, which was: How is it that of all the nations of the world, only China has had such a long and uninterrupted history? It is because of this age of faith, and this faith has been like a river that has flowed throughout the whole of Chinese civilization. It was this constant faith of the Chinese people toward Shang Di that supported the continuation of Chinese civilization. My second question was this: Are Chinese culture and Christianity at odds with each other? The answer: Absolutely not. The key is which period of Chinese history we look at. The faith that is the root of Chinese culture, from the age of the sages when 'the Great Way was in force over all the earth,' is actually spiritually compatible with Christian culture."

~ **Dr. Zhao Xiao,**
Professor, Management School, Beijing's Science and Technology University;
Former head, China State Council's Macro Strategy Department; and
Proponent of the role of God and faith in China's transition to a market economy

Other editions

Simplified Chinese: 先贤之信 (Beijing: Dong Fang Publishing House/China
Publishing Group Orient, 2005)
ISBN 7-80186-429-8

English: *Faith of Our Fathers: God in Ancient China* (Beijing: Dong Fang Publishing
House/China Publishing Group Orient, 2006)
ISBN 7-80186-506-5

English: *Faith of Our Fathers: Discovering God in Ancient China* (Singapore:
Campus Crusade Asia Limited, 2007)
ISBN 978-981-05-6302-8

Simplified Chinese: 先贤之信 (Singapore: Campus Crusade Asia Limited, 2007)
ISBN 978-981-05-8947-9

German: *Chinas wahre Größe* [The True Greatness of China] (Singapore: Campus
Crusade Asia Limited, 2009)
ISBN 978-981-05-7008-8

FINDING
GOD IN
ANCIENT
CHINA

Previously published as *Faith of our Fathers*

CHAN KEI THONG

with CHARLENE L. FU

ZONDERVAN.com/
AUTHORTRACKER
follow your favorite authors

ZONDERVAN

Finding God in Ancient China
Copyright © 2009 by Chan Kei Thong

Originally published in Simplified Chinese in the People's Republic of China by China Publishing Group, Orient Publishing Center, Shanghai, China.

Requests for information should be addressed to:

Zondervan, *Grand Rapids, Michigan 49530*

This edition: ISBN 978-0-310-29238-8 (softcover)

All photos unless otherwise noted are by Chan Kei Thong.

All illustrations unless otherwise noted are from the China Folk Arts Graphics Library. Used by permission.

All Scripture quotations unless otherwise noted are from the *New American Standard Bible*®. Copyright © 1960, 1962, 1963, 1968, 1971, 1972, 1973, 1975, 1977, 1995 by The Lockman Foundation. Used by permission.

Bible quotations marked NKJV are from the *New King James Version*. Copyright © 1982 by Thomas Nelson, Inc. Used by permission. All rights reserved.

Scripture quotations marked CEV are from the *Contemporary English Version* © 1991, 1992, 1995 by American Bible Society. Used by permission.

Scripture quotations from *THE MESSAGE* are copyright © by Eugene H. Peterson 1993, 1994, 1995, 1996, 2000, 2001, 2002. Used by permission of NavPress Publishing Group.

Any Internet addresses (websites, blogs, etc.) and telephone numbers printed in this book are offered as a resource. They are not intended in any way to be or imply an endorsement by Zondervan, nor does Zondervan vouch for the content of these sites and numbers for the life of this book.

Printed in China

09 10 11 12 13 14 15 • 24 23 22 21 20 19 18 17 16 15 14 13 12 11 10 9 8 7 6 5 4 3 2 1

This book is dedicated to

Lisa,

Charissa, Stefan, and Jonathan;

and to all the MTI/LDI staff,

my fellow pilgrims on this journey of discovery.

Acknowledgements

A project of this proportion cannot be accomplished by one person alone. Along the way, I have been supported and encouraged by many. I would like to specially thank a few who were most instrumental in making this dream a reality:

Ms. Charlene L. Fu, a journalist *par excellence*, for her undying belief in this project and for her many hours over the past four years of rewriting and editing numerous drafts of the entire work. Her insights are incorporated throughout this book, and she wrote most of Chapters 6 and 7.

Dr. Raymond Petzholt, a fellow researcher, who encouraged me to publish this book. He generously allowed me to incorporate extensively the material from his treatise, *China's Ancient Monotheistic Religious Roots in Shang Ti*, throughout this book, particularly in Chapters 3 and 5.

Ms. Tang Min, an accomplished writer, for her insights and expert knowledge of Chinese history, language, and culture which have been incorporated into this work.

Ms. Deng Xiao Mei and Mr. Qi Bin of Han Qing Design Company, for their creativity and artistic passion. Because of their labors, what you hold in your hands is much more than simply a book; it is also a work of art.

Mrs. Bev Swem, for coming from the United States to Beijing to do the all-important final editing. She helped clarify many of our thoughts and gave the book a clearer framework.

Mr. Chen Hui Lin, for his enthusiastic support of this project from the very first. His endorsement gave me the faith to believe that this could happen.

Dr. Phil Bassett, Rev. Malcolm Tan, Mr. Philip Poh, Mrs. Robyn Harris, and Mrs. Sandra Upton for their editorial input to an early draft.

Ms. Darrell Lee and Mr. David Ren for their meticulous proofreading of the final manuscript.

Mr. Lim Siong Guan, for giving me the idea of turning my oral presentation of this material into written form. His mentoring and his consistent support for the things I get myself into have been a source of great encouragement over the course of three decades.

My wife and three children, for their many sacrifices over the past seven years so that I could work on this project. They regularly pray for the success of this book.

Most of all, I am grateful to Shang Di, who is the reason for this book.

Chan Kei Thong
Beijing, China

CONTENTS

TIMELINE

Comparative Timeline

World History	Chinese History	Hebrew History
3500 B.C. first known writing, in Mesopotamia		
3000 "di" phoneme found in Middle East cuneiform tablets dating to this period		
3000 Sumerians in southern Mesopotamia build ziggurats		
c.2700-2400 Egypt's Old Kingdom period, era of pyramid-building	**c.2700 B.C.** beginning of Chinese writing	**c.2700-2600 B.C.** Tower of Babel
	2697-2599 reign of Huang Di, built altar to Shang Di at Mt. Tai	
c.2500 Development of the Indus River civilization in modern day India and Pakistan	**c.2500-2000** Long Shan Culture	
	2357–2258 reign of Emperor Yao	
	2255-2208 reign of Emperor Shun	**c.2100** Abram (later Abraham) moves from Ur to Canaan
	2207-2198 reign of Emperor Yu, tamed a great flood, unified his nomadic people, wrote Yu's Tributes, founder of Xia Dynasty	**c.1900** Joseph sold into Egyptian slavery by his brothers **c.1800-1400** Israelites in slavery in Egypt
	2070-1600 Xia Dynasty	
1792-1750 Babylonian king Hammurabi the Great, during his 20-year reign he issues the famous Law Code of Hammurabi. He may have begun building the tower of Babel	**c.1765-c.1122** Shang Dynasty **1766-1754 B.C.** reign of Emperor Tang, who offered self as human sacrifice to break drought	
1600-1200 Egypt's Empire period; also time of Israel's sojourn in Egypt		**1440** Moses leads Israelites out of Egyptian slavery (the Ten Plagues, crossing of the Red Sea, 40 years of wandering in the desert)
		Moses received God's Law and sacrificial code
c.1200 The Iron Age begins in Europe	**c.1200** earliest inscribed oracle bones	**c.1200-1020** Period of the Judges

World History	Chinese History	Hebrew History
	1121-249 Zhou Dynasty	**c.1100-1050** life of Prophet Samuel
	1134-1116 reign of Wu Wang, invoked Mandate of Heaven to topple Shang Dynasty, honored Shang Di	
c.1000 Zoroaster, an Iranian thinker who breaks from Indo-Iranian religious traditions in advocating monotheism	**1115-1108** regency of Duke of Zhou	**c.1020** Samuel anoints Saul king
		c.1020-1000 reign of King Saul
		c.1000-965 reign of King David **c.965-931** reign of King Solomon, **959** completion of Temple, built by Solomon **c.860** Elijah brings down fire from heaven **c.820** Jonah and the great fish
776 earliest records of Greek athletic games at Olympia **753** city of Rome founded	**894-771** corruption of Border Sacrifice ceremony by emperors Yi, Li, and You	**740-680** Prophet Isaiah's ministry **722** Israel goes into captivity in Babylon
		604-562 reign of Babylonian king Nebuchadnezzar
c.582-c.507 Greek philosopher Pythagoras	**6th century B.C.** philosopher Lao Zi, whose teachings give rise to Taoism	**586** Jerusalem falls to Babylon, Temple is razed, Daniel serves in Babylon
563-483 Siddartha Gautama, founder of Buddhism	**551-479** philosopher and sage Confucius **5th century B.C.** philosopher Mo Zi who opposed Confucians' skepticism towards Heaven	**536** first Jews return to Palestine from exile in Babylon, end of 70 years of exile
469-399 Greek philosopher Socrates, teacher of Plato	**475-221** Warring States period	**c.464-424** events in the book of Esther
431-404 The Great Peloponnesian War		**c.430** Malachi writes last book of the Old Testament
c.427-347 Greek philosopher Plato		

World History	Chinese History	Hebrew History
384-322 Greek philosopher Aristotle, a student of Plato, tutor of Alexander the Great	**c. 372-289** philosopher Mencius, altered and codified Confucian thought into Confucianism	
336-323 reign of Alexander the Great		
341-270 Greek philosopher Epicurus		**336** Alexander the Great conquers Judah
305-44 reign of the Ptolemies over Egypt		
287-212 Greek scientist and philosopher Archemides		
264 Rome goes to war against Carthage.		
218 Second war between Carthage and Rome begins. Hannibal leads Carthaginians from Spain through Gaul and over the Swiss Alps into Italy	**221-207** Qin Dynasty, founded by Qin Shi Huang (259-209 B.C.), who reunifies China after 400 years of civil war	
	213 "Fen-Shu, Keng Ru," Qin Shi Huang's great book burning and massacre of dissident scholars	
201 Rome defeats Carthage	**206-A.D. 220** Han Dynasty	
196 Rosetta Stone, key to Egyptian hieroglyphics, is inscribed in hieroglyphics and Greek	**145-85** life of grand historian Sima Qian, compiler of first comprehensive Chinese history	
100?-44 Julius Caesar, Roman statesman and general	**138** beginnings of the Silk Road	
69-30 Cleopatra, queen of Egypt	**105** Sima Qian takes over his father's project of writing grand history of China	**63** Rome annexes land of Judah, which it calls Judea
19 BC Roman poet Virgil writes the Aeneid, a story about the gods and the founding of the Roman race	**5-4 B.C.** comet in Alpha Aquilae recorded by imperial astronomers	**5-4 BC** birth of Jesus Christ

World History	Chinese History	Hebrew History
A.D. 37-41 reign of Roman emperor Gaius Caesar, nicknamed Caligula	**A.D. 31** major solar and lunar eclipse recorded by imperial astronomers, halo follows three days later	**A.D. 31** death and resurrection of Jesus Christ
43 Roman Emperor Claudius sends troops to conquer Britain		**35** Saul, fierce persecutor of Christians, becomes Apostle Paul on road to Damascus
64 Rome burns		
68 Emperor Nero commits suicide		**70** Temple in Jerusalem is destroyed
79 Pompeii buried by eruption of Mount Vesuvius		
121-180 Roman Emperor Marcus Aurelius		**c.100** John, the last surviving disciple, writes the Gospel of John, in which he calls Jesus "Logos"
	220-280 Three Kingdoms	
288-337 Roman Emperor Constantine	**265-420** Jin Dynasty	**70-1948** Jewish Diaspora
4th century Europe enters the Middle Ages		
444-453 reign of Attila the Hun	**420-581** Northern and Southern Dynasties	
570-632 Prophet Muhammad		
	581-618 Sui Dynasty	
	618-907 Tang Dynasty	
731 English historian and theologian, Bede, writes *Ecclesiastical History*		
768-814 rule of Charlemagne, crowned Holy Roman Emperor by pope in 800		
c.800 Vikings start to raid Europe	**907-960** Five Dynasties	
1095-1291 Crusades to the Middle East	**960-1279** Song Dynasty 1000 gunpowder developed	

World History	Chinese History	Hebrew History
1215 Magna Carta issued in England, forms basis of constitutional law	**1271-1368** Yuan Dynasty **1295–1307** reign of Emperor Cheng Zhong, built Altar of Heaven in Beijing	
15th century Renaissance period in Europe begins	**1368-1644** Ming Dynasty, reestablishes preeminence of Shang Di in the Border Sacrifice Ceremony	
1473-1543 Polish astronomer Nicholas Copernicus	**1421** Emperor Yong Le rebuilds Altar of Heaven in Beijing	
1492 Columbus sails to the New World		
1517 Reformation in Europe that resulted in Protestant movement		
1561-1626 English writer, statesman, scientific thinker Sir Francis Bacon		
1564-1616 English playwright William Shakespeare	**1582-1610** Jesuit Matteo Ricci's years in China, advisor in Emperor Wan Li's court	
1564-1642 Italian astronomer Galileo	**1623-1666** Jesuit Johann Adam Schall's years in China, served as Imperial Chamberlain to Qing Emperor Shun Zhi	
1620 Mayflower brings Pilgrims from England to America		
1632-1653 India's Taj Mahal built	**1644-1911** Qing Dynasty, China's last **1644-1661** reign of Emperor Shun Zhi, interested in spiritual matters, taught by Schall	
1643-1715 reign of Louis XIV in France		
	1654-1722 reign of Emperor Kang Xi, China's longest-reigning emperor and one of China's best rulers	
1689-1725 reign of Peter the Great in Russia		

World History	Chinese History	Hebrew History
	1658-1688 Jesuit Ferdinand Verbiest's years in China, trusted aide and tutor of Emperor Kang Xi	
1706-1790 American statesman, scientist, writer Benjamin Franklin	**1692** Kang Xi issues edict: Christians can teach and convert throughout China	
1756-1791 Austrian composer Wolfgang Amadeus Mozart	**1742** Kang Xi bans Christianity due to Rites Controversy	
1769-1821 French general, emperor Napoleon Bonaparte		
1776 America declares independence from Britain		
1789 French Revolution starts		
1809-1865 U.S. President Abraham Lincoln	**1807** Englishman Robert Morrison (1782-1834) arrives, first Protestant missionary to China	
1819-1901 Queen Victoria of Great Britain	**1858-1876** James Legge's years in Hong Kong; evangelist and translator of Chinese Classics, eminent Sinologist	
1861-1865 U.S. Civil War		
	1899 discovery of first oracle bones, in Beijing	
1914-1918 World War I		
1917 October Revolution in Russia	**1900** Boxer Rebellion, thousands of missionaries and Chinese Christians killed; Hanlin archives destroyed	**May 14, 1948** Jews returned to Palestine and Israel declared itself as an independent nation once again
1939-1945 World War II	**1911** Founding of the Republic; end of dynastic rule	
(Source: resources available at www.bartleby.com)	**1949** Chairman Mao declares founding of the People's Republic of China (Sources: *A Chinese-English Dictionary, The Encyclopedia of World History, 2001; The Columbia Encyclopedia, 6th Edition, 2001*)	(Sources: *Halley's Bible Handbook; Believers Bible Commentary; The Encyclopedia of World History*, 2001; *Timeline of the Bible* at http://mustardseed.net/timeline/ timeline-top.html [cited October 2006])

Introduction

WHY THIS BOOK?

    This is not the first book to consider the parallels between the ancient beliefs of the Chinese people and the teachings of the Bible and Christian faith. What I discovered in my personal study of this subject, however, has compelled me to write this book, which is a systematic examination of works by other scholars on this topic, along with new revelations and my own insights. As a result of my study, I have been able to reconcile my rich cultural heritage as a Chinese with a priceless personal Savior who has been associated throughout history with the Western world. My hope is that this book will be easy to read and will lead others to understand, through the perspective of Chinese culture, the truth of the Bible and the faithfulness of God. In particular, I hope that my fellow Chinese will see that the God spoken of in the Bible and now worshipped throughout the world is the same God that our ancient forefathers revered.

    Finding God in Ancient China is the result of my own discovery of this little-known truth. I am a fourth-generation overseas Chinese from Singapore, and, like most Chinese families of my generation, we held to many traditional beliefs and carefully observed traditional practices and rituals. As a required form of veneration, I faithfully offered sacrifices of fruit and meat at the altars of our ancestors on traditional holidays, such as Chinese New Year and the Mid-Autumn Festival. Each of us lived in deep fear of a netherworld filled with evil spirits and ghosts of all kinds. At the same time, my family also practiced the wonderful time-tested virtues valued in Chinese culture: respect for elders, modesty, humility, diligence, and commitment to the family. When I discovered the God of the Bible and became a Christian at age 19, I was made to believe that I had abandoned my roots and betrayed a rich Chinese heritage. My Christian spiritual journey of the past three decades has been a joyous one, but always in the far reaches of my consciousness was an irritant, like a pebble in my shoe: the feeling that I had turned my back on my culture by adopting a foreign faith.

Happily, that irritant was removed a few years ago, after our family moved to Beijing in 1995. Living in the Chinese capital, I had many opportunities to visit the Temple of Heaven, where Chinese emperors traditionally performed the annual sacrifice for good harvest. As I became aware of the fact that the ancient Chinese had a sacrificial system similar to that found in the Old Testament, my interest was piqued. I had heard about the redemptive analogies found in Chinese characters, but that interest was superficial. Like many others, I found these analogies titillating but initially unconvincing. I was intrigued, however, by what I learned about the sacrifice performed at the Temple of Heaven, and I began to pay attention.

As I learned more about the details and history of this sacrificial system, I started examining other aspects of Chinese history and culture. It was as if God had gone before me and had set up signposts or historical markers to direct me on this journey of personal discovery. These were the signposts that I found, left by a faithful God who desires us to know Him:

1. The composition of ancient Chinese characters suggests knowledge of the earliest events of human history as described in the Bible.

2. The Supreme Being venerated by the ancient Chinese as described in historical texts corresponds to the God revealed in the Bible.

3. The Border Sacrifice ceremony performed by the emperor at the Temple of Heaven for more than 4,000 years shows startling and meaningful parallels with the sacrificial system prescribed in the Bible.

4. The judgment of some eminent scholars from the 16th to 19th centuries supports the view that the ancient Chinese venerated a Deity who bears remarkable resemblance to the God of the Bible. These scholars were the intellectual giants of their time and devoted years to the study of classical Chinese historical texts, some of which are no longer available. These great men are still regarded today as among the greatest Sinologists in history and are esteemed for their intellect, scholarship, and virtue.

5. Striking similarities exist between the Hebrew and the Chinese approach to moral truth, particularly as it pertains to man's responsibilities to society and his relationship to the Divine.

6. The ancient rulers of China understood and set forth a godly way of ruling the people. Although the Chinese were not a "chosen nation" in the same sense as Israel, the rulers of China saw themselves as serving Heaven by serving the people. Since they understood their highest responsibility was to a righteous Supreme Being, they felt themselves obligated to rule the nation with goodness and humility.

7. Chinese historical records appear to confirm some key astral events spoken of in the Bible. This mutual corroboration lends credibility to the testimony of both the Hebrew Bible and China's historical records. Perhaps more significantly, the Chinese records were not merely a simple chronology of these cosmological events. They contained interpretations of these events that are astonishingly consistent with the stated intent of the Bible, which is to draw mankind to a deeper understanding of God.

When I put all these pieces together, I became convinced that the ancient Chinese worshipped the Creator of the Universe in a manner similar to that prescribed in the Old Testament. I have now come to the studied conclusion that the ancient Chinese were one of the many original nations dispersed after the confusion of languages at the Tower of Babel, described in Genesis 11 of the Bible. Some among these dispersed nations were alienated from God, while others wanted to follow His way. Like the Pilgrims who went to America to preserve the purity of their religious beliefs, the people group that went on to found the Chinese civilization was, I believe, a God-fearing race that desired to worship God appropriately.

These ideas may sound incredible, but I ask you to read this book with an open mind. Each of the "signposts" listed above may not, on its own, be strong enough to make a case, but taken together, they lead to the conclusion that the early Chinese forefathers worshipped God in a manner similar to that set forth in the Bible. As God continued to reveal His truth, these revelations that the ancient Chinese acknowledged were in many ways similar to those found in Genesis, the first book of both the Hebrew and the Christian Scriptures. God's plan of salvation and reconciliation was difficult for the Chinese to fully grasp, as it was for the Jews, but the puzzle was finally made clear with the incarnation of Jesus 2,000 years ago.

I firmly believe that God wanted the Chinese people to know Him and to love Him, and to that purpose, He left many markers or signposts scattered throughout Chinese history and culture. Jesus Christ, the Son of God born into a Jewish carpenter's family, was the One to whom the markers pointed, and He is therefore the fulfillment of the deepest longings of the Chinese people.

> *The God who made the world and all things in it, … made from one man every nation of mankind to live on all the face of the earth, having determined their appointed times and the boundaries of their habitation, that they would seek God, if perhaps they might grope for Him and find Him, though He is not far from each one of us….*
> Acts 17:24 – 27

The Chinese and Jewish peoples share the distinction of having the longest consecutively preserved cultures and histories in the world. China's more than four millennia of history shows what I believe to be the preserving hand of God and reveals an amazingly accurate knowledge of that One True God, whom the Chinese reverentially referred to as Shang Di. The Bible says that God honors those who honor Him. As it is true of individuals, surely it is also true of cultures. The material in this book is presented with a desire to raise the reader's sensitivity to the God who is active and intimately acquainted with the affairs of all human beings. It is my special hope that my fellow Chinese will see that believing in the God spoken of in the Bible is not a betrayal of our Chinese roots. Rather, it is a return to the foundations of our ancient cultural heritage. So, let me invite you to take this first step with me on this journey of discovery, by looking at: Roots.

壹

Roots

The most dangerous people are those who have been cut off from their cultural roots.

~ G. K. Chesterton, English critic and author

1

Roots

In a forest, the healthiest trees have the deepest and most extensive root systems. A tree draws nourishment through its roots, and the roots anchor it to the ground, preventing it from toppling over. The larger the tree and the farther its branches extend, the deeper its roots must be. Our own roots perform a similar function by providing stability in times of personal crisis and uncertainty; understanding who we are is an important first step to becoming the person we are meant to be. Perhaps this is why interest in genealogy is growing and why many people expend much time and effort on reconstructing their family trees.

Rather like the root systems of the healthy trees, our cultural roots can similarly ground us in today's turbulent and ever-changing world in which globalism is blurring cultural distinctions. By digging deep, we can find significant historical details and patterns to enlighten us, providing us with a greater understanding of the past and in turn of the present. This chapter is the beginning of a journey that will guide us to some amazing facts and startling similarities in the history of the world's two longest surviving civilizations: the Hebrew and the Chinese. These facts, founded on the truth of the past, offer us confidence for the present and a sure hope for the future.

RECORDING HISTORY

In the earliest era of human existence, before mankind learned to write and therefore before historical records could be kept, oral traditions were the only means of preserving cultural history. The written record we now possess of actual events that occurred in ancient times came into existence through the following four-step process:

- An event occurred.
- An account of the event was told and retold, repeated so often that it became widely known.
- The account of the event became fixed in the collective memory, so that it was retold in similar ways.
- Eventually, the event was recorded in written form.

Can these orally transmitted traditions and accounts be trusted? We may be inclined to doubt the reliability of oral traditions, an entirely reasonable response given the long passage of time between the beginning of human history and the time when these events were finally committed to writing. Many biblical and Chinese materials presented in this book fall into this category of oral traditions. Rather than dismissing these accounts as being totally unreliable, however, many scholars today acknowledge that extant ancient records contain an essential core of truth, some of which are well substantiated.[1]

MYTH, LEGEND, OR HISTORY?

In considering the validity of ancient tradition, whether it be oral or written, it is necessary first to clarify the terms myth, legend, and history as they are used in this book. Being precise about these distinctions is vital to avoiding confusion about what really happened in history.

Myths are narratives, usually of unknown origin, that ostensibly recount actual events that occurred at an unspecified time in the past. Myths are woven around extraordinary events or circumstances that, so far as human intelligence can tell, could not have happened. There is a myth about ten suns appearing in the heavens during the reign of Emperor Yao 堯帝, who commanded the great archer Hou Yi 後羿 to shoot nine of the suns out of the skies. Likewise, the equally implausible story of Nüwa 女媧, who patched up a gaping hole in the sky with

1. R. M. Fales, Ph.D., "Archaeology and History Attest to the Reliability of the Bible," *The Evidence Bible,* compiled by Ray Comfort (Gainesville, Fla.: Bridge-Logos Publishers, 2001), p.163. More information on the reliability of the Bible is available online at sites such as this page on Manuscript evidence for superior New Testament reliability by Christian Apologetics and Research Ministry, http:www.carm.org/evidence/textualevidence. htm. (Cited July 2006). The reliability of ancient Chinese writings will be dealt with later in this chapter.

Emperor Yao

Hou Yi

Nüwa

five colored stones, must also be considered a myth. These two stories are well known to the Chinese, but no one considers them to be true historical events. Nothing about Nüwa is recorded before 300 B.C., and none of the other Chinese myths can be traced to an earlier time: all appear similarly late in ancient history. Because of the lack of corroborating evidence, common sense tells us that events such as these likely were not actual historical occurrences.

Legends are embellished or exaggerated stories of real people known to have actually lived or of events that actually happened. Americans are familiar with the story of a young George Washington chopping down a cherry tree and then confessing the misdeed. Although this event may not have actually taken place, there is no dispute about the historical existence of George Washington and the universal recognition of his good character. The same is true of some Chinese stories. The origins of *zongzi* 棕子, the bamboo leaf-wrapped rice dumplings eaten on the day of the Dragon Boat Festival 端牛節 (duanwu jie), is one example. The story goes that *zongzi* originated from rice balls that people threw into the river to keep fish from eating the body of the beloved imperial advisor Qu Yuan 屈原, who committed suicide when invading forces captured the capital of his country. As with the story of Washington's cherry tree, the legend may not be accurate in every detail, but the historical existence of Qu Yuan and the fact of his love for his country are without dispute.

Therefore, a key distinction between a myth and a legend is that the former involves the outrageously improbable while the latter is grounded in historical plausibility. Though it may sometimes be difficult

壹

to separate real history from fabrication, we can still draw sound conclusions from acknowledged historical facts. This can be true even about people or events that have become mythologized. We know with some certainty that Emperor Yao of the ten suns was a real person and can place him at a specific time in history (c. 2357 – c. 2258 B.C.). Even though some of what is recorded about him appears to be myth, because it is "outrageously improbable," we can conclude from other historical material that Emperor Yao was a virtuous ruler and that over time he came to be viewed as a good model for other rulers to follow.

Qu Yuan

History is the study of the chronological records of events based on an attempt to objectively evaluate the available source materials. History that is trustworthy deals with real events and real people as preserved in oral traditions as well as recorded in written texts. It seeks to look beyond legendary embellishments to discover what really happened in the past. Both Jewish and Chinese history were recorded meticulously through the ages; however, early Jewish history was compiled more systematically and in a more God-focused way than was Chinese history. Most of the earliest recorded anecdotal Chinese histories extant today were compiled by the Chinese philosopher and sage Confucius (551 – 479 B.C.). It was, however, the great historian Sima Qian 司馬遷 (c. 145 – c. 85 B.C.), of the Western or Former Han Dynasty 西漢朝 (206 B.C. – A.D. 25), who began the systematic recording of Chinese history (Zheng Shi 正史). Every subsequent dynasty added to his grand work, thereby forming an authoritative history of China throughout its civilization.

Sima Qian's historical compilation starts with Huang Di 黃帝, or the Yellow Emperor, in the 27th century B.C. Many historians consider this earliest period of Sima Qian's account—from its beginning to 2205 B.C.—to be legendary because, though the people mentioned are real, certain stories may still have been exaggerated. We must take great care, however, in labeling ancient accounts as either myths or legends. Many perceived exaggerations in ancient writings can be traced to our own biased worldview that leads us to hastily dismiss parts of these histories as

Confucius

Sima Qian

embellished and unreliable. For example, many believe that the unusually long lifespan credited to ancient personages, such as the patriarchs in Jewish records or the early emperors in Chinese records, to be an exaggeration. There are, however, plausible explanations for why these ancients were able to live 40 to 50 years longer than the present-day lifespan of about 70 years. We will examine some of these explanations later in this chapter.

Modern archaeology and astronomy continue to confirm the general accuracy of Jewish and Chinese recorded history. The discovery of oracle bones from the Shang Dynasty 商朝 (c. 1765 – c. 1122 B.C.)[2] has verified a large portion of the history recorded by Confucius in the Chinese *Classics*. K. C. Wu, former mayor of Shanghai (1946 - 1949) and an acknowledged authority on Chinese history, concludes that "we may reasonably assume that the very first document in the Book of History may be used as a source for credible history."[3] Further confirmation came in the year 2000 when more than 200 Chinese historians, archaeologists, astronomers, physicists, and other scholars of ancient Chinese artifacts and records completed an exhaustive five-year study. Their findings led them to this conclusion: There is sufficient evidence to prove that the earliest Chinese dynasties, previously regarded by historians as legendary, did exist and, in fact, were culturally sophisticated and technologically advanced for their day.[4]

HEBREW and CHINESE HISTORICAL RECORDS

Extensive records exist to document the early history of both the Hebrew and Chinese cultures. Ancient Hebrew history was clearly and systematically recorded by the biblical patriarch Moses in the first five books of the Bible, known as the Pentateuch. The first book, Genesis, records the beginning of the world and the origin of the

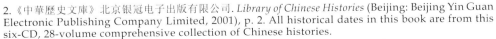

2. 《中華歷史文庫》北京银冠电子出版有限公司. *Library of Chinese Histories* (Beijing: Beijing Yin Guan Electronic Publishing Company Limited, 2001), p. 2. All historical dates in this book are from this six-CD, 28-volume comprehensive collection of Chinese histories.

3. K. C. Wu, *The Chinese Heritage* (New York: Crown Publishers, 1981), p. 465.

4. "Finding Clues to the Puzzle," *China Daily*, November 10, 2000. See also "Xia-Shang-Zhou Chronology Project," *The Journal of East Asian Archaeology*, Volume 4, No. 1 – 4 (2002), Brill Academic Publishers, Leiden, The Netherlands.

Hebrew people. Likewise, Confucius compiled the five-volume Chinese *Classics*, or *Wu Jing* 五經.

Because biblical apologetic materials are in abundance, we will not attempt in this chapter to explicate the biblical record as we do the Chinese *Classics*. Our intention in focusing on the Chinese *Classics* is simply to provide a basic overview of Chinese works with which some readers may not be familiar, because we will refer to them later in this book. In doing so, we do not intend to give more weight to the Chinese *Classics* than to Scripture. In fact, we firmly believe that the Bible is God's special revelation to the world and that it is completely true. Our desire is to use these two ancient historical sources—the Hebrew and the Chinese—to create a more complete picture of world history and to identify points where they shed light on and corroborate each other.

The Chinese Classics

Confucius made it very clear that he was not the author of the five *Classics*, but simply their compiler. In other words, the Chinese *Classics* were historical records written much earlier than the 6th century B.C. in which Confucius lived. They are:

The Classic of Changes or Yi Jing (I Ching) 易經

Many Chinese consider this the most important of the five. The main body of this work has traditionally been attributed to King Wen 文王 (c. 12th century B.C.), founder of the Zhou Dynasty 周朝 (c. 1122–249 B.C.), whose life we will look at in much greater detail in Chapter 7. Confucius said in his introductory commentary on *Yi Jing* that its purpose was to help people "pursue an exhaustive understanding of the universe in order to do God's will"[5]–very different from its current popular usage as a book for fortune telling.

The Classic of History or Shu Jing 書經 (also Shang Shu 尚書)

This is a compilation of documentary records of China's ancient history. Although some of its 58 chapters are considered unreliable, the generally acknowledged authentic parts constitute the oldest Chinese writing of its kind. The first five chapters provide the sayings and deeds of the emperors, including Yao 堯 and Shun 舜, who reigned during what Confucius considered to be China's Golden

5. "窮理盡性別 以至于命." Attributed to Confucius, "Shuo Gua Commentary 説卦傳" (Commentary on the Hexagrams), usually attached to and published along with *The Classic of Changes* and considered a part of it.

Age. The next four chapters are a history of the Xia Dynasty 夏朝 (c. 2207 – c. 1766 B.C.), while the following 17 chapters deal with the Shang Dynasty and its collapse in 1122 B.C. The final 32 chapters cover the Western Zhou Dynasty 西周, which ruled until 771 B.C.

The Classic of Poetry (also called Book of Odes) or Shi Jing 詩經

This first collection of Chinese poetry consists of 305 religious, court, and folk songs believed to range in date from the beginning of the Zhou Dynasty to the time of their compilation by Confucius in the 6th century B.C.

The Record of Rites or Li Ji 禮記

This book emphasizes the moral principles that underpin the development of rites, royal regulations, ritual objects and sacrifices, education, music, the behavior of scholars, etc. It is similar to the Book of Leviticus in the Bible.

The Spring and Autumn Annals or Chun Qiu 春秋

This is the first Chinese chronological history, and it covers the reign of 12 rulers of Lu 魯, the native state of Confucius, from 722 to 479 B.C. The title is a short form of Spring-Autumn-Summer-Winter, derived from the ancient practice of dating events by season as well as by year. As a result of this work, that portion of Chinese history is called the "Spring and Autumn" period.

These five *Classics* can be considered thematically in this way: the *Classic of Changes* is metaphysical; the *Classic of History* is political; the *Classic of Poetry* is poetic; the *Record of Rites* is social; and the *Spring and Autumn Annals* are historical. These five strands together weave a social pattern or fabric which Confucius hoped would foster harmony between man and his Creator as well as among men as they lived and worked together in their daily lives. Like Moses, Confucius was recording how man could live a peaceful and contented life if he lived according to the way that God had created him to live.

The Four Books

In A.D. 1190, the neo-Confucian philosopher Zhu Xi 朱熹 (A.D. 1130 – 1200) produced the *Four Books* 四書 as a primer to the five *Classics*. These are four ancient Confucian texts compiled for the first time as a unit. Much shorter than the five

Classics, it was used by scholars as an introduction to the more extensive *Classics*. The *Four Books* are:

The Analects, or Lun Yu 論語

Considered a most reliable compilation of the teachings of Confucius. It is an unsystematic and sometimes repetitive presentation of Confucius' ethical concepts.

Great Learning, or Da Xue 大學

Taken from a chapter of the *Record of Rites*, one of the five *Classics*. *Great Learning* states that international peace is impossible unless a ruler first governs his own country well. To do this, family units in a nation must be set in order, and order within the family requires self-discipline on the part of every individual family member. Thus, good government and world peace are founded on the personal virtue of a ruler and each of his subjects.

The Doctrine of Mean, or Zhong Yong 中庸

Another chapter taken out of the *Record of Rites*. The Chinese title *Zhong Yong* expresses the Confucian ideal of harmony and moderation. It is broad in scope and discusses almost every relationship and every activity of a person's life.

Mencius 孟子

The final of the *Four Books*, named for its author. Mencius, a 4th-century B.C. philosopher, was considered second only to Confucius in wisdom. This book deals with government affairs and contends that the welfare of the masses comes before every other consideration. It teaches that when a ruler is no longer virtuous, the Mandate of Heaven—the God-given right to rule—is withdrawn and such a ruler should be removed. Mencius also declared filial piety to be the cornerstone of good society.

While the Chinese five *Classics* and *Four Books* do not claim to be divinely inspired as the Bible does, they have points of correspondence with much in the Bible. In fact, discoveries in archaeology and astronomy have continued to bolster the reliability of both the Bible and many parts of recorded Chinese history. For example, the 1928 discovery of archaeological artifacts in Shandong province of the Neolithic Long Shan Culture dating back to c. 2500 to 2000 B.C. supports China's written records[6] that the Long Shan 龍山 had a sophisticated culture with a hierarchical class structure, advanced buildings, and an elaborate religious ritual using beautiful bronze vessels. Indeed, the Long Shan discovery also corresponds with the biblical account of a general dispersion of human families after the Tower of Babel, which serious Bible scholars estimate took place about 2600 B.C.[7]

Furthermore, scholars have been able to confirm and date ancient events by comparing the histories of ancient civilizations. Although the Bible record does not use the calendar we use today, scholars have correlated the biblical chronology with known dates of Assyrian and Babylonian rulers to arrive at reliable dates of some biblical events. Since these Middle Eastern kingdoms, like the Chinese, linked their historical records to astral occurrences, scholars have been able to plot biblical dates accurately according to the known movements of the stars.[8] Similarly, historians can cross-reference Hebrew and Chinese historical accounts to produce a fairly clear picture of the beginnings of human civilization.

CAN WE TRUST ANCIENT RECORDS?

The conclusions drawn in this book presuppose a trustworthiness in the ancient historical records that are consulted. We offer three reasons why Hebrew and Chinese oral traditions and written history contain much that is trustworthy: recent discoveries that confirm the general reliability of some ancient writings; a commitment to accuracy on the part of many of the writers of these histories; and the long lifespans of those who lived in ancient times, which promoted the accurate transmission to later generations of their memories of ancient events.

Ancient Writings Are Reliable

Modern people have an unfounded arrogance that presumes that we are more intelligent and more enlightened than our forefathers. Hence, modern scholars often assume the unreliability of ancient writings, including those of the Hebrew and Chinese peoples. As various authors have amply defended the authenticity and reliability of the Bible,[9] we will focus in this section solely on the question of the reliability of the Chinese *Classics*.

6. "Lung-shan Culture," Encyclopædia Britannica, from *Encyclopædia Britannica Ultimate Reference Suite 2004 DVD*. Copyright © 1994–2003 Encyclopædia Britannica, Inc. May 30, 2003.

7. An example of how astronomy confirms the reliability of ancient Chinese history is given later in this chapter.

8. Readers interested in learning more can consult sources such as *Nelson's Illustrated Manners and Customs of the Bible*, by J. Packer, M. C. Tenney, and W. White (Nashville, Tenn.: Thomas Nelson, 1997, c1995).

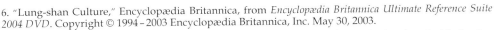

Finding God in Ancient China

Due to this prevailing modern bias, historical accounts of the very earliest periods of Chinese civilization are considered to be myths and legends rather than history. Early Chinese history is referred to as the "Legendary Period," and many dismiss Chinese writings from remote antiquity as unreliable sources of historical information. For nearly as long as academicians have studied China, the convention has been to regard as trustworthy only those Chinese historical records dating from the late Shang (or Yin 殷) Dynasty, 14th–12th centuries B.C. and later. Records of earlier dynasties were considered mythological because of a presumed paucity of supporting evidence. In fact, quite the opposite is true. Discovery of the so-called "oracle bones" at the turn of the 20th century dramatically turned the accepted view on its head.

The first several hundred of these bones—ornately carved tortoise shells and ox scapula—were discovered in 1899. In subsequent decades, some 150,000 were unearthed. They have generally been cited as evidence of a rich written language dating back some 4,800 years.[10] Called oracle bones because they were mainly used for divination, these bones were also used for other purposes as well. They are, therefore, a rich historical record that complements, confirms, and fills in the gaps in historical accounts of events and personages that scholars until recently had regarded as mythological. Such previously discredited accounts are being viewed in a new light. Historian K. C. Wu writes with great excitement of the oracle bones discovery in his book, *The Chinese Heritage*:

> ... *from their inscriptions we have learned anew of the 30 rulers of the Shang Dynasty and their relationship to one another. And the marvel is that they correspond entirely with the narrative text and the genealogical chart of the Historical Records both in the matter of names and in the order of historical sequence ... In addition, from a close study of the oracle bones, some of the gaps in the Historical Records which were formerly inexplicable seem now to have become explicable.*[11]

The text *Historical Records* 史記 referred to by Wu is the authoritative 2nd century B.C. compilation of China's first historian, Sima Qian. He completed this massive work after studying all the ancient writings of the time, some of which are no longer

9. See Josh McDowell's *Evidence That Demands A Verdict* (San Bernardino, Calif.: Here's Life Publishers, Inc. 1972, 1979).

10. "Oracle Bone Script," on website China the Beautiful. Available online at http://www.chinapage.com/oracle/oracle00.html. (Cited August 2006.)

11. Wu, *The Chinese Heritage*, p. 44.

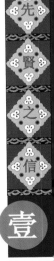

extant. Sima Qian's tome has been—and continues to be—one of the foundational sources for the study of Chinese history.

Historian Wu, in a lengthy appendix to *The Chinese Heritage*, argues convincingly for the reliability of these ancient written records. His points include the following:

- Writings that contain more complicated or sophisticated philosophical ideas are most logically of a later historical date; that is, documents that deal with the most elementary units of human existence (e.g., the five elements that Chinese consider the most basic: earth, water, fire, air, and ether) must predate documents that discuss the relationships among these elements and their relative strengths and weaknesses;

- Recent archaeological discoveries have proven the truth of some documents that had previously been thought unreliable because of seeming internal contradiction;

- Contentions that Confucius, in compiling historical texts into the *Classic of History*, had substantively altered the histories and idealized the ancient emperors to conform to his teachings are without basis. We now know that the texts from which Confucius drew his material were still widely available in his day and, therefore, any such drastic alteration would have quickly been discovered and brought to light. In fact, some of the direct quotes taken from those texts are still extant today and can be checked easily;

- Variances in the writing styles of historical documents claiming to be based on earlier writings can be explained by the need on the part of writers of the later documents to render the earlier writings understandable.

Finally, Wu refers with great joy to the work of Dr. William Henry Medhurst. As a 19th-century China scholar, Dr. Medhurst was the first to "acknowledge that the *Canon of Yao*, the first document in Confucius' *Book of History*, might be

carrying within its own text proofs of its antiquity."[12] In 1981, Medhurst's findings were brought to the attention of American-trained astrophysicist Dr. H. K. C. Yee, who confirmed, based on a comparison of the Chinese names for the stars and on modern precession formulas,[13] that the time period described in the *Canon of Yao* "is indeed around the year 2200 B.C."[14] Dr. Yee thus established with reasonable confidence the reliability and authenticity of this ancient foundational historical document. In this way, modern scholars have used ancient astronomy to confirm that this earliest of Chinese historical documents, which purports to be a factual record of emperors Yao and Yu, who reigned between c. 2357 B.C. and c. 2208 B.C., is a credible historical source.

Similarly, the hundreds of Chinese experts who participated in the special 1995–2000 project on the Chronology of Early Chinese History in the Xia, Shang, and Western Zhou Dynasties drew conclusions of equal historical import. The project involved experts working in nine different branches of research on 44 topics. Archaeologists worked some 15 sites in Beijing and the provinces of Henan, Hebei, and Shanxi. Historians studied dates on dozens of ancient bronze containers to determine the chronology of ancient rulers. Philologists scoured nearly 400 ancient Chinese annals and collected written records in which they found "clues" recording astronomical events and indicating the locations of early imperial capitals. Astronomers studied celestial phenomena from thousands of years ago, and, by correlating the astronomical data with the modern calendar, were able to create a rough timeframe for the reigns of the kings in the Xia and Shang dynasties. Physicists performed carbon dating tests on samples of human and animal oracle bones that came from tombs known to have dated to the Shang and Western Zhou dynasties to provide scientific confirmation of the historical timeframe that the other scholars had postulated.

After this extensive research across disciplines, the experts concluded that the earliest known Chinese dynasty, the Xia, existed for about 470 years between 2070 B.C. and 1600 B.C., followed by the Shang Dynasty, which the researchers divided into earlier (1600–1300 B.C.) and later periods (1300–1046 B.C.). The researchers also found evidence confirming the dates of the reigns of the 12 monarchs of

12. Wu, *The Chinese Heritage*, p. 465.

13. Precession formulas have to do with the "precession of the equinoxes, which is a slow westward shift of the equinoxes along the plane of the ecliptic, resulting from precession of the earth's axis of rotation, and causing the equinoxes to occur earlier each sidereal year. The precession of the equinoxes occurs at a rate of 50.27 seconds of arc a year; a complete precession requires 25,800 years." From *The American Heritage Dictionary of the English Language, Fourth Edition* (Houghton Mifflin Company, 2000). Available online at http://www.bartleby.com/61/2/P0510200.html. (Cited August 2006.)

14. Wu. *The Chinese Heritage*, p. 465.

the later Shang Dynasty and all the 13 monarchs of the Western Zhou Dynasty (1046 – 771 B.C.).

"We now have reason to believe that our ancestors in the Xia and Shang dynasties created and developed a far more sophisticated civilization than we previously thought," the project's chief historian, Li Xueqin, was quoted as saying by the English-language newspaper, *China Daily*.[15]

Motive of the Writers

Although recent discoveries like these bolster the reliability of the most ancient historical texts, we must acknowledge that historical accounts may be distorted if they were recorded by someone with an ulterior motive. Such a person may change the facts of a historical event to his advantage or to support his position and thus render the historical record unreliable or untrue. The nature of our journey of discovery, however, means we need not be overly concerned about this kind of distortion. We are seeking points of correlation between two cultures far removed from each other in space and experience, and there are factors inherent in the cultures themselves that would tend to minimize such distortion.

The material on which our study is based are the historical records of two of the oldest civilizations in the world; in both these cultures, virtue—that is, personal integrity and personal character—is emphasized over external standards and outward behavior. It is generally accepted that the Bible provides a standard for morality. The Chinese *Classics* present a remarkably similar standard of right and wrong, and demand that readers live by those standards. For example, the *Classic of History* places the blame for the collapse of the Shang Dynasty on the last Shang ruler, who is described as oppressive, murderous, extravagant, and lustful. On the other hand, it highly exalts the virtues and reverential attitude of emperors such as Yao, Shun, and Yu.

The great 6th-century B.C. philosopher Lao Zi 老子 teaches about morals in his immensely influential *Dao De Jing (Tao-te Ching)* 道德經:

> *When Dao [The Truth][16] is lost, we are left with morals; when morals are lost, we are left with benevolence; when benevolence is lost, we are left with justice; when justice is lost, we are left with protocol.*

15. "Finding Clues," *China Daily*.

16. 道 *Dao* is often translated as "The Way," and it corresponds with the Greek word "logos" which can be translated "The Expression." The New Testament uses "logos" to describe Christ as the expression of the Truth. *Dao* and *logos* will be compared in Chapter 9.

故失道而後德，失德而後仁，失仁而後義，失義而後禮。[17]

This passage shows the high priority that was placed on reverence for the Divine, which Lao Zi calls *Dao* (The Truth), as well as the inevitable downward spiral toward empty outward behaviors when that reverence for principle and morals is lost. The intention of the authors of the Bible and of the Chinese *Classics* was to teach virtue; these writers were not focused on meaningless deeds, nor were they primarily influenced by political agendas.

In the case of the Bible, its internal testimony bears strong witness to its reverence for truth. For example, the ninth of the Ten Commandments recorded by Moses states, "You shall not bear false witness." It is unlikely that the writers and compilers of the Bible, while seeking to promote morality and integrity, would consciously and deliberately bend the truth. Moreover, many biblical writers suffered persecution and great loss in their effort to preserve the knowledge of what they believed. Would they have made such a sacrifice for a fabrication?

In Chinese history, there were some who were similarly motivated. A dramatic example is the life of the historian Sima Qian. In 105 B.C., he undertook to continue his father's work of writing a definitive history of China's past. Before he could finish the work, however, he deeply offended the Han emperor, Wu Di 武帝, by speaking in defense of the disgraced general Li Ling 李陵. As a consequence, Emperor Wu Di condemned Sima Qian to die or be castrated. Sima Qian opted for castration, which is not only excruciatingly painful but also carries with it great shame and humiliation. In a letter to his friend Ren An 任安, Sima Qian explained why he chose this painful punishment rather than an honorable death:

> The reason I have not refused to bear these ills and have continued to live, dwelling among this filth, is that I believe that I have things in my heart that I have not been able to express fully, and I am shamed to think that after I am gone my writings will not be known to posterity.... I too have ventured not to be modest but have entrusted myself to my useless writings. I have gathered up and brought together the old traditions of the world [that] were scattered and lost. I have examined the deeds and events of the past and investigated the principles behind their success and failure, their rise and decay, in one hundred

17. 《道德經, 老子》 *Lao Zi*, Chapter 38, verse 5.

and thirty chapters. I wished to examine into all that concerns Heaven and man, to penetrate the changes of the past and present, completing all the work of one family. But before I had finished my rough manuscript, I met with this calamity. It is because I regretted that it had not been completed that I submitted to the extreme penalty without rancor. When I have truly completed this work, I shall deposit it in some safe place. If it may be handed down to men who will appreciate it and penetrate to the villages and great cities, then though I should suffer a thousand mutilations, what regret would I have? [18]

僕雖怯耎欲苟活，亦頗識去就之分矣，何至自湛溺累紲之辱哉！且夫臧獲婢妾猶能引決，況若僕之不得已乎！所以隱忍苟活，函糞土之中而不辭者，恨私心有所不盡，鄙没世而文采不表于後也。...僕竊不遜，近自托于無能之辭，網羅天下放失舊聞，考之行事，稽其成敗興壞之理，上計軒轅，下至于茲。爲十表，本紀十二，書八章，世家三十，列傳七十，凡百三十篇，亦欲以究天人之際，通古今之變，成一家之言。草創未就，適會此禍，惜其不成，是以就極刑而無慍色。僕誠已著此書，藏之名山，傳之其人通邑大都，則僕償前辱之責，雖萬被戮，豈有悔哉！

Clearly, Sima Qian was motivated by an honorable ambition. Notice too that his priority was "to examine into all that concerns Heaven and man." As we shall see in later chapters, Heaven 天 refers to the Creator God. If our conclusion is correct, then it would mean that Sima Qian was interested in presenting history because it gives insights into man's relationship with the Creator God and with one another, and that his motive was not to benefit himself but to make truth known.

18. William Theodore De Bary and Irene Bloom, *Sources of Chinese Tradition*, Volume 1 (New York: Columbia University Press, 1960), p. 372. This translation is an abridged version of Sima Qian's original lengthy letter giving the background to his castration and why he went along with it. The original unabridged letter is found in the *The History of the Han Dynasty*, Volume 62, Chronicle 32: Sima Qian 《漢書-卷六十二 -司馬遷傳》.

Long Life Spans of the Ancients

A third reason why ancient histories can be considered trustworthy is the existence and reliability of oral traditions. Facts of history can be distorted both intentionally and unintentionally. We have already shown that the intentional distortion of ancient Jewish and Chinese histories is not likely. What, then, of unintentional distortion, such as the corruption of facts as they pass through many intermediaries over a long period of time? In fact, even with the passage of time, an individual can remember some events quite clearly; people sometimes find that they actually have a far better long-term memory—remembering with great clarity events from their childhood, for instance—than short-term memory. The practice among preliterate societies of constant memorization of important matters also supports the view that oral traditions are often carefully preserved and can be considered reliable. When a story is told by one source to another, however, there is a tendency for distortion to occur. So, the problem here is not the passage of time itself, but rather of corruption through a large number of intermediaries.

Let us address then the problem of distortion through intermediaries. The chart on the next page shows the long lifespan of the biblical patriarchs. This chart is not a strict chronological timeline because the Bible account leaves some gaps in the early generations. It does, however, serve to illustrate an important point: early man lived much longer before the Flood.[19] If we take as a given these long pre-Flood lifespans, we can see how the longevity of Adam and the ten generations that followed allowed them to recount the creation story and God's plan of salvation to their offspring and descendants. Based on the biblical account, when Adam died, Lamech, his descendant to the eighth generation, was already 53 years old. In that time, Lamech would have had several decades to hear about the events immediately following creation, and he probably even heard from Adam himself about creation, original sin, the sin of Cain, and the necessity of a blood covenant to reconcile mankind with God.

19. One possible reason for these extraordinarily long life spans was that the physical impact of sin, which brought death into man's life, needed time to take its toll on Adam and his descendants. Though the result of Adam's sin in the Garden of Eden was spiritual as well as physical death, perhaps God delayed Adam's physical death by 930 years to allow him to propagate the human race and to tell the creation and salvation story to his descendants. Otherwise, the human race and the knowledge of these early events would have died with Adam. There is overwhelming scientific proof supporting the accuracy of these long life spans, and it is not our purpose in this book to argue this point. For those who are interested in learning more, www.answersingenesis.org and similar websites have thousands of articles researched and written by experts in many scientific fields confirming the accuracy of the Genesis account of creation and the early events of human history.

The Accumulation of Ancient Wisdom and Knowledge[20]

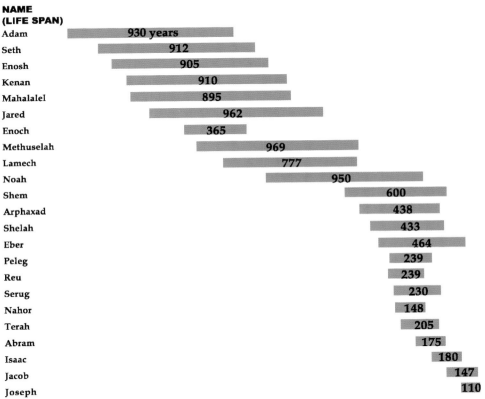

NAME (LIFE SPAN)	Life Span
Adam	930 years
Seth	912
Enosh	905
Kenan	910
Mahalalel	895
Jared	962
Enoch	365
Methuselah	969
Lamech	777
Noah	950
Shem	600
Arphaxad	438
Shelah	433
Eber	464
Peleg	239
Reu	239
Serug	230
Nahor	148
Terah	205
Abram	175
Isaac	180
Jacob	147
Joseph	110

According to the Bible, the lifespan of most pre-Flood patriarchs was about 900 years. This longevity allowed the patriarchs to accumulate wisdom, knowledge, and experience, which were in turn passed on to subsequent generations.

20. From Figure 49, "Patriarch Chart of Life Spans," in D. G. Lindsay, *The Canopied Earth: World That Was* (Dallas, Tex.: Christ for the Nations, 1999, c1991), np. See also Genesis 5:3–32; 11:10–32; 21:5–25:7; 25:26; 35:28; 47:28; 50:26.

Adam's stories were no doubt reinforced over the years by the many ancestors who preceded Lamech. Moreover, some of these early humans had the privilege of conversing with God directly. Some, such as Enoch, walked with God, who knows all things without any distortion. Even Cain, the first murderer, apparently had direct conversations with God himself because the Bible says he knew the proper way to please God but chose otherwise. We can, therefore, conclude that because of these long life spans, the early accounts of the human race were substantively transmitted with minimal distortion by intermediaries until the confusion of the languages at the Tower of Babel.

The ruins of the ancient tower of Samara on the Tigris River 70 miles (112 kilometers) northwest of Baghdad which native Moslems and Christians alike believe is the Tower of Babel.

Credit: Corbis

Chapter One Roots

As the nations were dispersed because of their rebellion at Babel, they carried with them these accounts of creation, the Garden of Eden, Noah and the universal flood as well as God's requirements for forgiveness and reconciliation. Although their languages became confused, their memories were not erased. God did not give them amnesia! God loves the people of the world and desires that they know Him and know how to draw near to Him.

When Moses wrote down the creation story and the history of the nation of Israel, he was not without help. God inspired him and helped him write what was accurate and pertinent. Apart from that inspiration, however, Moses, like his contemporaries, already had knowledge of the beginnings of the world which was passed down to him through oral tradition. This same knowledge was also carried into the rest of the world as the nations were dispersed from Babel. That would explain why many unevangelized, primitive societies have in their tribal traditions a concept of a Creator God who reigns supreme over all.[21] If we accept that there is a universally held body of knowledge about the Creator God, then we must conclude that the forebears of all the tribes and nations of the world had an equal chance to reconcile with God when His special provision for reconciliation was finally made in the person of Jesus Christ.

REVELATION

In many cultures, even those that are polytheistic, this Creator God — referred to in some cultures as the High God — is regarded as utterly remote and transcendent, removed from the world and the affairs of men. In part, this is because the mighty Creator God of the universe is a Spirit. Humans have no means of knowing God without His help, so He has to take the initiative in unveiling Himself to us. God's revelation may occur in a single, instantaneous act, or it may extend over a long period of time and may be understood by the human mind in varying degrees of fullness. It is important to understand that, because God is sovereign, unless He reveals Himself, there can be no way for man to discover Him. Happily, He is a loving God and has chosen to make Himself known in every age and in every culture.

21. *The Dictionary of the History of Ideas: Studies of Selected Pivotal Ideas* contains this entry: "Andrew Lang (1844–1912) in *The Making of a Religion* (London and New York: Longmans, Green and Co. 1898), stressing the fact that many 'primitive' peoples believed in a supreme creator-deity, a 'High God' or 'All-Father,' argued that monotheism was the earliest form of religion and that animism represented a degeneration from this original conception. This idea of a primeval monotheism found its most devoted exponent in

General Revelation

Since the earliest days, God has revealed Himself to all mankind in general ways. He has revealed Himself by intentionally leaving His fingerprints, so to speak, over His creation. All the peoples of the world have had the privilege of knowing God and His truth directly from Him, for He has revealed Himself to them all, without distinction of families and tribes. This general revelation occurs in at least these three ways: through nature, through history, and through man's conscience.

Nature is perhaps the most vivid demonstration of God's general revelation to mankind. In the Bible, the Psalmist says,

> *The heavens are telling of the glory of God;*
> *And their expanse is declaring the work of His hands.*
> *Day to day pours forth speech,*
> *And night to night reveals knowledge.*
> Psalm 19:1–2

This form of general revelation is continuous and never ceases; and exists even to our present age. It has been available to all, including to the Chinese from the beginning of their civilization. For example, this knowledge of the creative power of God is expressed in the following song found in *The Collected Statutes of the Ming Dynasty*,

> *Of old in the beginning, there was the great chaos, without form and dark.*
> *The five planets had not begun to revolve, nor the two lights to shine. In the*

Father Wilhelm Schmidt (1868–1954), who maintained his case in a twelve-volume work, *Der Ursprung der Gottesidee* (1926–55). He believed that this primeval monotheism also involved a primeval morality which included the practice of monogamy; he consequently saw both polytheism and polygamy as degenerate forms of the earlier faith and practice." Philip P. Wiener, ed., *The Dictionary of the History of Ideas: Studies of Selected Pivotal Ideas,* Volume 4 (New York: Charles Scribner's Sons, 1973–74), p. 96.

midst of it there existed neither form nor sound. You, O spiritual Sovereign, came forth in Your sovereignty, and first did separate the impure from the pure. You made heaven; You made earth; You made man. All things became alive with reproducing power.

于昔洪荒之初兮，混蒙，五行未運兮，雨曜未明，其中挺立兮，有無容聲，神皇出御兮，始判濁清，立天立地人兮，群物生生。[22]

Because God reveals Himself to everyone through nature, the Apostle Paul could say in the Bible's New Testament that those who reject God are without excuse,

> *For since the creation of the world His invisible attributes, His eternal power and divine nature, have been clearly seen, being understood through what has been made, so that they are without excuse.*
> Romans 1:20

Another form of general revelation is God's providence and intervention in human history. Daniel, a Jew who served as imperial advisor to the rulers of the Babylonian and Medo-Persian empires in the 7th century B.C., said of God,

> *It is He who changes the times and the epochs; / He removes kings and establishes kings; / He gives wisdom to wise men / And knowledge to men of understanding.*
> Daniel 2:21

Daniel was highly qualified even from a human standpoint to make this observation because he served the superpowers of the time for 65 years, watching the fortunes ebb and flow from the Babylonians to the Medes and then to the Persians.

The Chinese, as astute students of history, observed divine intervention in the rise and fall of their kingdoms as well. The *Classic of History* says,

> *But Di [God] sent down calamities on the Xia Dynasty. The ruler of Xia had increased his opulence. He would not speak kindly to the people, and became utterly immoral and foolish. He was unable for a single day to bring himself to follow the path marked out by Di.*

惟帝降格于夏，有夏誕厥逸，不肯戚言于民，乃大淫昏，不克終日勸于帝之迪。[23]

22. 《大明會典》 *The Collected Statutes of the Ming Dynasty*, Volume 82, p. 28.
23. 《fl!5胄國JS胄國乡力》 *Classic of History*, Chronicles of Zhou, Duo Fang, paragraph 3.

Di 帝 and Tian 天 are the two terms used by ancient Chinese to refer to the Creator God, and we will look at these in greater detail in the next chapter. The important thing to note here is that the Chinese were aware that God does intervene in human affairs according to His moral judgment. This divine providence and intervention is captured in the Chinese concept of the Mandate of Heaven, which will be discussed in Chapter 7.

A third form of general revelation by which God reveals Himself to us is conscience. Every human being possesses some degree of moral awareness. Mankind intuitively knows that God delights in goodness while abhorring evil, and knows that we are ultimately accountable to Him. Paul the Apostle puts it this way in the Bible:

> *For when Gentiles who do not have the Law do instinctively the things of the Law, these, not having the Law, are a law to themselves, in that they show the work of the Law written in their hearts, their conscience bearing witness and their thoughts alternately accusing or else defending them, on the day when, according to my gospel, God will judge the secrets of men through Christ Jesus.*
> Romans 2:14 – 16

Mencius (c. 372 – c. 289 B.C.), a Chinese philosopher credited with developing orthodox Confucianism, declared:

> *It is by the preservation of one's heart and the nourishment of one's character that man is able to serve Heaven [God].*
> 存其心，養其性，所以事天也。[24]

It is clear from this quote that Mencius understood that man has moral qualities that need to be developed in order to please God.

Although general revelation is foundational and does help us gain a general knowledge of God, it is not enough; we must not stop here. Doing so would be like attempting to launch a rocket into space with only high school physics! General revelation is meant to let us know that a sovereign, creator God truly does exist. Its purpose is to lead us to seek God and to discover His special revelation.

24. 《孟子-卷十三盡心章句上》 *Mencius*, Volume 13, Jin Xin Zhang Ju Part 1 (Wisdom on Commitment), paragraph 1.

Special Revelation

God, after He spoke long ago to the fathers in the prophets in many portions and in many ways, in these last days has spoken to us in His Son, whom He appointed heir of all things, through whom also He made the world.
Hebrews 1:1–2

As the human race grew in numbers, God set apart one family through which to reveal Himself more fully, choosing them from all the tribes and nations of the world. This was a strategic decision that provided a way for mankind, in times to come, to identify the Savior promised to Adam and Eve in the Garden of Eden. In this way, God built on His general revelation to give us specific—or special—revelation. He chose to reveal Himself to the world through the line of Abraham and his descendants, the Hebrews. Ultimately, He came to live among men in the incarnation of His only begotten son, Jesus of Nazareth. The Apostle Paul, author of much of the Bible's New Testament, said of this Jesus,

He is the image of the invisible God, the firstborn of all creation.
Colossians 1:15

The word translated as "image" here means "icon." In other words, Jesus is the icon of the invisible God; He is the physical expression of God, who is Spirit. Just as the icon on a computer screen represents an unseen and powerful program, Jesus is the physical expression of the all-powerful and all-loving God.

Special revelation comes to us through the Bible, the first part of which is the Scriptures of the Hebrew people. Beginning with Moses and through many generations of writers, God's special revelation to mankind has been put into writing. Everything that we know about Jesus is also from the Scriptures. The Bible provides us with objective statements about God, statements that originated not with man but from the mind of God. Therefore, it takes precedence over general revelation.

In our introduction to God's use of revelation, we noted that even though every culture has had the opportunity to know the One True Creator God through oral traditions passed down from the time of Babel, many of these cultures regarded Him as utterly remote and transcendent, having no influence in the daily affairs of man. In part, this is because God is a Spirit and we cannot see Him; but this is also true because of the impact of sin on man, which has compromised his ability to interpret general revelation. Look again at Paul's words in Romans 1, which was quoted on p. 36, but this time look at the verses before and after verse 20 for a better understanding of man's responsibility in "missing" God.

> *For the wrath of God is revealed from heaven against all ungodliness and unrighteousness of men, who suppress the truth in unrighteousness, because that which is known about God is evident within them; for God made it evident to them.*
>
> *For since the creation of the world His invisible attributes, His eternal power and divine nature, have been clearly seen, being understood through what has been made, so that they are without excuse.*
>
> *For even though they knew God, they did not honor Him as God, or give thanks; but they became futile in their speculations, and their foolish heart was darkened.*
> Romans 1:18–21

General revelation can bring us only to the threshold of understanding; special revelation is clear enough to guide us through the door. General revelation is like a bronze mirror: it gives us an image, but one that is blurred by self and sin. Special revelation is like a glass mirror, giving us a sharp and clear image of the invisible God. General revelation gives us an idea of who God is, but it is insufficient to bring us to a saving knowledge of Jesus. Special revelation guides us without doubt into salvation and a secure eternal relationship with God, through His Son. A

saying from an enduring Chinese classic, *The Chronicles of the Three Kingdoms*, is appropriate here: 妻不操燭, 日有餘光 (zhou bu cao zhu, ri you yu guang), which can be paraphrased as, "Put out the candles, the sun has risen."[25]

In the next few chapters, we will show that there is sufficient light peeking through the windows of general revelation in Chinese history, records, literature, and practices to convince one to take the next step, into the sunlight of God's special revelation.

REFLECT and RESPOND

God loves all the people of the world. He desires that you know Him. Have you gained knowledge of Him by experiencing His creation or by observing His righteous judgments in history? Perhaps He has spoken to you through your conscience. Seek Him and you will see Him at work in your life and in your world.

25. More literally, the translation should be, "There is no need to use the candles in the daytime, the sun has sufficient light." 《三國志》 *The Chronicles of the Three Kingdoms*, Volume 38, History of Shu, Book 8.

Grand historian Sima Qian (in the foreground) writing the Historical Records, as depicted in the "Tribute to Chinese History" mural at the Millennium Monument in Beijing.

貳

Words
2
Have Meaning

Language, literary language, is the greatest artistic creation of a civilized nation.

~ Bernhard Karlgren, Swedish Sinologist

現代漢語的獨特性表現在眾人所知的三個重要方面第一漢字最早形成于三千五百多年以前它是迄界上唯一從起初流傳下來沿用至今的文字第二漢語不是表音文字而是一種象形文字和會意文字如今迄界上超過五分之一的人使用漢字特別有意思的是第三點無論哪裏的中國人盡管他們說着不同的方言可能彼此聽不懂對方說的話但却能够使用大家都認識的文字來彼此溝通這一章將從另外一個角度一個鮮爲人知的方面來探討中國文字的字源在這方面漢字是獨特的而且它簡直是奇異的文字反映出中國幾千年悠久歷史中上帝對中國人的親手引領。

2

Words Have Meaning

More people in the world today speak Chinese than any other language. Chinese is also widely acknowledged as one of the most difficult languages for non-native speakers to learn, in part because it relies on tone as well as pronunciation to distinguish one word from another. That means that a seemingly small mistake in tone can result in a word with a totally different meaning from the one intended.

Written Chinese is perhaps even more worthy of notice because it is unique in a number of important ways. First, it is the only script that has been in continuous use since its inception, between 3,500 to 5,000 years ago. Second, it is pictographic and ideographic rather than phonetic. Third, it allows Chinese everywhere—more than 1 billion people, accounting for almost one-fourth the world's population—to communicate using a single recognizable written form even though they may speak one of many different dialects. Now, a fourth unique aspect of the Chinese language has come to light. Recent studies have found evidence that seems to show in a remarkable way that China's ancient written language reflects God's guiding hand over the Chinese people throughout their centuries-long history.

These new studies on the origin and formation of ancient Chinese characters were the first signpost along my journey of discovery.

Evidence of ancient Chinese writing was first discovered in Beijing in 1899. A scholar noticed that some bones sold for medicinal use in a Beijing pharmacy had inscriptions, later called "oracle bone" script, carved on them. Although earlier

Photo at left shows the Chinese character for "word" written in calligraphy style.

writing was subsequently found on Neolithic pottery dating back to c. 4000 B.C., these oracle bones from the Shang Dynasty 商朝 (c. 1765 – c. 1122 B.C.) contain the earliest writing that modern scholars have been able to decode, albeit only partially.

The inscriptions on these bones are evidence that by the Shang Dynasty, which is roughly from about the time of Joseph's death through Moses' lifetime, China already had a highly developed, complex, and sophisticated system used to write a language quite similar to classical Chinese. Although the origins of this writing system are still lost to history, there is this account recorded by Xu Shen 許嗨 in his preface to *Shuowen Jiezi* 説文解字, the oldest surviving Chinese dictionary: "The Yellow Emperor's Court Recorder, Cang Jie 盒頜, looked down and saw the marks left by the tracks of birds and animals. He realized that by distinguishing their patterns he was able to differentiate one thing from another. Thus he created the script." This story would place the beginning

A block print of Cang Jie creating Chinese writing.

of China's written language at about 2700 B.C., about 200 years before the Egyptians started building their pyramids.

The next stage of development in Chinese writing was bronze inscriptions — texts cast or carved onto the surfaces of bronze vessels used mainly for ceremonial purposes. These inscriptions date as far back as the Shang Dynasty but the vessels did not come into wide use until the Western Zhou 西周 Dynasty (c. 1121 – c. 771 B.C.), about the time of the divided kingdoms of Israel and Judah in the Old Testament and the growth of city-states in Greece. In language and calligraphic style, these inscriptions were similar to those on the oracle bones.

Beginning about the 5th century B.C., wooden tablets, silk cloth, and most commonly, bamboo strips tied together to form long rolls came into use as media for the written language. The content changed as well; in addition to historical and administrative writings, the bamboo texts contain some of the earliest manuscripts of the famous Chinese philosophical texts, such as the *Dao De Jing* 道憲經, also called *Lao Zi* 老子.

During the reign of Qin Shi Huang Di 秦始叟帝, who reunified China in 221 B.C. after 500 years of warfare, the written language was standardized. Until then, written characters had varied from state to state in style or other peculiarities. Qin Shi Huang Di introduced the Qin script as the official writing form and required that it be used by all the unified states. Following this standardization, the characters soon evolved into the "classical Chinese" that remained in use until the late 19th century.

Much has been written about the evolution of the Chinese language from early pictures to today's characters. In the traditional linguistic theory known as *Liushu* 六書 (six writings), characters are grouped into six categories based on their composition: pictographs, indicatives, ideographs, phonetic compounds, manipulated irregular derivatives, and phonetic loans. We will consider just three of these groups later in this chapter.

Linguistic theory, however, does not explain why the Chinese language has endured through the ages relatively unchanged. The *Encyclopedia Britannica* attributes this continuity to the pictographic nature of this language: "It is the use of characters, not letters as in Western languages, that is most important in the Chinese language .... The characters stand for things or ideas and so, unlike groups of letters, they cannot and need never be sounded. Thus, Chinese could be read by people in all parts of the country in spite of gradual changes in pronunciation, the emergence of regional and local dialects, and modification of the characters." While foreign students of Chinese may bemoan the challenge of having to learn thousands of characters through sheer memorization, the "pictures" embedded in these characters have actually served to preserve the meaning of the characters with little change for thousands of years.

THE MEANING OF WORDS

Language, however, is not static. It changes and develops with history and reflects the cultural context of the time.

The English language, for example, is replete with phrases and sayings that demonstrate the great influence Christian writings and other literary classics, such as Shakespeare's plays, have had on it. Although many English-speakers today may not be aware of the origin of references to "the writing on the wall," everyone understands that it means an obvious, clear, and unmistakable sign or an imminent disaster. In fact, this saying comes from the biblical account of Daniel's prophecy in Daniel 5 concerning the imminent capture of Babylon by the attacking Medo-Persians. Similarly, not everyone may realize that it was Jesus who taught the virtues of "turning the other cheek," but this saying is regularly used today to encourage forgiveness rather than revenge in response to an affront or an injustice. Likewise, people today speak of "washing (one's) hands" of some unsavory act but may not recall that this comes from Shakespeare's *Macbeth*, which itself refers to the New Testament account of the ruler Pontius Pilate attempting to cleanse himself of the guilt of condemning an innocent man, Jesus Christ, to death.

What these examples demonstrate is that at some point in history, people were so well acquainted with the Bible and with Shakespeare's works that these references were readily understood without need for explanation or elaboration. Once words or phrases become part of common usage, their origin might be forgotten through the passage of time, but their usefulness remains.

Language is also enhanced by cross-pollinization. While this happens most often between close families of languages, it has even happened between the vastly different languages of Chinese and English. Wok—鍋, kumquat—金桔, kung-fu—功夫, ketchup/catsup—琉汁, and, of course, to shanghai—上海, to name just a few, all came from Chinese words. In the other direction, the Chinese words for tin can—聽, media—媒體, logic—邏輯, and romance—羅叟史, again naming just a few, are all borrowed from English.

While many English-speakers may know that "wok" and "kung-fu" are Chinese words because they are associated with things distinctively Chinese, the assertion that "ketchup/catsup" is a Chinese word may be a surprise. Non-Cantonese Chinese speakers may be equally surprised and may even challenge the suggestion that this word in English comes from the Cantonese words for tomato sauce. This fact however is immediately and unmistakably clear to a Cantonese speaker: "ketchup/catsup" is an extremely close transliteration of the Cantonese pronunciation for tomato, 统—ket, and sauce, 汁—chup. There can be no better explanation for the derivation of this English word.

Similarly, the Chinese words for "can," as in "a soda can," and for "media" are clearly borrowed from English. In Chinese, "can" is "ting,"clearly phonetic in nature and probably derived from the British word for "can," which is "tin"—although that derivation may not be obvious to someone who is not familiar with British English. The Chinese word for "media" is "mei-jie" 媒介, and for "the media" is "mei-ti" 媒體. Mei-jie has implicit Chinese meanings within it. *Mei* (as in *mei ren* 媒人, match-maker) and *jie* (as in *zhong jie* 中介, intermediary) both carry the idea of a medium of interface. Despite this, however, it is obvious that the coinage of "mei-jie," and even more clearly that of "mei-ti," is inspired by the English word "media." As for the example of the verb "to shanghai," although no one is really sure how this came to mean kidnapping someone and pressing him into service on a ship, there is no dispute that it is related to the Chinese city of Shanghai, and certainly no documentation is needed to link the verb to the unique name of this world-renowned city.

It is logical and equally as valid to draw the same conclusions when we find reflected in ancient Chinese characters details of the unique accounts of the origin of the earth and mankind as presented in Genesis, the first book of the Bible. Although there is no irrefutable explanation for such a correlation between Chinese words and the Genesis account, it is reason enough to accept that there is, in fact, a connection, especially in light of the other evidences that will be presented in this book.

Graphic Interface

To borrow an illustration from today's world of information technology, it is as though the Chinese written language has kept the icon-based "Windows Operating

FINDING GOD IN ANCIENT CHINA

System" while the rest of the world has switched to the text-based "DOS" or "Disk Operating System." Of course, in reality, the development of computer technology has been exactly the reverse. In the case of language development, however, Chinese has bucked the trend of development worldwide and has remained a language based on pictographs or icons. Written languages of all ancient cultures started with pictographs and ideograms, but over time, these icons were transliterated to aid recall and to facilitate writing. When these icons were transliterated into a phonetic alphabet, they gained the advantage of easy recall, which in turn promoted literacy, but the rich meaning behind the words was lost.

We still use icons, however, when universal understanding is needed, such as in situations or locations where the meaning of a symbol is more important than the need for recall. For instance, in public places, we use icons to indicate restrooms and escape routes. On expressways, we use various symbols to guide and give instructions because it is important for drivers to understand warnings and directions even if they do not know the language of the host country. At home, we use symbols to communicate important information; for example, a skull-and-crossbones on containers of poisonous materials shouts danger even to someone who cannot read.

In the 1960s, Chinese leader Mao Tse-tung, in a misguided effort to improve literacy, tried — but failed — to Romanize the Chinese language by doing away with characters entirely and replacing them with *pinyin* 拼音 (phonetic transcription or transliteration). Had this or any other similar attempt succeeded, the Chinese language would have lost its graphic interface, and we would have lost the ability to understand its original meaning.

Fortunately, that did not happen, and Chinese characters today still carry, embedded in them, the stories and meanings of the original pictographs from which they are formed. This is a great boon for students of history, because over time characters may undergo stylistic changes and changes in pronunciation, but the "icon" — the character's original meaning as captured in picture form — has remained. These "icons" are like "snapshots" frozen in time even if general knowledge of the original meaning or story is lost with the passage of time. Just like the icons on your computer that are universally recognized regardless of whether the user's language is English, Chinese, French, or Arabic, so the pictographs in Chinese also can be easily understood.

50

This embedding of meanings and stories also makes Chinese writing, especially ancient or classical Chinese writing, succinct. The observant reader will have quickly noticed that the Chinese passages quoted in this book, when rendered in English, often require many more words to explain. Just as the icons on your computer screen are windows to unseen but powerful software programs, many Chinese characters are windows to powerful insights about the past. We will "click" open a few for you in this chapter.

First, though, let us consider three major classifications of Chinese characters.

Pictographs, which number about 600, are used to depict material objects, and they form the basis of China's written language. For instance, 口 (kou) means "mouth," and 木 (mu) means "tree." There is, however, a fundamental difference between pictographs and pictures: pictographs are generally nothing more than rough sketches of objects (e.g., 日 "sun" ☉, 月 "moon" ☽, 山 "mountain" ⋀, 川 "river" ⫴, 人 "man" ⼈, 大 "big" ⼤) or depict only a characteristic part of an object (e.g., 牛 "ox" ⼤, 羊 "sheep" ⼤), and hence are much simpler than pictures. As pictographs evolved, they became more abstract, and today may be merely symbolic.

Nonetheless, the illustrations below show vividly how those first pictures dating from about 250 B.C. are still recognizable in the characters used today.

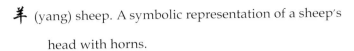

羊 (yang) sheep. A symbolic representation of a sheep's

head with horns.

龜 (gui) tortoise.

鱼 (yu) fish.

Ideographs number more than 700 and are used to convey abstract ideas that pictographs, though very graphic, cannot represent. They are compounds composed of two or more existing characters or pictographs. For instance, a "mouth" over a "tree" suggests a wooden mouth 呆 (dai), hence, someone who is slow-witted or who is dumbfounded and struck speechless. More obviously, the single character 木 stands for a "tree," two trees together 林 denotes a group of trees, hence "grove," and the character made up of three trees 森 means a place full of trees, hence, "forest." The character consisting of 人 — man and 木 — tree shows a man leaning or resting against a tree, hence "rest" 沐 (xiu).

Phonetic characters make up the bulk of the Chinese language, totaling some 20,000. As compared with pictographs and ideographs, these characters are more like phonetic languages such as English in that sounds are employed to convey meaning. For instance, the word for "cat" is 继 (mao), which uses both pictographs and phonetics to convey the meaning. 苗 is pronounced "miao" and the radical 犭(犬) is the pictograph that is used in almost all characters of animals' names. Other phonetic characters may use pictographs and/or ideographs for the sound and add a radical, which is the classifying part of the word, for meaning.

FIRST THINGS FIRST

Now, back to our journey of discovery and those Chinese characters that reflect details of the first experiences of mankind as told in Genesis. Because of their long history and the fact that they can be traced back to their original forms, Chinese characters can corroborate the history of the Hebrew people, and vice versa. By selectively examining some Chinese characters, we can see that embedded in them are stories that tell us about the problem of sin and God's plan for dealing with it. These characters show that the Creation story, as recorded in Hebrew history, that is, biblical history, must have been common to both the Hebrew and the Chinese cultures for these elements of the Hebrew story to be reflected in Chinese characters. In other words, ancient Chinese characters often referred to the first things in the world in the same way as these events were recorded by the Hebrews.

We are not suggesting that these words were originally designed to convey a Christian message. What they seem to suggest, however, is that what is now

known as the biblical story of Creation was at one point in ancient history also the Creation story known in Chinese culture. It was so commonly accepted as truth that elements of that story are reflected in the symbols chosen to represent key ideas in the formation of the written Chinese language.

It is also significant to note that the appearance of Chinese characters in the timeline of Chinese history was approximately the same time that the races were dispersed after the debacle of the Tower of Babel as recorded in Hebrew history. Hence, the following scenario is entirely plausible. Those who fled the chaos of Babel and settled in the river valleys of what was to become China formulated a written language using symbols influenced by and in some cases based on the oral traditions that were common to all mankind at that point in time.

There are, in fact, many more characters than those presented in this chapter that can be traced to the biblical Creation story. The purpose here is not to present an exhaustive list, to which others have devoted entire books (see, for instance, C. H. Kang and Ethel R. Nelson, *Discovery of Genesis*, St. Louis: Concordia Publishing House, 1979). Rather, we will look only at those characters that demonstrate how God's plan for redemption is embedded in the characters that Chinese have used throughout their centuries-long written history. With each character, we provide excerpts from the Bible to show it relates to the Hebrew account or teaching.

True Happiness

Then the LORD *God took the man and put him into the Garden of Eden to cultivate it and keep it.*
Genesis 2:15

How blessed are the people whose God is the Lord!
Psalm 144:15

福 (fu), ancient form 福, means "blessing" or "happiness." Chinese people love this word because it means "good fortune." This character is often pasted on doors of Chinese homes and businesses in hopes that "fu" or good fortune will come or has already arrived. The word means much more than simply material wealth, though. The ancient form of the word has the "god" radical (示)

to indicate that the word is related to God or spiritual matters. 字 literally means "to reveal," and when used on its own is written 示 (shi). 示 is a pictograph of an altar, that is, the place the ancients approached when seeking God's direction or divine revelation; hence, the meaning of "to reveal," and when used in radical form, it refers to God. This reflects God's nature as the Self-revealing One: no one can know Him unless He reveals Himself. As recounted in the previous chapter, God has revealed Himself through general revelation, such as the natural order of the universe, and through special revelation, which is contained in the Bible and ultimately in His Son, Jesus Christ.

The right side of this character is formed by a jar of wine ⊗ at the top and a pair of hands ⊭⊰ below it. Both are suggestive of worship: the wine because it was used in acts of worship and the hands because they appear to be raised in worship. This composition clearly suggests that blessedness is closely correlated with one's relationship with God; that is, the ancient Chinese concept of blessedness is a spiritual condition, not entirely centered on material possessions. The modern form of this character is missing the pair of worshipping hands, reflecting the modern Chinese concept of "fu" or blessing as being in possession of food and land (口 — kou means mouth and 田 — tian means field). A superstitious practice that continues even today in Chinese communities worldwide is to post the "fu" character upside down. This practice is the result of a play on words: the word for "arrived" and the word for "upside down" are pronounced the same way — "dao." Therefore, saying, "'Fu' is upside down" can sound like "blessing has arrived." This symbolic topsy-turvy understanding of blessing actually is very revealing of how the concept of blessing has become distorted. In ancient times, the Chinese understood that responding in worship to God, who loves us and wants to live in harmony with us, brings unmatched peace and joy — that is, blessing. Nothing else can give us the sense of wellbeing and blessedness that being united again with Him in spirit does.

A Spiritual Community

社 (she) means society as in 社會 (she hui). 社 is made up of two pictographs: 字 (shi) or the altar/God radical on the left and 土 (tu), which means "earth" or

"place," on the right. Its pictorial meaning is a place where God is worshipped. In the past, 社畜 referred to the large spring and autumn religious gatherings, usually of entire villages and communities, for the purpose of worship. The modern usage of 社會 has lost this ancient meaning and now simply refers to a group of people, i.e., a society. A similar example in the English language is "holiday," the derivation of which is "holy day," meaning a day set aside for worship. Now it just means a day off from work.

社 reveals that God was very much at the center of ancient Chinese society, where communities were held together by the corporate worship of God. That the word today has lost that meaning reflects an existing reality: God is no longer a part of Chinese society. This reality, however, runs counter to God's purpose for communities, that is, He should be at the very center of each community; only then can society experience His fullest blessings.

> *I will put My Spirit within you and cause you to walk in My statutes, and you will be careful to observe My ordinances. And you will live in the land that I gave to your forefathers; so you will be My people, and I will be your God.*
> Ezekiel 36:27 – 28

The Test

> *The LORD God commanded the man, saying, "From any tree of the garden you may eat freely; but from the tree of the knowledge of good and evil you shall not eat, for in the day that you eat from it you will surely die."*
> Genesis 2:16 – 17

> *It's the child he loves that he disciplines; the child he embraces, he also corrects.*
> Hebrews 12:6 (The Message)

禁 (jin), ancient form 林示, means "to forbid." It is formed by "two trees" on top, with 示 (shi) or "to reveal" below (this is the same radical representing God in the "fu" 福 character above). The two trees refer to the Tree of the Knowledge of Good and Evil and the Tree of Life. The 示 refers to God telling, or revealing to, Adam that he was not to eat of the first tree. God's command was the first restriction

FINDING GOD IN ANCIENT CHINA

put on man and the first time he was forbidden to do something. This was done so that he would have an opportunity to exercise his free will.

This restriction or test must be seen in light of God's intention for Adam and Eve. When God created man, He made man in His own image so that man could relate to Him in His fullness, which consists of intellect, emotion, and will. He made mankind with these same attributes along with the capacity to grow in these areas. To develop Adam's intellect, God gave him a job: to take care of the garden and to name all the animals.

Behind the simple task of naming the animals were several objectives. In carrying out this task, Adam learned to study God's creation in detail, and in the process, he learned to appreciate God's creativity, which in turn expanded his own intellectual capacity. Recall Confucius' saying, quoted in the previous chapter, that the purpose of the Book of Changes is 窮理盡性, 以至于命 (jiu li jin xing, yi zhi yu ming), that is, the exhaustive study of nature is for the purpose of understanding God's will. The task of naming the animals also made Adam aware of a need within him, and that was the need for someone like him—someone to whom he could relate and with whom he could share his emotions and experiences. None of the animals could meet this need, so God created another person, Eve, to satisfy this human longing and fulfill this need.

God did not stop there. Besides his intellectual and emotional development, Adam also needed to exercise his volition, or free will. So God created a situation for Adam and Eve in which they had to make a simple decision. It was a very straightforward situation: you may eat of all the fruits of the garden, but not from this one tree. God's goodness can be seen in the simplicity of this test. Until they were faced with this simple test, Adam and Eve had never had to make any choices, and therefore their righteousness—that is, their right-ness before God—could not be confirmed.

束 (shu), ancient form 朿, means to "restrain." The explanation for this character is very interesting. If we were to devise a character today to mean "restrain," we probably would try to depict two hands tied together. Yet, that is not at all how this character is written. In fact, it is a 口 "mouth," superimposed over

a 木 "tree." This Chinese character further confirms the Genesis account described above. It refers to the first restraint placed on man, that is, when God told Adam, "Do not eat from the Tree of the Knowledge of Good and Evil." To exercise power over their will, Adam and Eve were to restrain themselves from eating from one of the many trees in the Garden of Eden. So, when the Chinese designed an ideogram to mean "restrain," they thought of the first instance in which mankind had to exercise restraint. And that was when they were commanded not to eat from the forbidden tree.

The Tempter

> *Now the serpent was more crafty than any beast of the field which the* LORD *God had made.*
> Genesis 3:1

> *Be of sober spirit, be on the alert. Your adversary, the devil, prowls around like a roaring lion, seeking someone to devour.*
> 1 Peter 5:8

它 (ta) and 蛇 (she), ancient form 它, are related to each other in that both originally meant "serpent." 它 (ta) was the original pictograph for "serpent." In the course of time, however, it lost its pictographic meaning. It is now used exclusively to mean "it" or the third person non-human pronoun. The character for "serpent" or "snake" is now written with 虫 (chong) next to 它 (ta) to form 蛇 (she). 虫 means "insect" and gives the meaning of an animal or insect to any character using it as a radical. Again, the Genesis story sheds light on these characters and their meaning, in this case, on the connection between the "third person" and the serpent. While Adam and Eve were undergoing the test involving the forbidden fruit, a "third party," who was not a human being, came along to tempt them. Unlike God, who placed the tree in the middle of the garden to test Adam and Eve in order to build them up, Satan came along, in the form of a serpent, to tempt them in order to destroy them. The Chinese characters show that the third party in the garden was the serpent.

tree of the Knowledge of Good and Evil. Eve made God look unreasonable by embellishing the restriction and saying that they were forbidden even to touch the tree. Often, a series of distortions and deceptions are interwoven into the process of temptation to sin. Satan's first distortion led Eve to rationalize her forbidden desire.

Once Eve was hooked, Satan moved in with a bigger contradiction, "*You surely will not die!*" (Genesis 3:4). This is the third falsehood. God's command and the consequences for disobedience were very clear. Yet Satan cunningly pointed out that they would not die immediately. God had spoken of an immediate spiritual death or spiritual separation, accompanied by a breakdown of the created order. Sin brought with it physical pain, suffering, and other evil consequences to the world, including ultimately physical death. Although Adam and Eve did not immediately die a physical death, they began to die from the day they sinned because they had died spiritually. Recall that spiritual death is separation from God. Satan's deceptions are still powerful today; foolish men and women are still following his ways by living for the treasures of this world, thereby surrendering their long-term purpose and ultimately their eternal life.

The fourth contradiction followed swiftly, "*For God knows that in the day you eat from it your eyes will be opened, and you will be like God, knowing good and evil*" (Genesis 3:5). Satan delivered his *coup de grace* with a characteristic half-truth. Indeed their eyes were opened, indeed they became like God, and indeed they gained knowledge of good and evil. The irony was their eyes were opened, but it was to see their shame. God's good intention was that they would become more like Him, through a practical knowledge of good and evil; that is, that they would gain this knowledge through duty and obedience. God wanted them to gain experiential knowledge of good or happiness and evil or misery. Satan perverted the whole situation by offering a shortcut when God's intention was for mankind to become more like Him through sensible compliance to a simple command.

The Result of Sin: Death

When the woman saw that the tree was good for food, and that it was a delight to the eyes, and that the tree was desirable to make one wise, she took from

a 木 "tree." This Chinese character further confirms the Genesis account described above. It refers to the first restraint placed on man, that is, when God told Adam, "Do not eat from the Tree of the Knowledge of Good and Evil." To exercise power over their will, Adam and Eve were to restrain themselves from eating from one of the many trees in the Garden of Eden. So, when the Chinese designed an ideogram to mean "restrain," they thought of the first instance in which mankind had to exercise restraint. And that was when they were commanded not to eat from the forbidden tree.

The Tempter

Now the serpent was more crafty than any beast of the field which the LORD
God had made.
Genesis 3:1

*Be of sober spirit, be on the alert. Your adversary, the devil, prowls around like
a roaring lion, seeking someone to devour.*
1 Peter 5:8

它 (ta) and 蛇 (she), ancient form ⌂, are related to each other in that both originally meant "serpent." 它 (ta) was the original pictograph for "serpent." In the course of time, however, it lost its pictographic meaning. It is now used exclusively to mean "it" or the third person non-human pronoun. The character for "serpent" or "snake" is now written with 虫 (chong) next to 它 (ta) to form 蛇 (she). 虫 means "insect" and gives the meaning of an animal or insect to any character using it as a radical. Again, the Genesis story sheds light on these characters and their meaning, in this case, on the connection between the "third person" and the serpent. While Adam and Eve were undergoing the test involving the forbidden fruit, a "third party," who was not a human being, came along to tempt them. Unlike God, who placed the tree in the middle of the garden to test Adam and Eve in order to build them up, Satan came along, in the form of a serpent, to tempt them in order to destroy them. The Chinese characters show that the third party in the garden was the serpent.

FINDING GOD IN ANCIENT CHINA

The Temptation

> *Let no one say when he is tempted, "I am being tempted by God"; for God cannot be tempted by evil, and He Himself does not tempt anyone. But each one is tempted when he is carried away and enticed by his own lust.*
> James 1:13–14

婪 (lan), ancient form 婪, means "to covet" or "to desire something forbidden." It is made up of "two trees" on top with a 女, which means "woman/female" on the bottom. The "two trees" as we have already seen, refer to the two trees in the Garden of Eden—the Tree of Knowledge of Good and Evil and the Tree of Life—and the woman is Eve in front of the trees. It was Eve who committed the first act of coveting in human history, by desiring the fruit of the Tree of the Knowledge of Good and Evil.

The composition of this character is even more interesting when one recalls that in ancient China, women had no place in society: they were not involved in public affairs; they had no role in social transactions; in some cases, they were not even allowed to leave their rooms. Yet, the ancient Chinese chose to use the character for "woman" rather than the one for "man" in constructing this 婪 "covet" character. This shows that the ancient Chinese had some knowledge of the story of the first act of disobedience against God, which resulted in sin entering the world. It was not only the woman who was guilty, though. The man, Adam, was not blameless; he also was responsible because not only did he not stop her from disobeying, he joined her in eating the fruit she coveted.

The Process of Temptation and Sin

罪 (zui), ancient form 辠 means "sin." The ancient form is made up of two parts. The top part is 自 (zi), ancient form 自, depicting a nose to represent "self." The bottom is 辛 (xin) which means "bitter." Sin as understood by the ancients meant "self-centeredness," and the result is bitterness. Sin is a condition of the heart, when one puts oneself at the center of the universe. The result is always the opposite of what is sought, and we will taste the bitter fruit of

sin. This character was changed to its present form by Qin Shi Huang Di, the first emperor of the Qin Dynasty 秦朝 (248 – 207 B.C., unified nation 221 B.C.), who is best known for building the Great Wall and for the terra-cotta soldiers guarding his mammoth tomb in Xi'an. His connection to this character is very interesting because Qin Shi Huang Di was one of the most self-centered men in all of history. As we shall see in Chapter 8, when we examine his life, Qin Shi Huang Di certainly experienced the bitter fruit of his self-centeredness.

The character now used for "sin" is made up of the character for "four" 四, over the character 非 for "contradiction" or "counter to" as in fei-fen 非分, "over-stepping one's bounds." The pictograph for "fei" looks like two wings flying in opposite directions. "Fei" can also mean "evil" or "wrongdoing." In modern China, the concept of sin has been watered-down, and the more common meaning of 罪 is "crime," "guilt," or "offense." The character has lost the concept of a moral transgression, much less a moral transgression that is punishable by death, as is taught in the Bible. Nonetheless, the character shows that the ancient Chinese were familiar with the events leading up to the first sin. The two parts of the character refer to the four false or contradictory statements or four falsehoods that Satan, in the form of the serpent, used to persuade Eve to eat the forbidden fruit, thereby leading her to commit the first sin.

These are the four contradictions or falsehoods.

"Indeed, has God said, 'You shall not eat from any tree of the garden?'" (Genesis 3:1). Satan, in asking this question, contradicted God's directive by switching just one word: from "one tree" to "any tree." Satan's tactics are always deceptive. Our moral dilemmas are not as black and white as we would like them to be because deception often is clothed in some semblance of truth. Yet, Satan's intent was malicious to the core. God's generous provision (all but one tree) was subtly and cunningly made to look stingy and unreasonable.

Eve, unwittingly, engaged in this dangerous discussion. In so doing, she also contradicted God's word, by saying, *"From the fruit of the trees of the garden we may eat; but from the fruit of the tree which is in the middle of the garden, God has said, 'You shall not eat from it or touch it, or you will die'"* (Genesis 3:2-3). This was the second contradiction. God's only restriction was: Do not eat the fruit of this

tree of the Knowledge of Good and Evil. Eve made God look unreasonable by embellishing the restriction and saying that they were forbidden even to touch the tree. Often, a series of distortions and deceptions are interwoven into the process of temptation to sin. Satan's first distortion led Eve to rationalize her forbidden desire.

Once Eve was hooked, Satan moved in with a bigger contradiction, "*You surely will not die!*" (Genesis 3:4). This is the third falsehood. God's command and the consequences for disobedience were very clear. Yet Satan cunningly pointed out that they would not die immediately. God had spoken of an immediate spiritual death or spiritual separation, accompanied by a breakdown of the created order. Sin brought with it physical pain, suffering, and other evil consequences to the world, including ultimately physical death. Although Adam and Eve did not immediately die a physical death, they began to die from the day they sinned because they had died spiritually. Recall that spiritual death is separation from God. Satan's deceptions are still powerful today; foolish men and women are still following his ways by living for the treasures of this world, thereby surrendering their long-term purpose and ultimately their eternal life.

The fourth contradiction followed swiftly, "*For God knows that in the day you eat from it your eyes will be opened, and you will be like God, knowing good and evil*" (Genesis 3:5). Satan delivered his *coup de grace* with a characteristic half-truth. Indeed their eyes were opened, indeed they became like God, and indeed they gained knowledge of good and evil. The irony was their eyes were opened, but it was to see their shame. God's good intention was that they would become more like Him, through a practical knowledge of good and evil; that is, that they would gain this knowledge through duty and obedience. God wanted them to gain experiential knowledge of good or happiness and evil or misery. Satan perverted the whole situation by offering a shortcut when God's intention was for mankind to become more like Him through sensible compliance to a simple command.

The Result of Sin: Death

When the woman saw that the tree was good for food, and that it was a delight to the eyes, and that the tree was desirable to make one wise, she took from

its fruit and ate; and she gave also to her husband with her, and he ate.
Genesis 3:6

Therefore, just as through one man sin entered into the world, and death through sin, and so death spread to all men, because all sinned.
Romans 5:12

(sang), ancient form , means "death." The classical and ancient form of the Chinese word for "death" clearly shows that death is associated with two mouths eating from a tree. The simplified version of this character replaces the "mouth" component with two short strokes, weakening its implied meaning.

God had a covenant or a contract with Adam and Eve, one that was quite simple: as long as Adam and Eve refrained from eating the fruit of the forbidden tree, they would live in harmony with God in His presence. This exercise of restraint should be regarded as the outward sign of an inner condition, that of choosing God as their Master. By breaking this covenant and eating the forbidden fruit, they were saying in effect that they did not regard God as their Master. As God had warned, the consequence of this choice and their disobedience was death. When Adam and Eve chose not to let God be Master of their lives, they died spiritually; that is, their hitherto uninterrupted intimate relationship with God was severed.

They also immediately experienced emotional separation between themselves; as soon as they lost their spiritual connection with God, they lost their connection with each other. Rather than confessing their disobedience and seeking forgiveness, they blamed each other, demonstrating that man could no longer live in perfect harmony. They also immediately experienced personal emotional dissonance, in the form of shame, insecurity, fear, and guilt. Physical separation occurred many years later, when Adam and Eve experienced the death of the body and its separation from the soul, as God had warned.

The Result of Sin: Shame

Then the eyes of both of them were opened, and they knew that they were naked; and they sewed fig leaves together and made themselves loin coverings.
Genesis 3:7

FINDING GOD IN ANCIENT CHINA

My people are destroyed for lack of knowledge. / Because you have rejected knowledge, / I also will reject you from being My priest. / Since you have forgotten the law of your God, I also will forget your children. / The more they multiplied, the more they sinned against Me; / I will change their glory into shame.

Hosea 4:6–7

裸 (luo) means "naked." This character is made up of 衤 (yi) "clothing" and 果 (guo) "fruit." The 衤 radical designates it as a word to do with clothing, or, in this case, the lack of it. Immediately after Adam and Eve ate the forbidden fruit, their eyes were opened and they realized that they were naked. Nakedness is a graphic expression of the shame they experienced due to their disobedience. Only from the Genesis account can such a correlation between nakedness and fruit as depicted in this Chinese character be explained.

羞 (xiu), ancient form 𦍋, now means "shame"; however, it evolved from an ancient word that meant "something tasty." That original word is now written as 饈 (xiu), with the addition of the "food" radical, 食 (shi), to classify it as a word related to food. The ancient form of the word was simply made up of the symbol for "lamb" 羊, which has been modified into the upper left part of the modern character, and the symbol for a hand, now at the lower right of the character. The resulting character symbolized the offering of lamb in a sacrifice. By extension, the original word meant "good taste" or "sacrificial food that is acceptable." Most Chinese words that contain the "lamb" component are good and auspicious words, for instance, 祥 (xiang) meaning "auspicious," and 美 (mei) meaning "beautiful." The Chinese, like the Hebrews, understood that the lamb represents gentleness, innocence, and purity. It is the most "human" of all animals because it is fully dependent on its human owner. Because of these qualities, the lamb is the preferred sacrificial animal. So, what is the connection between a good or tasty sacrifice and the concept of shame?

It is not entirely clear how a word that originally meant "tasty" or "good sacrifice" has come to mean "shame." Some examples in modern English, however, will help explain how this kind of mutation happens in languages. Today, the brand name Xerox is used interchangeably with the verb "to photocopy," so that one is just as likely to say, "Let me Xerox that letter" as "Let me photocopy that letter." Similarly, the brand name Kleenex has become synonymous with "facial tissue."

In the case of 羞, a similar mutation happened in ancient times: Man sinned and God provided a good or acceptable sacrifice—a lamb—to cover his sins. The sacrifice was in the form of a lamb, which people associated with tasty food. They also recognized, however, that this "tasty food" was connected with the "shame" of a sinful act that required this food to become a sacrificial offering. The first time mankind experienced shame was after Adam and Eve ate the forbidden fruit and became aware of their nakedness, which they immediately tried to cover up. Shame, objectively, was the moral state that resulted from the reprehensible nature of their sinful act of doubting and disobeying the good intentions of the loving God. Subjectively, shame was the painful feeling that resulted from their transgression and guilt.

The Result of Sin: Guilt

For all of us have become like one who is unclean, / And all our righteous deeds are like a filthy garment; / And all of us wither like a leaf, / And our iniquities, like the wind, take us away.
Isaiah 64:6

愧 (kui) means "guilt." The word is made up of the words for heart 忄 (xin) and devil 鬼 (gui). Guilt is the state of having violated or broken a law. Therefore, guilt is not primarily or solely an inward feeling. People generally feel guilty because they are! The Chinese word graphically depicts this state of moral violation by showing that the devil is in one's heart. When Adam and Eve sinned, or violated God's simple command, they allowed the devil to occupy the place that once belonged to God alone. They had lost their original state of innocence and perfection! They were guilty because they allowed Satan to gain a foothold within the heart of man.

The Result of Sin: Crimes

Cain told Abel his brother. And it came about when they were in the field,

that Cain rose up against Abel his brother and killed him. Then the Lord
said to Cain, "Where is Abel your brother?" And he said, "I do not know.
Am I my brother's keeper?"
Genesis 4:8–9

兄 (xiong), ancient form 𗧪, and 凶 (xiong), ancient form 𗧪, have a common element and are pronounced exactly the same way. These two characters also further develop the Genesis account. After mankind's first transgression, sin became a part of human nature; the devil was now in the hearts of all men to prompt them to more transgressions.

The first character 兄 means "older brother" and the second character means "violence" or "murder." First, let's look at "older brother," which comprises a "mouth" over a "son" or "person." This comes from the status of the firstborn son or elder brother in a family as the family's spokesman or mouthpiece. But why should the character for "violence" or "murder" have as one of its components the word for "brother"? The ancient form of the character for "violence" cannot be more graphic as it depicts one brother holding down the other to commit the murder.

The explanation is clear in light of the biblical story of Cain and Abel, in which Cain, the older brother, kills Abel. This was mankind's first murder. When the two brothers presented their sacrifices to God, God was not pleased with Cain's offering. We can assume that God, because He is just, had made clear to both brothers what would be considered an acceptable sacrifice. Cain, however, even though he spoke face to face with God, did not follow God's instructions. That is always the root of sin: willful disobedience. When God told him that his offering was unacceptable while Abel's was pleasing, Cain in anger killed his brother—a violent, murderous act. When Cain pleaded with God to spare his life, God agreed and, to protect him from being put to death by others who knew he had committed murder, God placed a mark on Cain's forehead. Hence, the "×" in this character for murder 凶, refers to Cain's mark. When the Chinese designed an ideogram to represent violence or murder, what they came up with told the story of the first murder in history, one in which brother killed brother.

God's Provision for Sin: Sacrifice

All of us like sheep have gone astray, / Each of us has turned to his own way;
/ But the Lord has caused the iniquity of us all / To fall on Him. / He was
oppressed and He was afflicted, / Yet He did not open His mouth; / Like a lamb
that is led to slaughter, /And like a sheep that is silent before its shearers, / so
He did not open His mouth.
Isaiah 53:6 – 7

祭 (ji) is the character for "sacrifice." On the upper left is a radical that means
"flesh" 肉, referring to what is most commonly used as a sacrificial offering, that is,
the flesh or meat of various animals. This shows that life of some kind is involved
in a sacrifice. In the upper right is a symbol representing a hand, and below the two
is the symbol for God, 示, which we've seen in several previous characters. This
character with a radical meaning "city" or "mound" 阝, added to the left has resulted
in a character, pronounced exactly the same way, that means "border": 際. Although
the relationship is not immediately clear between 際 and 祭, the close correlation
is the result of the border sacrifices that the emperor was expected to perform on
a mound outside the border of the city. The significance of the border sacrifice in
China's history will be explored in Chapter 4.

God's Provision for Sin: The Sacrificial Lamb

The next day he saw Jesus coming to him and said, "Behold, the Lamb
of God who takes away the sin of the world!"
John 1:29

羔 (gao) means "young lamb." As far back as the oracle bone inscriptions,
the two components of this character are the symbol for "sheep" 羊, and the
radical for "fire" 灬 (huo). Originally, this combination meant "to roast sheep or
lambs over a fire." As lambs were generally the preferred animals for sacrifice,
however, this combination came to mean specifically "lamb" or "kid." This
character relates to the meaning of sacrifice that God wanted to convey to man:

貳

sin must be paid for and an innocent and perfect life must be offered to cover sin and remove the guilt. We have seen why the lamb is the preferred sacrifice from the explanation for 羞 (xiu) "shame." Only the innocent can pay for the guilt of those who have sinned. In all of history, there was only one innocent and perfect man, Jesus Christ. The sacrifices, performed by the Hebrews and the Chinese in the past, foreshadowed God's plan: sending His Kid 羔羊 (gao yang), as the ultimate sacrifice to die for our sins.

The Requirement of Sacrifice: Blood

For the life of the flesh is in the blood, and I have given it to you on the altar to make atonement for your souls; for it is the blood by reason of the life that makes atonement.
Leviticus 17:11

In Him we have redemption through His blood, the forgiveness of our trespasses, according to the riches of His grace, which He lavished on us.
Ephesians 1:7–8

血 (xue), ancient form ⽊, means "blood." From the verses above, it is clear that blood is both God's requirement and His provision, for it represents life. This correlation between blood and sacrifice is clearly seen in the Chinese character for "blood," which shows a drop of blood in a vessel used for sacrifice. The Chinese character for "vessel" is 皿 (min), ancient form ⽊. Chapters 4 and 5 of this book discuss sacrifice and blood covenants and show that the Chinese language and the Bible both use a similar symbol to depict blood and the act of sacrifice that is required to remove and make restitution for sin. At the Last Supper, Jesus also used this symbol when he took a cup of wine and said, "This is My blood of the covenant, which is poured out for many" (Mark 14:24).

The Result of Sacrifice: A Covenantal Relationship

[Jesus said:] "Drink from it, all of you; for this is My blood of the covenant, which is poured out for many for forgiveness of sins."
Matthew 26:27–28

(meng), ancient forms and , means "covenant." The first ancient form simply shows a cup with a drop of blood. The second ancient form and the current form both have 明 (ming) which means "bright" or "to declare" on top of the symbol for "cup" or "vessel" 迎 (min) below. The first ancient form shows that the ancient Chinese sealed their covenants with blood. The second ancient form shows that blood (the symbol of the cup containing blood at the bottom of the character) was a necessary part of a covenant, and that the covenant is proclaimed (明) to all, particularly before God, to ensure compliance by all parties involved. Although the word can be defined simply as "a contract," the dictionary also defines "covenant" as "God's promises to man." Therefore, the word connotes something far more serious than a simple contract. The Chinese character fully reflects the import of the word with its component parts: blood, cup, and a public declaration before witnesses, including God, who were expected to hold the covenant-makers accountable to their promises.

The ultimate covenant was the one proclaimed by Jesus at the Last Supper the night before His crucifixion. His words are quoted in the Bible verse above; Jesus announced that He was sealing His covenant with mankind with His own life, sealing His commitment to us with the shedding of his own blood! He gave Himself for the forgiveness of our sins, so that man might once again enjoy an intimate relationship with God.

The Result of Sacrifice: Righteousness

For not knowing about God's righteousness, and seeking to establish their own, they did not subject themselves to the righteousness of God. For Christ is the end of the law for righteousness to everyone who believes.
Romans 10:3–4

義 (yi), ancient form , means "righteousness." In this character, we can see the good news God has been trying to convey to man since the fall of Adam and Eve. That is, even though man sinned, God had a plan to rescue and restore him. This plan, simply stated, is the provision of a "scapegoat" on man's behalf: God would provide His own Lamb to pay the penalty for our sins. Some, like Abel,

chose to follow God's plan and accept His gift; others, like Cain, refused. God's plan is the way of the sacrificial lamb, and it can be clearly seen in the character for "righteousnes."

This character has three forms, and although they differ quite significantly, the core meaning is captured and retained. The ancient form shows a dagger slicing or piercing a lamb, suggesting the killing and sacrificing of a lamb. This shows that the ancient Chinese understood that righteousness comes with a price, and that price is the life of the sacrificial lamb because a person on his own cannot attain or achieve righteousness. The lamb was considered the finest sacrifice because it was viewed as pure and undefiled; it is a precursor to the ultimate sacrifice, God Himself in the form of His Son Jesus Christ.

In the traditional or complex form, the bottom half of the character shows a "hand" 手 on the left and a "spear" 戈 on the right, forming the word for "me": 我. In this form, the symbol representing "lamb" 羊, with its tail chopped off, sits over the symbol representing "me." Embedded within this ideogram is the idea of sacrifice. The "lamb above me" indicates that when people see "me" they first see the "lamb" above or over me. This suggests that the ancient Chinese understood that righteousness is not a personal character trait; rather, it is imputed. That is, they had the idea that righteousness or "right-ness" is the acceptance of the sacrificial lamb on one's behalf, as indicated by the "lamb" above "me." This concept is entirely consistent with the biblical teaching that righteousness cannot be earned, it is imputed; it is a legal state, not a personal trait. When God sees me, a sinner, through the shed blood of the Lamb that is Jesus Christ, He sees me as righteous; that is, I am righteous only because of the Lamb.

When Chairman Mao Tse-tung undertook a major overhaul of the Chinese language in the 1960s, thousands of characters were simplified, fundamentally altering much of China's written language. Unlike most of the simplified characters now in use, however, the modern form of "righteousness" used today was not a Maoist invention. His team of language experts recalled that this simplified form was already in use as a variant form in ancient times. During earlier times, this form was not popular because righteousness was then considered far too important a concept to be conveyed in such a simplistic manner. The simplified

form of "righteousness" is written this way: 义. Nonetheless, even this simplified form captures the same idea: the dot is a symbol for blood, which can be a reference to the blood involved when an animal sacrifice is made, foreshadowing the blood shed by Jesus Christ when He died on the Cross. The two crossed strokes can mean one of two things. First, it can be a pictograph of a cup, especially one that is used in a sacrifice. Or, it can be of "firewood," symbolizing the wood used for a burnt offering. So, even in this simplified form, the idea of righteousness that is attainable only through sacrifice still manages to come through.

Quite remarkably, this idea that righteousness always involves sacrifice is consistent in all three forms of this character preserved through the centuries of China's very long history.

A Special Sacrifice

> *He made Him who knew no sin to be sin on our behalf, so that we might become the righteousness of God in Him.*
> 2 Corinthians 5:21

> *For by one offering He has perfected for all time those who are sanctified.*
> Hebrews 10:14

犧 or 犠 (xi), means "a solid colored or perfect sacrificial animal, usually a calf or a lamb." It is used with 牲 (sheng) to form 掛牲, meaning "to sacrifice." This word further confirms the Chinese understanding of the biblical concept of righteousness through a sacrifice. The 牜 (niu) radical, which means "bull," was added to the Chinese word for righteousness 義 to form the ideogram for "a perfect sacrifice." Emperors used unblemished bulls for their sacrifices because these animals were more costly than all others and because the imperial sacrifices were made to cover the sins of the entire nation. Officials and ordinary people could use lesser sacrificial animals because these people were atoning only for their own individual offences. Clearly, the ancient Chinese understood that righteousness is imputed through an acceptable sacrifice, usually that of a perfect bull.

特 (te) in ancient times referred to a three-year-old bull in robust health,

the pick of the herd. This word in conjunction with 牲 (sheng), forming 特牲 (te sheng), appears in many places in the *Record of Rites* to indicate that the animal sacrifice offered by the emperor had to be this kind of special bull.[1] In time, 特 (te) took on a generalized meaning of being special, as in 特別 (te bie). Chapter 4 is devoted to a closer examination of the annual special sacrifice required of each emperor.

Acceptance of the Sacrifice by Faith

船 (chuan) means "big boat." From the concept of righteousness, we move to the story of Noah, who was considered a righteous man.

As in all ancient cultures, the Chinese too have a story of a great flood covering the earth. The Chinese character for "big boat" or "ark" tells exactly what happened during this great flood. The character is comprised of three parts: the left side is the symbol for "vessel" 舟 (zhou); in the upper right corner is the character for "eight" 八 (ba); and in the lower right corner is the character for "mouth" 口 (kou), which also means "person" or "people." So the implied meaning of this character is "eight people in a boat." When the ancient Chinese wanted to come up with a character to represent a big boat, they thought of the biggest boat that existed up to that time—and that was the boat that held eight people and pairs of all the animals. This correlates precisely with the biblical story of Noah: Noah and his wife, their three sons with their wives were the eight people who survived the worldwide deluge by taking refuge in the enormous ark that Noah built, in obedience to God's commandments and warning (Genesis 6:18; 7:7).

The Bible summarizes Noah's act of faith and resulting righteousness this way,

> *By faith Noah, being warned by God about things not yet seen, in reverence prepared an ark for the salvation of his household, by which he condemned the world, and became an heir of the righteousness which is according to faith.*
> Hebrews 11:7

Since the days of Adam and Eve, man has been in rebellion against God. God, however, wants us to return to Him and He has provided the way. Unfortunately,

1. Examples: 《禮記》 *The Record of Rites*, No. 10 Sacrificial Articles; 《復漢書》 *Record of Latter Han,* Annals No. 4.

during Noah's time, only Noah and his family accepted God's gracious offer. Today, this offer is still open to everyone. We need to get into the "boat." We can accept His offer or reject it. This is much more than an intellectual or emotional decision: It is a life choice. Those who accept it, do so by faith. It is a faith that believes in the character and nature of God, that He will do what He promises. It is also a faith that takes action, like the faith of Noah who built the boat in response to God's instructions. Finally, it is a faith that carries a reward; for Noah, it was a new life, not just for him but for his entire family. The choice is yours.

CONCLUSION

The fact that a few significant Chinese characters correlate to the Genesis record of man's sin and God's provision might be dismissed as circumstantial evidence. These characters by themselves may not prove that the ancient Chinese had a concept of the God of the Universe or that they were knowledgeable about the beginning of history and knew the Creation account. These characters should, however, compel us to seek further evidence within the Chinese culture to see if, in fact, the ancient Chinese worshiped the One True God. To not pursue this journey of discovery is to deny oneself the possibility of uncovering great truths with life-changing consequences.

The special message, embedded in the first Chinese characters by the ancient people who created them, is truly one of China's greatest treasures! It is, therefore, most appropriate to conclude this chapter with a quote from Swedish Sinologist Bernhard Karlgren, who was the first to use European-style principles of historical linguistics to study the Chinese language,

> *Language, literary language, is the greatest artistic creation of a civilized nation; it is not shaped by philologists at their desks, but by the giants of thought who have something to say to their contemporaries, and who carve their monuments from the solid granite of the spoken language.*[2]

2. Bernhard Karlgren, *Philology and Ancient China* (Philadelphia: Porcupine Press, 1926, 1980), p. 167.

FINDING GOD IN ANCIENT CHINA

REFLECT and RESPOND

God is an active Communicator. His "fingerprints" are all over the world. He has not stopped speaking to us. Have you seen Him in Chinese characters? Have you seen Him around you today? If not, ask Him to open your eyes to His active participation in your life.

Chinese block printing as depicted in the "Tribute to Chinese History" mural at the Millennium Monument in Beijing.

叁

3

A Name Above All Names

The Chinese stand out distinctly from all other heathen nations in that their representations of Shang Di are consistent throughout. And no other is ever made "equal or second" to Him. He has no rival.

~ James Legge, first Professor of Chinese at Oxford University

3

A Name Above All Names

In the Hebrew and Chinese cultures alike, parents pick names for their children based primarily on the meaning of a name rather than on how it sounds. This chosen name often reflects the parents' hopes and aspirations for their child, whether in terms of worldly success or good character. The name "Jesus" is perhaps the best example of this, because it means "Savior." In the Bible story about Jesus' birth, God told Joseph, "You shall call His name Jesus, for He will save His people from their sins."[1] Also in both cultures, a person may change his name to match an apparent change in his character or position in life. For example, Abram, the forefather of the Jews and the Arabs, was renamed Abraham, which means "father of a multitude." The Chinese had a similar practice: when an emperor ascended the throne, he assumed a new name.

With this understanding of the importance placed on the meaning of a person's name in both the Hebrew and Chinese cultures, it behooves us on our journey of discovery to study the names that the Hebrews and the Chinese gave to their supreme deity, the one who was the primary object of their worship. These names reflect the attributes of this Creator of the Universe, who has no physical form and cannot be represented in any physical way. That being so, He can only therefore be known and worshipped through an understanding of His nature and His attributes. The Hebrews often were mocked by idol worshipers, who could not comprehend this unseen God, and challenged them to "Show us your God." In response, the psalmist wrote,

1. Matthew 1:21.

Photo at left shows the *Huang Tian Shang Di* (Supreme Lord of the Great Heaven) tablet inside the Prayer Hall for Good Harvest at the Altar of Heaven complex in Beijing.
Credit: Dong Yali

Finding God in Ancient China

Not to us, O LORD, not to us,
But to Your name give glory,
Because of Your lovingkindness, Because of Your truth.
Why should the nations say,
"Where, now, is their God?"
But our God is in the heavens;
He does whatever He pleases.
Their idols are silver and gold,
The work of man's hands.
They have mouths, but they cannot speak;
They have eyes, but they cannot see;
They have ears, but they cannot hear;
They have noses, but they cannot smell;
They have hands, but they cannot feel;
They have feet, but they cannot walk;
They cannot make a sound with their throat.
Those who make them will become like them,
Everyone who trusts in them.
Psalm 115:1 – 8

The attributes of the Creator God are among the most important truths we can learn in this life. The reason, as stated by the psalmist, is that we become like the object of our worship: If we worship dumb idols, we will become dull in our senses — spiritual, mental, emotional, as well as physical!

The Creator God, as revealed in the Bible, is an invisible yet personal and living Spirit. He is distinguished from all other spirits by attributes that can be categorized in these ways. Metaphysically, God is self-existent, eternal, and unchanging. Intellectually, He is all-knowing and wise. Ethically, God is just, opposed to evil, and merciful. Emotionally, He is loving, compassionate, and patient. Relationally, God is active in human affairs and in guiding and reconciling people to Himself. He is without limits, all-powerful, and ever-present.

Chapter Three  A Name Above All Names

The ancient Chinese knew and worshipped One with similar attributes. Among all the beings that the Chinese worshipped over a period of several thousand years, there was One who stood out, One who was so preeminent in His attributes that we today can recognize Him as the same God revealed in the Bible. Incredibly, the Chinese people did not attempt to make an image of this One whom they worshipped. Although many idols can be found in Chinese society, nowhere is there a single image or physical form of this Supreme Being. God in the Hebrew Scriptures proscribed such images; the Chinese evidently adhered to the same ban.

This was another signpost in my journey of discovery, where I learned important details about this One whom the ancient Chinese acknowledged as "A Name Above All Names." Here, I discovered even more points of correlation between the Chinese and Hebrew historical records.

THE CONCEPT OF GOD IN ANCIENT CHINA

Archaeological evidence has confirmed the existence of the earliest Chinese dynasties, which previously were believed to be mythical. Oracle bone inscriptions and other artifacts from archaeological excavations have traced the Shang Dynasty 商朝 (c. 1765 – c. 1122 B.C.), to the period of Emperor Wu Ding 武丁 (c. 1352 B.C.), which is contemporaneous with the period of biblical history when Joshua led the nation of Israel. These findings also show that the Shang had a well-developed religion even at the very beginning of their history. Artifacts reveal that they believed in three classes of spirits:

> Di 帝 – Lord, or Shang Di, 上帝 — Lord on High;
> shen 神 nature, spirits; and
> zu xian 祖先 — ancestors.

The concurrent existence of these three classes of spirits seems to contradict theories suggesting that the Shang religion evolved progressively from worship of gods of nature to ancestral worship and finally to worship of the one Supreme God.[2] In fact, Shang Di was from the very beginning revered by the Shang people as the all-powerful and supreme Deity.[3] It is true that there were times in China's history when the people forgot Shang Di, the God who gave them life as a nation, but His supreme position in Chinese history is without question.

2. Much research exists to refute this theory that religion evolved from polytheism to monotheism. See, for example, *The Dictionary of the History of Ideas: Studies of Selected Pivotal Ideas*, edited by Philip P. Wiener (New York: Charles Scribner's Sons, 1973, 1974), Volume 4, p. 96.

3. It is important to note that the Shang 上 in Shang Di is a different character from the Shang 商 in Shang Dynasty; therefore, Shang Di 上帝 is not the earliest human ancestor of the Shang Dynasty 商朝 as some have erroneously suggested.

The oracle bone inscriptions confirming the existence of the Shang Dynasty also reveal attributes credited to Shang Di by the Shang people. These writings suggest that the Shang people believed He could command enemies to invade a degenerated Shang nation as punishment. This indicates that Shang Di was not merely seen as the ruler of the Shang people only, but was regarded as the Sovereign of the surrounding nations as well. These inscriptions have also corroborated what we know about the Shang Dynasty from Confucius' five *Classics* 五經 and Sima Qian's *Historical Records* 史記. The Shang people acknowledged that Shang Di governed the wind, clouds, thunder, drought, and rain; thus He also governed the success or failure of agriculture.

A classic illustration of this is the Hong Fan chapter of the Zhou History in the *Classic of History*. "Hong Fan" 洪範, literally means "Great Model," and scholars consider it a key text from which to gain insights into ancient Chinese politics, culture, and philosophy. In this chapter, King Wu 武王 of the Zhou Dynasty 周朝, conqueror of the Shang Dynasty, sought advice from an able former Shang minister Ji Zi 箕子 known for his wisdom in governance. Ji Zi's instruction includes the observation that Shang Di is sovereign and governs the natural elements and that Shang Di's displeasure is provoked when mankind destroys the environment.

> Ji Zi [箕子] answered saying, "I understand that in antiquity, Ji [鯀] was responsible for stopping the floods but he did so by haphazardly rearranging the five natural elements. His acts provoked the anger of Di. [Di] withheld the Great Model consisting of nine principles [from Ji]. Therefore the principles of government were corrupted. Ji died in exile. Yu [禹] was raised up. Heaven gave the nine principles of the Great Model to him. The nine principles of government were thus established."

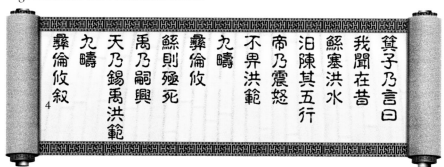

彝倫攸敘 九疇 天乃錫禹洪範 禹乃嗣興 鯀則殛死 彝倫攸 九疇 不畀洪範 帝乃震怒 汩陳其五行 鯀堙洪水 我聞在昔 箕子乃言曰

4. 《尚書-周書-洪范》 *Classic of History*, Zhou History, Hong Fan, paragraph 3.

Compare this understanding of Shang Di with the God of the Hebrews,

> *In the generations gone by He permitted all the nations to go their own ways;*
> *and yet He did not leave Himself without witness, in that He did good and*
> *gave you rains from heaven and fruitful seasons, satisfying your hearts with*
> *food and gladness.*
> Acts 14:16 – 17

The Shang people also believed Shang Di governed the construction of cities, the outcome of wars, and the well-being and misfortune of human beings. Amazingly, despite such powers, Shang Di received no cultic or manipulative worship. This suggests that His will was too inscrutable to be influenced by mankind.[5] Shang Di was the Sovereign One. Shang Di had the ultimate authority over the human world. For Shang Di to exert such influence on Shang society, He must have been very real to them and thus very immanent.

The Shang Dynasty was conquered by the Zhou Dynasty (c. 1122 – 249 B.C.), which replaced them as the ruling dynasty. The Zhou also worshipped a supreme Deity, but they knew Him by the name Tian 天 (Heaven). When the Zhou people compared Shang Di to their Tian, it was clear to them that they worshipped the same God as the Shang people. Hence, they for a long time used the two terms interchangeably, but toward the end of their dynastic reign, the Zhou used Tian almost exclusively.

Like the Shang, the Zhou people believed that the Creator God was near and active in their midst. The *Encyclopaedia Britannica* confirms that this is a deep-rooted worldview in its entry on "Confucianism: The Historical Context,"

> *They believed that the mandate of Heaven (the functional equivalent of the will*
> *of the Lord-on-High) was not constant and that there was no guarantee that*
> *the descendants of the Chou royal house would be entrusted with kingship,*
> *for "Heaven sees as the people see and Heaven hears as the people hear"; thus*
> *the virtues of the kings were essential for the maintenance of their power and*
> *authority. This emphasis on benevolent rulership, expressed in numerous*
> *bronze inscriptions, was both a reaction to the collapse of the Shang dynasty*
> *and an affirmation of a deep-rooted worldview.*[6]

5. "China, History of: State and Society." Encyclopædia Britannica, from *Encyclopædia Britannica Ultimate Reference Suite 2004 DVD*. Copyright © 1994 – 2003 Encyclopædia Britannica, Inc. May 30, 2003.

6. "Confucianism: The Historical Context." Ibid. "Lord-on-High" is the translation of Shang Di, and Chou is another way to transliterate Zhou.

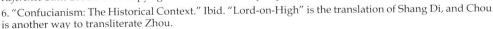

Currently, we have no conclusive evidence from archaeology or ancient literature as to the origin of the concepts "Tian" and "Di." This is perhaps because the ancient Chinese considered the Supreme Being, Shang Di, to be eternal, having no beginning or end: whether known as Shang Di or Tian, He has always existed.[7]

THE NAME SHANG DI, DI, and TIAN

So who is this Shang Di, Di, or Tian?

A single root word, "di" or "ti" can be isolated in languages and language families worldwide. It is a language factor or morpheme that indicates:

- the name of God.
- a common noun for deities.
- sacred concepts.
- an honorific title for ancestors or kings.

As a morpheme, it is present in the early "cuneiform" clay tablets (dating back to 3000 B.C.) that were excavated in the Middle East. It is common in the Indo-European family of languages as well. English uses "deity" as a generic term to refer to a God supreme as well as to gods. "Deity" is derived from the Latin word *Deus*, which immediately suggests the Italian *Dio*, the French *Dieu*, the Spanish *Dios*, the old Irish *Dia*, the Welsh *Duw*, the Breton *Doue*, the Lithuanian *Dievas*, the Lettish *Dieus*, the Sanskrit *Dyu*, the Greek *Theos*, etc.[8]

The language factor "di" or "ti" is present as a complete word both in isolating languages[9] such as Chinese and inflectional languages such as English. It is used as a prefix, suffix, or infix in languages as diverse as Finnish and Navajo. Certainly, its ubiquity is strong evidence that this linguistic factor spread worldwide from a single, common source.[10]

The three names used for the supreme deity in China—Shang Di, Di, and Tian— all contain this same universal morpheme for "deity." These three terms cannot be easily separated for discussion because they often are used interchangeably.[11] Shang

---

7. K. C. Wu in *The Chinese Heritage* (New York: Crown Publishers, 1981), pp. 7, 45, documented evidence that Tian was known in China even before the Zhou Dynasty and was not just the Supreme Being of the Zhou. See his footnote 17.

8. Gordon Holmes Fraser, "The Gentile Names of God," in *A Symposium of Creation (Volume V)*, ed. Donald W. Patten (Grand Rapids, Mich.: Baker Book House, 1975), pp. 22–27.

9. An isolating language is one in which each word form consists typically of a single morpheme.

10. This calls to mind the account in the Hebrew Scriptures of the confusion of languages at the Tower of Babel. It was from this single spot that mankind, which had until then spoken one language, was dispersed to the far reaches of the world.

11. James Legge, *The Religions of China* (New York: Charles Scribner's Sons, 1881), pp. 8–11.

Chapter Three  A Name Above All Names

Di was the most common name for God during the Shang Dynasty. 上 (Shang) in Shang Di means "above" or "supreme" and 帝 (Di) means "Lord," "Emperor," or "God." Thus, Shang Di would mean "the Sovereign above all other rulers" — wholly appropriate to refer to the supreme God!

The *Kang Xi Imperial Dictionary*[12] reveals more of the richness of these names. It gives the first meaning of 上 (Shang) as "above, upon, to honor, to esteem highly." The second meaning given is "sovereign" or one "most high" or "most honorable"; the third is "first in order." Therefore, when this term is applied to a ruler, it means "most high" and "most honorable"; when applied to Heaven's potentate, it is correct to translate it as "supreme."

The same dictionary reveals another interesting aspect of the Chinese terms for deity. The word 帝 (Di) is related to "諦," which is also pronounced "di." This "di" has a "speech" radical 言 (yan) to differentiate it from its root word. As we saw in Chapter 2, a radical in written Chinese is a part of a character that narrows or further defines the word. This "di" 諦, with a "speech" radical means "to judge," "to examine carefully," "to inspect precisely," "to separate between right and wrong," and it is primarily used as a noun, "a judge."[13] This shows that embedded in the Chinese word for "a judge" is a reference to a moral God who defines for man the standard of right and wrong, just and unjust. This same attribute is shared by the God of the Bible, who is called "the Judge of all the earth."

> *"Far be it from You to do such a thing, to slay the righteous with the wicked, so that the righteous and the wicked are treated alike. Far be it from You! Shall not the Judge of all the earth deal justly?"*
> Genesis 18:25

Here is another clue about this character 帝 (di) and why it means the Creator God in Chinese. Recall the pictographic and ideographic basis of the Chinese language. The pictogram for 帝 (di) has two possible origins.[14] First, it looks like the bud of a flower, and indeed originally was the word for "bud." As this character is now used to mean "deity," the original word for bud has been given a "flower" radical, hence, 蒂. If this interpretation is accurate, then the inventor of this character was depicting the creating power of God: a flower bud is the beginning of a new life. Indeed, Di is the Creator of the Universe and the Giver of Life. Another explanation is that the

12. Published by Emperor Kang Xi 康熙, in 1716.
13. W. H. Medhurst, *A Dissertation on the Theology of the Chinese with a View to the Elucidation of the Most Appropriate Term for Expressing The Deity, in the Chinese Language* (Shanghai: The Mission Press, 1847), pp. 257–59.
14. 王宏源：《字裏乾坤》華語教學出版社 2000. Wang Hong Yuan, *The Origins of Chinese Characters Zi Li Qian Qun* (Beijing: Sinolingua, 2000), p. 56.

pictograph shows a burnt offering with a stack of wood and a sacrifice. Such an association between this act of worship and the earliest form of the character for Di lends further credence to the view that the Chinese have been worshipping Di since the very beginning of their civilization.

As for the name 天 (Tian), or Heaven, few would dispute that it can be used to refer to God. Not only is this done quite frequently in the Bible itself,[15] it is common even in spoken English today, as in "Oh, heaven help us." For the Chinese, Shang Di has come to be used as a personal name for God, while Tian seems to be more of an abstraction. According to *The Great Chinese Electronic Encyclopedia*, the use of Tian to refer to the sovereign Ruler of the Universe goes as far back as the Xia Dynasty 夏朝 (c. 2207 – c. 1766 B.C.), China's very first dynasty! This encyclopedia also points out that while it may refer to the physical sky, in its most ancient usage and its usage in a large number of cases in the Chinese *Classics* the term can only mean "deity."[16]

Tian was often used in the *Classics* in a broad, indefinite sense, similar to the way "Heaven" is substituted for "God" in English when saying such things as, "Heaven helps those who help themselves." According to *Ci Yuan* 辭源, a dictionary of the etymology of Chinese words, Tian was listed as "head," in the sense of "leader" or "chief" or "person in charge," in *Shuo Wen Jie Zi* 説文解字, the first Chinese dictionary.[17] Such a meaning is reflected in the original pictograph of the character Tian, which is comprised of "one" — who is over or above "great" 大. In other words, Tian is the One above the greatest of all. The *Classic of History* states that Tian destroyed the Xia Dynasty because of its accumulation of sins, suggesting that Tian is the Sovereign, the Head, who executes judgment on the nations of the world.

Though Shang Di and Tian are two different terms used to refer to God, they point to the same Person. Zheng Xuan 鄭玄, a scholar of the Han Dynasty 漢朝 (206 B.C. – A.D. 220), puts it very simply in a commentary in the *Historical Records*,

> *Shang Di is another name for Tian. The spirits do not have two Lords.*

> **上帝港，天之別名也，神無二主。**[18]

---

15. See Psalm 73:9; Daniel 4:26; Matthew 21:25; Luke 15:18; 20:4; etc.

16. "Philosophy: Tian" *The Great Chinese Encyclopaedia* (Beijing: Dong Fang Ding Electronic Publisher, 2000), Volume 1, Version 1.1.

17. "Tian," *Student Ci Yuan* (Beijing: Beijing Electronic Publisher, 1991, electronic version 2000).

18. 《史記-卷二十八-書六-封禪書》 Sima Qian, Historical Records, Volume 28, Book 6, p 624. Throughout this book, we refer to 《中華歷史文庫》 (*Library of Chinese Histories*, Electronic ed.) as our source for *Historical Records, Han History,* and *Zi Zhi Tong Jian.*

Chapter Three A Name Above All Names

Shen or Spirits

The Chinese use another term for deities: 神 (shen). In one English-Chinese dictionary, the Chinese word "shen" is given in the entry for "god" (lower case "g"). For the entry "God" (capital "G"), it gives the Chinese word Shang Di or Di. Under the English word "Almighty," it also lists Shang Di.[19] Another dictionary gives this definition for 神 (shen): "any being regarded as or worshipped as having power over nature and control over human affairs; image in wood or stone, etc., to represent such a being." Under 上帝 (Shang Di), however, the definition is "creator and ruler of the universe."[20] Herbert A. Giles, considered one of the greatest Sinologists, gives this definition of 帝 (Di) in his 1912 dictionary: "God; the Supreme Ruler of the universe; a god; a deified being, such as a deceased emperor. The emperor; the supreme ruler on earth or vice-regent of God."[21] So we see that the word Di by itself can refer to gods, emperors, or God, but Shang Di always refers to the Creator God. While the Chinese recognized that there are many spiritual beings, i.e. "shen," only One is Supreme in their mind, and that One is Shang Di, also at times called Tian.

It is important to point out that in English there is also a major distinction between "God" and "gods" or a "god"; these terms also reflect a difference in rank between "God" and "god." Likewise, in the Bible, there is one Almighty God as well as other spiritual beings, and their relationship is clear in biblical psalms and poetry such as these:

> *Your people grow stronger, / and you, the God of gods, / will be seen in Zion.*
> Psalm 84:7 (CEV)

> *Remember the former things long past, For I am God, and there is no other;*
> *I am God, and there is no one like Me.*
> Isaiah 46:9

It appears, then, that the dictionaries are in agreement about the definition of "Shang Di" and "shen." In light of the accepted premise that dictionaries reflect the understanding and common usage of the general public, we can conclude that there is a general understanding among the Chinese people of Shang Di as the supreme Creator God and of "shen" as lesser spirits. As we shall see below,

85

19. A. P. Crowie and A. Evison, *Concise English-Chinese, Chinese-English Dictionary* (Hong Kong: Oxford University Press, 1986), pp. 186, 385, 391.
20. 《牛津高級英英, 英漢雙解辭典》 A. S. Hornby, E. V. Gatenby and H. Wakefield, *The Advanced Learner's Dictionary of Current English,* Second Edition with Chinese translation.
21. Herbert Allen Giles, *Chinese-English Dictionary* (London, Shanghai: A. H. de Carvalho, 1912).

Shang Di is the same Creator God worshipped by the Hebrews as Yahweh and by the Christians as Jesus. He has not left Himself without witness in China!

THE ATTRIBUTES OF GOD

When we look at what the ancient Chinese knew of Shang Di and at the kind of relationship they had with Him and He with them, we can say with confidence that Shang Di parallels the Creator God of the Hebrews and Christians. The picture that emerges dovetails so neatly and corresponds so closely with the One described in the Hebrew and Christian Scriptures that we can recognize Him as one and the same.

That picture is created by comparing Shang Di's attributes as recorded in the Chinese *Classics* with the biblical revelation of God's attributes. These attributes are the distinguishing characteristics of His divine nature that form the basis for His interactions with mankind. Only by taking all these attributes together can we gain a proper understanding of the nature and person of the One True God. It is important to understand that His attributes are not the same as His works or manifestations. They do not "add" anything to Him; rather they reveal His nature. Though we consider individual attributes below, it is the totality of them that reveals His complete nature, and we do not give any single attribute precedent over another.

Our attempt to compare these divine attributes as revealed in the Chinese *Classics* and the Bible cannot, in the limitations of this brief chapter, be exhaustive. Nor will we be able to provide the context for the passages from which we are quoting. Thus, some readers may object that what we cite here are only those texts that support our supposed preconceived ideas. It is our hope that those who question the validity of these comparisons would themselves study the context of the passages quoted to determine whether our conclusions have sufficient basis.

Others may object that these quotes from the Chinese *Classics* do not represent the concept of God that is common among Chinese today. Indeed, that is precisely our point: this classical knowledge of God in many ways perfectly mirrors the biblical revelation of God's attributes; the fact that Chinese today have misconceptions about these divine attributes does not nullify the knowledge the ancient Chinese once had of the One True God.

Chapter Three  A Name Above All Names

According to Dr. William Henry Medhurst, a leading Sinologist in the early 1900s, Shang Di is mentioned 175 times in the Chinese *Classics*. In only one instance is the term used in reference to human rulers. In all the other cases, it is a reference to the Creator God, and in only one of these references is anything disparaging said of the Creator God. From these references, it is possible to determine whether Shang Di possesses the same attributes as the God revealed in the Bible. Medhurst goes on to say,

> In no case do we find Shang-ti exhibited under any figurative representations; indeed, we are warned against confounding him with the images in the temples; while the Supreme Ruler is declared, again and again, to be distinct from the visible heavens. The main idea attached to Shang-ti is universal supremacy, uncontrollable power, justice, glory, majesty, and dominion.[22]

Another widely respected authority on China, James Legge, whose translations of the Chinese *Classics* are quoted throughout this book, came to the same conclusion as Medhurst. In 1852 he wrote,

> But the Chinese stand out distinctly from all other heathen nations in these two points–that their representations of Shang-Te are consistent throughout, and that they never raise any other being to an approximation to Him. He is always the same–the Creator and Sovereign Ruler, holy and just and good. And no other is ever made "equal or second" to Him. He has no rival.[23]

There are several ways to categorize the attributes of God. For our purposes, we will divide them into natural attributes and moral attributes. God's natural attributes are those that He alone possesses. His moral attributes are those that He has communicated to mankind, the crown jewel of His creation. We share in His moral attributes, but only as a distorted image or poor representation. Our responsibility is to grow in these attributes by the regenerating power that comes from knowing Him personally and intimately:

(The translations below from the Chinese Classics *are all adapted from James Legge's original English translation completed in the mid-1800s. We have*

22. W. H. Medhurst, *A Dissertation on the Theology of the Chinese with a View to the Elucidation of the Most Appropriate Term for Expressing The Diety in the Chinese Language* (Shanghai: The Mission Press, 1847), pp. 273–74. Shang-ti and Shang-Te are older transliterations of Shang Di, the modern standard.

23. James Legge, *The Notions of the Chinese Concerning God and Spirits* (Hong Kong: Hong Kong Register, 1852; reprinted by Ch'eng Wen Publishing Company, Taipei, 1971), p. 33.

revised this authoritative translation to make the language more accessible to modern readers. The Chinese that follows the English translation below is the text as found in the Classics. *The meaning of many of the words of this ancient text is quite different from the written Chinese in use today. Though most people will not be able to understand this ancient text, we provide it here to show that these passages indeed are part of the* Classics. *Many of the modern Chinese translations of these ancient texts have excised the passages that mention Shang Di. This is one reason why so many Chinese themselves, even scholars of these texts, are ignorant of the truth of the prevalence and the dominance of the belief in Shang Di in ancient times.)*

God's Natural Attributes

God Is Sovereign: God is sovereign in that He has a will and nothing can happen unless He allows it. While we are free moral agents, we are, nevertheless, subject to His sovereign will and purposes. He is ultimately in control, although He may work silently and indirectly. The Bible, in speaking of Jesus, says,

> *From His mouth comes a sharp sword, so that with it He may strike down the nations, and He will rule them with a rod of iron; and He treads the wine press of the fierce wrath of God, the Almighty. And on His robe and on His thigh He has a name written, "KING OF KINGS, AND LORD OF LORDS."*
> Revelation 19:15–16

The Chinese concept of the Mandate of Heaven is the best reflection of their understanding that Shang Di or Tian has a sovereign will. This concept will be examined in detail in Chapter 7, but simply stated, this mandate is the undeniable will of God in the choice of human government. The Chinese *Classics* further reveal that the ancient Chinese understood Shang Di or Tian to be sovereign in His appointment of human government.

> *The conclusive appointment of Heaven rests on your person; you must eventually ascend the throne of the great sovereign*
> 天之歷數在汝躬，汝終陟元後。[24]

24. 《尚書-虞書-大禹謨》 *Classic of History*, Book of Yu, Counsels of Great Yu, end of paragraph 14.

O bright and high Heaven
Who enlightens and rules this lower world!

明明上天，照臨下土。²⁵

Di establishes the kingdoms and rulers,
from Tai Bo to King Ji.

帝作邦作對，自太沾、王季。²⁶

The Mandate was from Heaven,
Mandating the throne to King Wen,
establishing his capital and the Zhou Dynasty.

有命自天，命此文王，于周于京。²⁷

Therefore Shang Di gave the right to rule to King Wen.

瞻時上帝，集厥命子文王。²⁸

God Is Eternal: The word "eternal" has two meanings. The first is figurative, denoting existence that has a beginning but no end; this is the case for angels and human souls. The second is literal, referring to an existence that has neither beginning nor end. God's existence is of the second type, for He is without beginning or end. God is not limited nor bound by time: He is before time and beyond time; He is above all temporal restraints. The psalmist expresses His eternity this way:

Before the mountains were born
Or You gave birth to the earth and the world,
Even from everlasting to everlasting,
You are God.
Psalm 90:2

The Chinese have a concept of eternal life as well. The *Book of Poetry* says of the emperor, "May the Son of Heaven live forever 天子萬年."²⁹ The Chinese believed that virtuous rulers would live in the presence of Shang Di; hence, they must have considered Shang Di to be eternal. Consider this, for example:

King Wen lives above,
his virtues shine in heaven.

25. 《詩經-小雅-北山之什-小明》 *Classic of Poetry*, Xiao Ya, Anecdotes of Beishan, Xiao Ming.
26. 《詩經-大雅-皇矣》 Ibid., Da Ya, Huang Yi, paragraph 5.
27. 《詩經-大雅-文王之什-小明》 Ibid., Anecdotes of King Wen, Da Ming, Chapter 11, verse 1.
28. 《尚書周書-文侯之命》 *Classic of History*, Book of Zhou, The Charge to Prince Wen, middle of paragraph 1.
29. 《詩經-大雅-荡之什-江漢》 *Classic of Poetry*, Da Ya, Anecdotes of Tang, Jiang Han, Chapter 5, verse 4.

FINDING GOD IN ANCIENT CHINA

Though our Zhou nation is old,
God's Mandate is still with us.
The Zhou nation was not established
when the time of Di's mandate had not arrived.
King Wen's soul is active
and he lives in the presence of Shang Di.

文王在上，於昭于天。周雖舊邦，其命維新。有周不
顯，帝命不時。文王陟降，在帝左右。[30]

Sima Qian's authoritative *Historical Records* covers a period of history from c. 2400 B.C. to c. 721 B.C. and nowhere does it attempt to explain the origin of Shang Di or Tian. Therefore, it would not be illogical to conclude that the ancient Chinese believed Shang Di to be without beginning or end and that they always considered Him the Supreme God.

God Is Immutable: God is immutable in that He does not change; He does not need to change because He is perfect. He does not change in His Being, His perfections, His purposes, and His promises. The Bible quotes God saying,

> *For I, the LORD, do not change; therefore you, O sons of Jacob, are not consumed.*
> Malachi 3:6

The Chinese *Classics* show an understanding of the immutability of Shang Di. This understanding forms the basis of trust and stability in generations of Chinese society.

> *Only Shang Di is inscrutable. He will shower blessings on those who do good. He will pour down calamities on those who do evil. We must not neglect to do small acts of righteousness because it is by the accumulation of these that the nations celebrate. We must not neglect to avoid small acts of unrighteousness because it is by the accumulation of these that an entire generation is corrupted.*

惟上帝不常，作善降之百祥，作不善降之百殃，爾惟德，
罔小，萬邦惟慶，爾惟不德，罔大，墜厥宗。[31]

Shang Di is constant in His principles, but He is flexible in how He deals with men. As He is consistent, He expects us to remain faithful in all things.

90

30. 《詩經-大雅-文王之什-文王》 Ibid., Anecdotes of King Wen, King Wen, verses 1–2.
31. 《尚書-商書-伊訓》 *Classic of History*, Book of Shang, Instructions of Yi, paragraph 8, verse 2.

Chapter Three  A Name Above All Names

God Is All-Powerful: God is all-powerful in that He is able to bring to pass all that He wills. God's power accepts no bounds or limitations unless He establishes limitations for His own purposes. That which He intends to do, He will accomplish. His omnipotence implies His ability to control entire nations and domains. The biblical Job said of God,

> *I know that You can do all things,*
> *And that no purpose of Yours can be thwarted.*
> Job 42:2

Shang Di warned the people of coming calamities by "signs" in the heavens.[32] When the rulers of the Xia Dynasty became corrupt, He replaced them with the Shang Dynasty. Then He exhibited His power again when He removed from power the more numerous Shang people and handed the kingdom to the Zhou Dynasty.

> *The descendants of the Shang [Dynasty]*
> *were in number more than hundreds of thousands;*
> *But when Shang Di gave the command*
> *they became subject to the Zhou [Dynasty].*

商之孫子，其麗不億。上帝既命，侯于周服。[33]

Almighty Heaven has given this middle kingdom with its people and territories to our ancestral kings. Our present ruler must use virtue to rally and to guide the obstinate remnant of the [Yin] people.

皇天既付中國民、越厥疆土于先王，肆王惟德用和懌先後迷民。[34]

We also find this in the *Classic of Poetry*:

> *Mysteriously Almighty Heaven*
> *is able to strengthen anything*

藐藐昊天，無不克固。[35]

God Is All-Knowing: As God is perfect, so He knows all things perfectly well. He knows all things actual and possible, past and present and future. God's knowledge

32. 《尚書-夏書-胤征》Ibid., Book of Xia, Punitive Expedition of Yin, paragraphs 1–4.
33. 《詩經-大雅-文王之什-文王》 *Classic of Poetry*, Da Ya, Anecdotes of King Wen, end of Chapter 4.
34. 《尚書-周書-梓材》 *Classic of History*, Book of Zhou, Timber of Zi Tree, paragraph 6.
35. 《詩經-大雅-蕩之什-瞻仰》 *Classic of Poetry*, Da Ya, Anecdotes of Tang, Homage, Chapter 7, verse 4.

is intuitive and immediate; it is not acquired and does not come through His senses. He knows all things at once. The psalmist expressed his awe of God's knowledge this way:

> *O LORD, You have searched me and known me.*
> *You know when I sit down and when I rise up;*
> *You understand my thoughts from afar.*
> *You scrutinize my path and my lying down,*
> *And are intimately acquainted with all my ways.*
> *Even before there is a word on my tongue,*
> *Behold, O LORD, You know it all.*
> *You have enclosed me behind and before,*
> *And laid Your hand upon me.*
> *Such knowledge is too wonderful for me;*
> *It is too high, I cannot attain to it.*
> Psalm 139:1 – 6

Since God is all-knowing, there is no running from His judgment, as these passages from the *Classics* acknowledge:

> *Heaven is all-intelligent and observing, let the godly [emperor] imitate Him, then his ministers will honor him and the people will be governed well.*

粮天聰明，粮聖時憲，粮臣欽若，粮民從。[36]

> *Heaven sees as my people see; Heaven hears as my people hear.*

天視自我民視，天聽自我民聽。[37]

> *O almighty Shang Di,*
> *You come to us in Your majesty,*
> *You discern all that is happening*
> *for the peace of the people.*

皇矣上帝
臨下有赫
監視四方
求民之莫[38]

36. 《尚書-商書-説命中》 *Classic of History,* Book of Shang, The Charge of Yue, Middle Section, paragraph 3.
37. 《尚書-周書-泰誓中》 Ibid., Book of Zhou, The Great Declaration, Middle Section.
38. 《詩經-大雅-文王之什-皇矣》 *Classic of Poetry*, Da Ya, Anecdotes of King Wen, Huang Yi, verse 1.

God Is Ever-Present: God is present everywhere; that is very different from those who say that God is in everything, which is pantheism. Put another way, God is not present everywhere in a bodily sense; His presence is a spiritual rather than a material presence. Nonetheless, it is a real presence. His ever-presence speaks of His immanence, filling all space, including the planet earth. His center is everywhere and His circumference is nowhere. There is no escaping God's presence. This is how God Himself expressed it to the Old Testament prophet Jeremiah:

> *"Am I a God who is near,"* declares the LORD, *"and not a God far off?*
> *Can a man hide himself in hiding places / So I do not see him?"* declares the LORD.
> *"Do I not fill the heavens and the earth?"* declares the LORD.
> Jeremiah 23:23 – 24

A common Chinese saying goes, "The net of Heaven is vast but loose, yet nothing can escape from it 天網恢恢，疏而不漏." In the *Classic of History*, God's ever-presence is expressed this way:

> *Shang Di is revered because His will extends to the nine limits [i.e., everywhere].*
>
> 上帝是祖，帝命式于九圍。[39]

God Is Infinite: God is beyond measure. He transcends all spatial limitations. There is a distinction between God's ever-presence as explained above and His infiniteness. His ever-presence emphasizes His immanence, while His infiniteness emphasizes His transcendence of space. Unlike creatures that are defined by space, the Creator is beyond these limitations and localizations. When the Hebrew king Solomon finished building a massive, ornate temple for God, he exclaimed,

> *But will God indeed dwell on the earth? Behold, heaven and the highest heaven*
> *cannot contain You, how much less this house which I have built!*
> 1 Kings 8:27

The fact that the Chinese already recognized Shang Di as all-powerful, all-knowing, and ever-present implies that they considered Him to be infinite as well. The Chinese *Classics* recognize this specifically by saying,

> *Heaven gave birth to the multitudes,*
> *and is vast enough to govern all creation with rules and principles.*
>
> 天生桑民，有物有則。[40]

39. 《禮記–孔子–閑居》 *Record of Rites*, Confucius, Xian Ju, verse 29.
40. 《詩經–大雅–蕩之什–蒸民》 *Classic of Poetry*, Da Ya, Anecdotes of Tang, Multitudes of People, top of paragraph 1.

Only the mandate of Heaven
is absolute and eternal, majestic and infinite.

維天之命，于穆不已。[41]

O vast and great Heaven,
who is called our parent.

悠悠昊天，曰父母且。[42]

God's Moral Attributes

While God's natural attributes are uniquely His, He has shared His moral attributes with human beings. The Bible tells us that we are made in the image of God and according to His likeness (Genesis 1:26, "Then God said, 'Let us make man in our image, after our likeness …'").

God is Love: God is love in that He is eternally moved to communicate His affections to His creatures. This love is not an impulsive emotion but a rational and voluntary affection that is grounded in His righteousness and truth. God's love does not consider the worth of the object of His love, even if His love is not reciprocated. His love is objective rather than emotionally based; yet, it is not devoid of emotions. Jesus' disciple John wrote this of God's love,

> *The one who does not love does not know God, for God is love. By this the love of God was manifested in us, that God has sent His only begotten Son into the world so that we might live through Him. In this is love, not that we loved God, but that He loved us and sent His Son to be the propitiation for our sins.*
> 1 John 4:8–10

That kind of love is unknown to those who worship idols; in their religions, fear is used to bring submission to the gods. Although God's kind of love is hardly seen in traditional Chinese society today, the *Classics* do speak of His love for His creatures. This is rather amazing and runs counter to the tenets of popular Chinese religions, which require supplicants to placate an array of petty, temperamental, and fickle gods. These religions also demand that worshippers present the gods

41. 《詩經-頌-周頌清廟之什-維天之命》 Ibid., Praise, Anecdotes of Zhou Praise of Qing Miao, Wei Tian Zhi Ming, beginning of Chapter 1.
42. 《詩經-小雅-小旻之什-巧言》 Ibid., Xiao Ya, Anecdotes of Xiao Min, Qiao Yan, beginning of Chapter 1.

and spirits with pleasing and sometimes costly offerings. In general, these religions operate on a system of rewards and punishments rather than on unconditional love and grace.

Heaven loves the people, the ruler should honor Heaven.

粮天惠民，粮辟奉天。[43]

Heaven protects and establishes you ... that you may enjoy every happiness.

天保定爾，亦孔之固，俾爾單厚，何福不除。[44]

God Is Holy: The basic meaning of holiness in the Bible is "set apart" or "separation." God is completely apart from all that is evil and all that contaminates. His holiness speaks of His perfection, purity, and the absolute sanctity of His nature. His holiness pervades all other attributes because it sets Him apart from us and reveals Him in His majestic splendor. This is the one attribute that God seems to want us to remember more than any other. That is because our view of Him and our perception of our need for Him are greatly influenced by our view of His holiness. A low view of His holiness will result in a careless relationship with Him. In truth, God is so holy that we cannot reach Him through our own means. The Hebrews said of their God,

> *Who is like You among the gods, O Lord? / Who is like You, majestic in holiness, / Awesome in praises, working wonders?*
> Exodus 15:11

And the prophet Isaiah said,

> *For thus says the high and exalted One / Who lives forever, whose name is Holy, "I dwell on a high and holy place, / And also with the contrite and lowly of spirit / In order to revive the spirit of the lowly / And to revive the heart of the contrite."*
> Isaiah 57:15

The Chinese *Classics* greatly exalt virtue, especially virtue in the rulers. When a ruler was not virtuous, it was a sign that he had lost the Mandate of Heaven. It was said of Yu 禹, the first emperor of the Xia Dynasty (whose reign began about 2207 B.C.),

> *It is virtue which moves Heaven. There is no distance to which it does not reach.*

43. 《尚書-周書-泰誓中》 *Classic of History*, Book of Zhou, The Great Declaration, Middle Section, paragraph 4.
44. 《詩經-小雅-鹿鳴之什-天保》 *Classic of Poetry*, Xiao Ya, Anecdotes of Lu Ming, Tian Bao, Chapter 1.

Pride brings loss, humility brings rewards. This is the way of Heaven.

惟德動天， 無遠弗屆， 滿招損， 謙受益， 時乃天道。[45]

Speaking of him, the *Classic of History* says,

*Among the ancients who exemplified this fear there was the founder of Xia Dynasty.
When his house was at its strength, he sought for able men to honor Shang Di.*

古之人迪惟有夏， 乃有室答兢， 吁俊尊上帝。[46]

So we see here that Emperor Yu, who was called Great Yu and was the first emperor of China's very first dynasty, maintained a holy fear of God. The following passages from the *Classics* speak of this same holy fear:

The king twice bowed low, then arose and said, "I am utterly insignificant and but a child; how can I govern the four quarters of the empire with such a reverent awe of the dread majesty of Heaven?"

王再拜興， 答曰， 眇眇予末小子， 其能而亂四方， 以敬忌天威。[47]

If you find no evidence on examination, do not listen to the case any further. In everything stand in awe of the dread majesty of Heaven.

無簡不聽， 具嚴天威。[48]

But Heaven was not with him because he did not seek to exemplify His virtue. Throughout the world, regardless of whether a nation is big or small, its demise is a judgment of its disobedience.

惟天不， 不明厥德， 凡四方小大邦喪， 罔非有辭于罰。[49]

*My illustrations are not taken from things long past;
Great Heaven makes no mistakes.
If you go on to corrupt your virtues,
you will bring great distress to the people.*

取譬不遠， 昊天不忒。 回遹其德， 俾民大棘. [50]

The bright and glorious Shang Di,

45. 《尚書-唐書-大禹謨》 Classic of History, The Book of Tang, The Counsel of Great Yu, middle of paragraph 21.
46. 《尚書-周書-立政》 Ibid., Book of Zhou, Establishment of Government, paragraph 2, verse 2.
47. 《尚書-周書-顧命》 Ibid., Book of Zhou, The Testamentary Charge, end of paragraph 25.
48. 《尚書-唐書-呂刑》 Ibid., The Book of Zhou, Punishment of Prince Lü, end of paragraph 17.
49. 《尚書-唐書-多士》 Ibid., Book of Zhou, Numerous Officers, verse 11.
50. 《詩經-大雅-蕩之什-抑》 Classic of Poetry, Da Ya, Anecdotes of Tang, Yi, paragraph 12, verse 4.

He will provide us with an abundant year.

明昭上帝，迄用康年。 [51]

God Is Full of Grace: Grace can be described as the unmerited favor of God to those who deserve punishment. Specifically, this grace is shown in God's gift of salvation through Jesus Christ, who enables us now to freely enter into an eternal relationship with God Himself. The grace of Jesus gives us life instead of the death that we deserve because of our sins. Though grace is unearned favor, it must be accepted through faith in Jesus. As the Apostle Paul explains,

> *Therefore, having been justified by faith, we have peace with God through our Lord Jesus Christ, through whom also we have obtained our introduction by faith into this grace in which we stand; and we exult in hope of the glory of God.*
> Romans 5:1–2

An emperor is expected to exhibit grace; hence, the phrase "隆恩浩大" (long en hao da) or "abundant grace," which was used only in reference to the sovereign. In fact, everything he did was supposed to be done with grace, benefiting his subjects. Such grace can only come from the Creator God, as shown in the passages below (in each example, "grace" has been translated as "favor" for a smooth reading in English).

> *Great Heaven has graciously favored the House of Shang, and granted to you, O young king, at last to become virtuous, this is truly a great thing for generations to come.*
>
> 曁天眷佑有商，簿嗣王克終厥婕，窗萬世無疆之休。 [52]

> *There is peace throughout our numerous regions, there has been a succession of plentiful years, Heaven does not weary in its favor.*
>
> 餒萬邦，遷豐年，天命匪解。 [53]

> *Shang Di regarded her with favor, without injury or hurt, her months were complete. She gave birth to Hou Ji,*

51. 《詩經-頌-臣工之什-臣工》 Ibid., Praises, Anecdotes of Chen Gong, Chen Gong, paragraph 1.
52. 《尚書-商書-太甲中》 *Classic of History*, Book of Shang, Tai Jia, Part 2, verse 2.
53. 《詩經-頌-閔于小之什-桓》 *Classic of Poetry*, Tribute, Anecdotes of a Child, Wen Yu, Huan, verse 1.

who received all His blessings.

上帝是依， 無災無害， 彌用不遲。 是生后稷， 降之百福。[54]

God Is Faithful: God is faithful in that He will not fail us nor does He break any of His promises. His faithfulness is established from everlasting to everlasting; it is also established in His eternal covenant. While unfailing in keeping His covenantal promises, He lovingly overlooks our failures and forgives us. The Book of Lamentations in the Bible expresses God's faithfulness beautifully,

> *The LORD's lovingkindnesses indeed never cease, / For His compassions never fail. They are new every morning; / Great is Your faithfulness.*
> Lamentations 3:22–23

The Chinese have this common saying, "Good will return good, evil will return evil. If we do not receive what we deserve, it is because the season has not yet arrived 善有善報， 惡有惡報， 不是不報， 詩辰未到." The following selections from the Chinese *Classics* show the confidence of the Chinese people in God's faithfulness.

> *Heaven took notice of his virtue, and entrusted His great mandate on him, that he should calm and settle the great number of regions.*
> 天監厥德， 用集大命， 撫綏萬方。[55]

> *The ordinances of Heaven, –*
> *how deep are they and unceasing!*
> 維天之命， 于穆不已。[56]

> *Faithfulness is the way of Heaven, to be faithful is a man's way.*
> 誠者， 天之道也。誠之者， 人之道也。[57]

These passages show that the ancient Chinese understood that faithfulness is one of God's intrinsic attributes, and that it is man's responsibility to pursue faithfulness.

God Is Good: To be good means to have the disposition to promote happiness in others. The goodness of God is revealed in all of nature: The world around us is full of life designed to bring us enjoyment. Though sin has corrupted God's perfect creation, not a single thing exists in nature that was designed to bring pain for the

54. 《詩經-頌-魯頌-閟宮》Ibid., Tribute, Tributes of Lu, Palace of Bi, verse 3.
55. 《尚書-商書-太甲上》 *Classic of History,* Book of Shang, Tai Jia, Part 1, middle of paragraph 2.
56. 《詩經-頌-周頌-清廟之什-維天之命》 *Classic of Poetry,* Tribute, Tributes of Zhou, Anecdotes of Qing Miao, Wei Tian Zhi Min.
57. 《中庸》 *Book of Means,* Chapter 20, verse 18.

sake of pain! It is impossible for us to count all the ways God has designed this universe for our good and our happiness—the air we breathe, the water we drink, the fruit we eat, the beauty of nature, etc. God has shown us in a multitude of ways that He is good to us. The psalmist speaks of this goodness.

> *You prepare a table before me in the presence of my enemies;*
> *You have anointed my head with oil;*
> *My cup overflows.*
> *Surely goodness and lovingkindness will follow me all the days of my life,*
> *And I will dwell in the house of the* LORD *forever.*
> Psalm 23:5–6

Emperor Yu, the founder of the Xia Dynasty, attained the throne because

Almighty Heaven regarded him with His favoring mandate, Giving him all the four seas so that he reigns as ruler of all under heaven.

皇天眷命， 奄有四海， 爲天下君。[58]

This statement from the *Classic of History* reveals the goodness of Shang Di in blessing Emperor Yu and, through Yu's leadership, blessing the Chinese people. When the Xia Dynasty became corrupt and its rulers no longer exhibited the virtues desired by Shang Di, He raised up another ruler, Tang 暴, to reflect His character. This was said of Tang, the first emperor of the Shang Dynasty:

Tang, rising to the throne, greatly administered the bright ordinances of Shang Di.

亦越成汤陟， 丕厘上帝之耿命。[59]

God is good in that He also provides peace, comfort, and abundant grains for the people, as these passages from the *Book of History* show:

I have heard that God leads men to tranquil peace, but the Xia Dynasty did not pursue this kind of peace, so God sent down His judgment, indicating His mind to the Xia.

我聞曰， 上帝引逸， 有夏不適逸， 則惟帝降格， 向于時夏。[60]

What have you to seek for? How to manage the new abundant crops? How

58. 《尚書-唐書-大禹謨》 *Classic of History*, Book of Tang, The Counsel of Great Yu, end of paragraph 4.
59. 《尚書-周書-立政》 Ibid., Book of Zhou, Establishment of Government, paragraph 4, verse 2.
60. 《尚書-周書-多士》 Ibid., Book of Zhou, Numerous Officers, beginning of verse 5.

beautiful are the wheat and barley. Whose bright produce we shall receive!
The bright and glorious Shang Di will in them give us an abundant year.

亦又何求？ 如何新畬？ 于皇來牟。 奖受厥明， 明昭上帝， 迄
用康年。 [61]

The *Clasic of Poetry* also speaks of God blessing His creation.

Receive the blessing of Heaven.

受天之祜。 [62]

Receive the blessing of Di.

既受帝祉。 [63]

God Is Merciful and Compassionate: God's mercy and compassion speak of His goodness towards us in the midst of our misery or distress. It emphasizes His faithfulness despite our unfaithfulness. Mercy is usually expressed in connection with the guilt of the one who receives mercy. God is a God of second chances, and He will sacrifice at great cost for our temporal and spiritual well-being. His compassion guides Him to share in our sufferings, whether we suffer for good reasons or because of wrong acts. The psalmist says,

> *The LORD is compassionate and gracious,*
> *Slow to anger and abounding in lovingkindness.*
> *He will not always strive with us,*
> *Nor will He keep His anger forever.*
> Psalm 103:8 – 9

In dynastic China, family and friends of convicts were allowed to wait at the Imperial Palace gate used by the emperor in hopes of securing a pardon for the convicted friend or relative. Chinese of the imperial period expected the emperor to rule with justice, but they also expected that he would be merciful, giving his subjects second chances. This expectation extended to all levels of government, down to the very lowest, and it reflects their knowledge of the grace of Shang Di and Tian, as these passages show:

> *Oh! Heaven had compassion on people everywhere. His favoring mandate fell*
> *on our founding fathers. Let the king cultivate virtue and reverence.*

61. 《詩經-頌-臣工之什-臣工》 *Classic of Poetry*, Tribute, Anecdotes of Chen Gong, Chen Gong, Middle Section.
62. 《詩經-小雅-北山之什-信南山》 Ibid., Xiao Ya, Anecdotes of North Hill, Xin Nan Shan, Chapter 4.
63. 《詩經-大雅-文王之什-皇矣》 Ibid., Da Ya, Anecdotes of King Wen, Huang Yi, end of Chapter 4.

嗚呼。天亦哀于四方民。其眷命用懋。王其疾敬德。[64]

Great and discerning Heaven,
how could He not show compassion on us?

悼彼皇天，寧不我矜?[65]

God Is Just and Righteous: Righteousness and justice are extensions of God's holiness. They speak of His moral excellence. God will always do right. He executes His judgments impartially, and He does not have second thoughts. He does not act irrationally or with the whims and fancies characteristic of false gods, such as those in Greek and Roman mythology. God hates sin because of His righteousness and justice. This is why, to satisfy His own requirement for restoring man's broken relationship with Him, He had to send His Son to die in payment for our sins. With that, His righteousness and justice were satisfied. King David put it this way,

The Lord is in His holy temple;
the Lord's throne is in heaven;
His eyes behold,
His eyelids test the sons of men.
The Lord tests the righteous and the wicked,
And the one who loves violence His soul hates.
Upon the wicked He will rain snares;
Fire and brimstone and burning wind will be the portion of their cup.
For the Lord is righteous,
He loves righteousness;
The upright will behold His face.
Psalm 11:4–7

The Chinese *Classics* repeatedly teach that God judges rulers and kingdoms by their morals. His standard of right and wrong is absolute and unquestioned.

For the many sins of the Xia Dynasty, Heaven has given the charge to destroy them.

有夏多罪，天命殛之。[66]

During the Shang Dynasty, they also knew that a man must be righteous before God if he was to receive His blessing.

64. 《尚書-周書-召誥》*Classic of History*, Book of Zhou, Announcement of Duke Zhao, end of paragraph 10.
65. 《詩經-大雅-蕩之什-桑柔》*Classic of Poetry*, Da Ya, Anecdotes of Tang, Sang Rou.
66. 《尚書-商書-湯誓》*Classic of History*, Book of Shang, The Speech of Tang, end of verse 1.

In Heaven's inspection of men below, He first considers their righteousness. He bestows on them length of years or otherwise. Heaven does not cut short men's lives — they cut short their lives themselves.

惟天監下民，典厥義。 降年有永有不永。 非天禾民，民中絕命。[67]

The mandate [of Heaven] is not easily [preserved].
Do not cause your own destruction.
Proclaim and exhibit righteousness,
seeing how the fall of the Yin Dynasty was brought about by Heaven.

命之不易，無遏爾躬。宜昭義問，有虞殷自天。[68]

Surely those of whom Great Heaven disapproves
shall flow as waters from a spring,
drifting down together to ruin.

肆皇天弗尚，如彼泉流，無淪胥以亡。[69]

Of course, there were times when people would question God's justice. The book of Job in the Bible addresses that. That same tendency still exists today. When things go wrong, God is the first to be blamed. The following is a response from the *Classics* to those who questioned God's justice:

It is not Shang Di that has caused this evil time,
but it arises from Yin's not using the proven [ways].
Although you do not have old and experienced men,
there are still classic models [to guide you].
But you will not listen to them,
so the great mandate is overthrown!

匪上帝不時，殷不用舊。雖無老成人，
尚有典刑。曾是莫聽，大命以傾！[70]

God Is Wise: God's knowledge and His wisdom are intricately related. His wisdom allows Him to choose the proper ends and to accomplish those ends through proper means. His wisdom is declared by all creation, which abounds with remarkable examples of His perfect design. From the miniscule to the mammoth, nature displays

67. 《尚書-商書-高宗-日》 Ibid., Book of Shang, Day of Sacrifice of Gao Zong, beginning of verse 3.
68. 《詩經-大雅-文王之什-文王》 *Classic of Poetry*, Da Ya, Anecdotes of King Wen, King Wen, paragraph 7.
69. 《詩經_大雅-蕩之什-抑》 Ibid., Da Ya, Anecdotes of Tang, Yi, beginning of paragraph 4.
70. 《詩經-大雅—蕩之什-蕩》 Ibid., Da Ya, Anecdotes of Tang, Tang, paragraph 7, verse 2.

wonderful, marvelous designs—designs that reflect the best means to reach the best ends. Likewise, His perfect control in making all things work together for the best interests of His people has been displayed throughout history. The Apostle Paul thus exclaimed when he considered God's wisdom,

> *Oh, the depth of the riches both of the wisdom and knowledge of God! How unsearchable are His judgments and unfathomable His ways! For who has known the mind of the Lord, or who became his counselor? Or who has first given to Him that it might be paid back to him again? For from Him and through Him and to Him are all things. To Him be the glory forever. Amen.*
> Romans 11:33–36

A similar view is found in the way the *Classic of Poetry* describes Heaven or Tian, which we earlier established was another name for Shang Di:

> *Great Heaven is very intelligent.*
> 昊天孔昭。[71]

> *O intelligent and high Heaven, Who enlightens and rules the people below.*
> 明明上天，照臨下土。[72]

In both the Bible and the *Classics*, the desired virtue of wisdom is regarded as coming from God; it is not an innate human quality. The Bible says,

> *But if any of you lacks wisdom, let him ask of God, who gives to all generously and without reproach, and it will be given to him.*
> James 1:5

These excerpts from the *Classics* show that good rulers were regarded as having been given by God the wisdom to rule well:

> *Heaven gifted our king with valor and wisdom to govern the vast nation.*
> 天乃錫王勇智，表正萬邦。[73]

> *Examining the men of old, there was the founder of the Xia Dynasty. Heaven guided his mind, allowed his descendants to succeed him, and protected them. He acquainted himself with Heaven and was obedient.*
> 相古先民有夏。天迪從子保。面稽天若。[74]

71. 《詩經-大雅-蕩之什-抑》 Ibid., Da Ya, Anecdotes of Tang, Yi, paragraph 11, verse 1.
72. 《詩經-小雅-北山之什-小明》 Ibid., Xiao Ya, Anecdotes of North Hill, Xiao Ming, Chapter 1, verse 1.
73. 《尚書-商書-仲虺之誥》 *Classic of History*, Book of Shang, Announcement of Zhong Hui, middle of verse 2.
74. 《尚書-周書-召誥》 Ibid., Book of Zhou, Zhao Gao, beginning of verse 11.

FINDING GOD IN ANCIENT CHINA

This King Ji
was gifted by Di
with the power of judgment,
so that the fame of his virtue spread quietly.
His virtue was highly intelligent —
highly intelligent and discerning, able to lead
and rule such a great nation.

維此王季，帝度其达。貊其德畜。其德究明，
克明究類，克長究君，王此大邦。[75]

GOD OF OUR FATHERS

What riches this journey of discovery has already produced from a careful review of the writings that tell of China's ancient knowledge of Shang Di!

First, we established that Shang Di or Tian is the name by which the Creator God revealed Himself to China throughout her long history, whereas "shen" is a general term applied to many other spirits, including false gods. We saw that religion in China did not evolve from the lower forms of idolatry and nature-worship to monotheism and then to the worship of one benevolent and loving God. Rather, exactly the reverse is true. The eternal, sovereign God, Shang Di, is not a figment of people's imagination. Shang Di is a good, powerful, loving, and just Creator who revealed Himself to the founding fathers of the Chinese civilization before they fled the Tower of Babel in search of a homeland. He is the only eternal, ever-present God who has been revealing Himself throughout history to all the peoples of the world. He has revealed Himself through general revelation and special revelation, but has most clearly and powerfully revealed Himself through the Bible.

We have also seen that the good news of God's provision to reconcile mankind to Himself is not solely a Christian concept. It has roots in China's ancient past as well. God revealed Himself to the early Chinese by the name Shang Di, and the truth of that name is a call to return to God. In the same way, the Bible in many places refers to the Creator God as the God of our fathers, for He truly is the Father of all. When we are willing to return to our true spiritual roots in the Creator God,

75. 《詩經-大雅-文王之什-皇矣》 *Classic of Poetry*, Da Ya, Anecdotes of King Wen, Huang Yi, beginning of Chapter 4.

we will come to know Him personally through His special revelation in the Bible and in the person of the Lord Jesus Christ.

> *God, after He spoke long ago to the fathers in the prophets in many portions and in many ways, in these last days has spoken to us in His Son, whom He appointed heir of all things, through whom also He made the world.*
> Hebrews 1:1–2

Finally, we saw an abundance of references that strikingly show how the attributes of Shang Di (Tian) match those of the One True God of the Bible, leading us to the conclusion that Shang Di (Tian) is the general revelation to the Chinese people of the same God worshipped by the Hebrews of the Old Testament and the Christians of the New Testament. The English missionary James Legge, considered even by the Chinese themselves to be one of the leading scholars of the Chinese *Classics*, concluded, "The God whom they worship, we learn from His attributes, is the same whom we adore, as He has been pleased in much larger measure to reveal Himself to us."[76]

It is unfortunate, therefore, that the Chinese have not worshipped this God alone; they have also worshipped a multitude of other beings. Indeed, despite their knowledge of this true God, many Chinese all around the world have fallen under the power of a host of fearful superstitions and syncretistic religious beliefs. Just as in many other societies, there is among the Chinese a propensity to worship false gods. We say this not to criticize but simply to point out that the ancient Chinese once venerated the One True God, and to invite everyone, Chinese and others alike, to worship this God alone, as He demands, and to enjoy the blessing that results.

In the light of these truths about Shang Di, how unfortunate is the Chinese misconception that Christianity is a Western religion and that Jesus is a Western God! Now, however, with this new knowledge of Shang Di readily available, dismissing Christianity as a Western religion is no longer an acceptable excuse for not believing in Jesus.

> *Therefore having overlooked the times of ignorance, God is now declaring to men that all people everywhere should repent, because He has fixed a day in which He will judge the world in righteousness through a Man whom He has*

76. Legge, *Notions*, p. 33.

appointed, having furnished proof to all men by raising Him from the dead.
Acts 17:30 – 31

As I continued along my journey of discovery, the evidence mounted that the Shang Di of my native culture was the same Father God of my Christian faith. It was not, however, until God led me to the signpost of "The Great Sacrifice" that this mounting evidence was secured to a cultural construct that is an integral part of my Chinese heritage. God is ever faithful to reveal Himself if we truly seek Him. As I studied the Great Sacrifice, I became convinced that as I worship the Creator God of my Christian faith, I am indeed sharing in the faith of my fathers.

REFLECT and RESPOND

As wonderful as it is to know God, also called Shang Di, in all His divine attributes, we would be missing the point of it all if we remain at the threshold of entering into His family. Certainly, the attributes of God are most important to our knowledge of God. We can know Him intellectually in the way we may know many famous people and heroes. We can even imitate heroes and strive to be like them. But the question is: Do they know me? More important is the question, "Am I known by God?" If you do not know Shang Di personally, you can take the first step, by accepting Him into your heart. God's name is the name above all names. And the name that saves us is the name of Jesus, God's special revelation. We need to agree with God that Jesus is His Son and that apart from Jesus we cannot be forgiven of our sins. One day, at the name of Jesus, every knee will bow and every tongue confess that He is the King of kings, and Lord of lords. Why not do that now?

China's three most prominent ancient philosophers—Lao Zi, Mo Zi, and Confucius (foreground)—as depicted in the "Tribute to Chinese History" mural at the Millennium Monument in Beijing. These three 5th and 6th century B.C. Chinese philosophers all attempted to explain Shang Di, the Creator God, to their many followers.

肆

4 The Great Sacrifice

For an emperor, the most important task is to follow the principles of Heaven. In following Heaven, nothing is more important than the sacrifice at the border.

~From *The History of the Han Dynasty*

4

The Great Sacrifice

Although the imperial palace is the finest architectural ensemble in the capital, it is in the Temple of Heaven, or as the Chinese call it, "The Happy Year Hall," where the emperor used to offer annual supplication to Heaven for a prosperous new year, that we find a single building in which the simple dignity of Chinese architecture is at its best.[1]

This accolade, from a 1920 issue of *National Geographic* magazine, describes the Prayer Hall for Good Harvest 祈年殿 (Qi Nian Dian), the central feature of the Temple of Heaven complex in Beijing. This hall was the place where the emperors of the Ming 明 (1368–1644) and Qing 清 (1644–1911) dynasties prayed each spring for a bountiful harvest. The umbrella-like structure of three tiers stands on a six-meter-high (20-feet-high) white marble circular terrace; it is 32 meters (105.5 feet) tall and has a circumference at the base of 32.72 meters (108 feet). The passage of time has not eroded the architectural splendor of this masterpiece, which has been designated a World Heritage site by the United Nations Educational, Scientific and Cultural Organization (UNESCO). More important, however, than the awe-inspiring qualities of this unique architecture is its profound significance, a significance that can affect the destiny of individuals as well as of nations. What I learned at the Temple of Heaven was an epiphany, and set me on this journey of discovery.

1. "Peking: the City of the Unexpected," *National Geographic*, November 1920, Volume XXXVIII, No. 5, p. 341.

Photo at left shows the Prayer Hall for Good Harvest at the Altar of Heaven complex in Beijing.

Birds'-eye view of the Altar of Heaven, looking from south to north. Credit: Altar of Heaven Administration

ALTAR OF HEAVEN

The English name "Temple of Heaven " is actually a misnomer. The Chinese name, 天壇 (Tian Tan), should properly be translated "Altar of Heaven" as 天 (tian) means "heaven" and 壇 (tan) means "altar." Tian Tan was not built as, nor was it ever used as, a temple for Tian or Shang Di. This is an important distinction to understand at the outset. A temple, 廟 (miao), is used to house 神 (shen), that is, spirits, ancestors, and gods of Chinese folk religion. The word "miao" comes from 貌 (mao) or "image."[2] A "miao" is a place where the images of "shen" are kept.

The Altar of Heaven is entirely different. It was built for and was dedicated to the worship of Shang Di, who does not dwell in any structure built by man. Tian Tan does not contain a single image of Shang Di. The fact that the Chinese have never tried to contain Shang Di or Tian in any kind of building or other structure suggests

2. 《宋書上-志第七-禮四》 *The History of Song,* Volume 1, explains: "The *Book of Rites* says, 'Miao (temple) is as mao (image); the dwelling place of spirits.'" 《禮》曰，朝者，貌也；神靈所憑依也。

that they knew God to be infinite and ever-present. The ancient nation of Israel had a similar understanding. After King Solomon completed the building of a grand and ornate temple for God, he proclaimed in praise,

> *But will God indeed dwell with mankind on the earth? Behold, heaven and the highest heaven cannot contain You; how much less this house which I have built.*
> 2 Chronicles 6:18

The Altar of Heaven complex that still stands today is a tangible legacy of China's oldest religious practice—one that lasted 4,000 years. Not a single one of the eighteen dynasties[3] that ruled throughout China's long history failed in its obligation to worship Shang Di in this manner. Although there were long periods when portions of the ceremony were corrupted, every ruling family acknowledged the supremacy of Shang Di through this ceremony. As dynasties rose and fell and as the imperial capital was moved from place to place, the site where the emperors carried out this most important duty followed those moves. In the ancient capital of Xi'an, famous today for its partially excavated army of terra-cotta soldiers, an altar mound—a precursor to Beijing's Altar of Heaven—was discovered in 1999 and has been under restoration for several years with plans to eventually open it to the public. Xi'an was the imperial capital of at least five different dynasties; it is therefore not surprising that such an altar, central to the worship of Shang Di, was found there.

Altar Mound in Xi'an, under restoration.   Credit: Benny Yang

3. Historians disagree on the total number of dynasties because of differences in counting the dynastic houses that ruled during the periods when China was divided into warring states.

FINDING GOD IN ANCIENT CHINA

When Emperor Yong Le 永樂 (reign A.D. 1402–1424) of the Ming Dynasty moved the imperial capital from Nanjing to Beijing in the early 1400s, he constructed the Imperial Palace 故宮 (the Forbidden City) as well as the Altar of Heaven, both of which are among China's top tourist sites today. The site he chose for the Altar was close to the site of the previous Altar constructed by Emperor Cheng Zhong 成宗 (reign A.D. 1295–1307) of the Yuan Dynasty 元朝.[4]

The Altar of Heaven complex in Beijing measures 1.7 km (just over 1 mile) from east to west, and 1.6 km (1 mile) from north to south. With an area of about 273 hectares (674 acres), it is the largest place of Chinese religious activity and is the site of the world's largest altar dedicated to the worship of the Creator God. This complex was originally at least three times the size of the Forbidden City,[5] but the area today is only two-thirds of its Qing Dynasty size.

Completed in 1421, the Altar complex was repaired and expanded many times in the subsequent 400 years. The most extensive work was done during the reigns of two emperors: Ming Emperor Jia Jing 嘉靖 (reign A.D. 1522–1566) and Qing Emperor Qian Long 乾隆 (reign A.D. 1735–1796). According to records provided at the Altar complex, over a period of some 500 years, 22 emperors made 654 sacrifices to Shang Di at the Altar of Heaven, which today attracts hundreds of tourists daily.

West Entrance to the Altar Mound.

4. "Arts: Tian Tan," *The Great Chinese Encyclopedia* (Beijing: Dong Fang Ding Electronic Publisher, 2000), Volume 1, Version 1.1.

5. Ibid.

The Border Sacrifice

The vastness and unique quality of this architectural wonder suggest the great importance the emperors placed on the act of worship performed there. Confucius, who highly esteemed these rites in the worship of Shang Di, said,

> *The ceremonies of the celestial and terrestrial sacrifices are those by which men serve Shang Di.*

郊社之禮，所以事上帝也。⁶

This most important of ceremonies was performed by the emperor and was called the Border Sacrifice 郊祭 (jiao ji), because it usually took place on the southern outskirts (border) of the imperial city. It was also called the Ji Tian, that is, the Ceremony of Sacrifice to Heaven 祭天大典. The *History of the Han Dynasty*, one of the 26 volumes of the official dynastic histories dating back to approximately 1100 B.C., underscores the profound importance of this ceremony:

> *To an emperor, the most important thing is to follow the principles of Tian [Heaven].*
> *In following Tian, nothing is more important than the sacrifice at the border.*

帝王之事莫大乎承天之序，承天之序莫重于郊祀。⁷

This all-important ceremony can be traced to the most ancient of Chinese emperors. Grand Historian Sima Qian 司馬遷 confirmed in the *Historical Records* that sacrifices were performed at Mount Tai in coastal Shandong province by many ancient rulers.⁸ He also explained why it was called the Border Sacrifice:

> *In ancient times, the Son of Heaven [i.e., the emperor] of the Xia Dynasty personally and reverentially sacrificed to Shang Di at the border, that's why it is called the Border [Sacrifice].*

古者天子夏躬親禮祀上帝于郊，故曰郊。⁹

China's own historical records show that active worship of the supreme God, Shang Di, goes back to some of the earliest Chinese emperors and continued

6. 《中庸》*The Doctrine of Mean*, Chapter 19, verse 6.
7. 《二十六史–漢書二十五卷下—郊祀志第五下》*Twenty-Six Histories, History of Han Dynasty*, Volume 25, *History of the Border Sacrifice*, Volume 5, Part II, paragraph 3, verse 2. *The Twenty-Six Histories* is a collection of systematic histories of all Chinese dynasties from the Zhou Dynasty to the Qing Dynasty.
8. These emperors included Wu Huai 無懷氏, Fu Xi 伏羲, Shen Nong 神農, Emperor Yan 炎帝, Huang or Yellow Emperor 黃帝 (reign 2697–2599 B.C.), Zhuan Xu 顓頊 (reign 2514–2437 B.C.), Emperor Yao 堯 (reign 2357–2258 B.C.), Emperor Shun 舜 (reign 2257–2208 B.C.), Emperor Yu of the Xia Dynasty 夏禹 (reign 2207–2198 B.C.), Emperor Tang of the Shang Dynasty 商湯 (reign 1766–1754 B.C.), Emperor Cheng of the Zhou Dynasty 成王 (reign 1115–1079 B.C.). From Historical Records, Volume 28, Book 6, Feng Shan. 《史記–卷二十八–書六–封禪書》Sacrifices performed on Mount Tai were called Feng Shan, 封禪.
9. 《史記卷十本紀十孝文本紀》*Historical Records*, Volume 10, Chronicle 10, Xiao Wen and 《史記卷二十八書六封禪書》Volume 28, Book 6, Feng Shan.

through several thousand years until the collapse of the last dynasty in 1911. Not every emperor, however, was faithful in how he carried out this ceremony, and some added ideas of their own invention to this divine worship. Volume 25 of the *History of the Han Dynasty*, which is quoted above, gives a history of the Border Sacrifice. This historical account shows that corrupt emperors, that is, those rulers who failed to faithfully fulfill their obligations to the Chinese people, were also the ones who neglected the Border Sacrifice. This neglect was most likely indicative of an overall venal attitude that permitted and even encouraged a widespread corruption that consistently resulted in the collapse of that emperor's reign and the ascension to the throne of a virtuous ruler. The most serious recorded corruption occurred during the reign of Qin Shi Huang Di 秦始皇帝 of the Qin Dynasty (259–210 B.C.) and lasted for 1,500 years. During this long period, worship of several other gods was included in the ceremony.

A revival of the original religious practices took place at the beginning of the Ming Dynasty, that is, in A.D. 1368, when the emperor commissioned two committees to investigate the most ancient practices and rites related to the Border Sacrifice. As a result, sacrifices to false gods were abolished, thus reinstating the preeminence of Shang Di in this most sacred of Chinese religious ceremonies.[10]

THE BORDER SACRIFICE CEREMONY

The emperor was expected to sacrifice at the Altar of Heaven three times a year: at the beginning of spring to pray for a good harvest; at the beginning of summer to pray for rain; and at the winter solstice to sacrifice to Heaven. Of course, not every emperor was faithful in carrying out each of these three ceremonial responsibilities.

The most important of these sacrifices was the Border Sacrifice or Ji Tian, meaning "Sacrifice to Heaven," which was offered at the winter solstice, the shortest day of the year, that is December 21 or 22. Only the emperor could perform this sacrifice, which was the most sacred of all his religious responsibilities. Not only that, this was one duty the emperor could not and did not want to delegate, for this sacrifice confirmed him as the one who held the Mandate of Heaven, that is, the divine appointment to the throne.

10. James Legge, *The Notions of the Chinese Concerning God and Spirits* (Hong Kong: Hong Kong Register Office, 1852; reprint, Taipei: Ch'eng Wen Publishing Company, 1971), pp. 43–45.

Chapter Four   The Great Sacrifice

Some details of this sacrifice, particularly the prayer songs, are recounted below to highlight the profound significance of this ritual and to draw parallels with the worship of the Hebrew God of the Old Testament. It is important to point out that the origins of this ceremony predate the accounts recorded in the Old Testament of the sacrifices prescribed for the Israelites. So, although we are drawing parallels with the divinely inspired instructions recorded by Moses, we are not suggesting that the ancient Chinese were similarly instructed.

We do believe, however, that, as the account of Cain and Abel in Genesis suggests, the earliest generations of mankind had an understanding of the kind of worship and sacrifice that was acceptable to God. In Genesis 7, Noah, who lived long before Moses, did not question God about the difference between clean and unclean animals when God instructed him on the numbers of animals to carry into the ark; he already knew that certain animals were acceptable for sacrifice and others were not. His first act upon leaving the ark, as recorded in Genesis 8:20, was to build an altar and to sacrifice clean animals and birds. This understanding of appropriate worship and sacrifice was therefore likely to have been carried by those who fled the Tower of Babel to settle in the river valleys of China. The core principles of that understanding could have endured through the centuries in China and been preserved in the Border Sacrifice.

Recounted here is the Ming Dynasty (A.D. 1368 – 1644) version of the ceremony as recorded in *The Collected Statutes of the Ming Dynasty* 大命會典 (Da Ming Hui Dian).[11] Although specific details of the ceremony differed somewhat from dynasty to dynasty, it is instructive to note that the statutes of China's last dynasty, the Qing (A.D. 1644 – 1911), included documentation of this ritual that is identical to the Ming ceremony, except for slight alterations in the names of the songs. The invading Manchurian founders of the Qing Dynasty likely were motivated by the need to validate their claim to the Mandate of Heaven. Therefore, they not only continued to observe this ritual, but they also stayed faithful to the established prayers and rites. Furthermore, it is reasonable to presume that this was the case from very early in China's history; as each new dynasty came to power, its founders had a similar need to authenticate their claim to the Mandate and would have faithfully adhered to the details of this all-important ceremony, maintaining it relatively unchanged through thousands of years. The records of this Border Sacrifice and,

---

11. This is a historical collection of 228 volumes of the statutes, ceremonies and policies of the Ming Dynasty starting in 1497. The Qing Dynasty followed the example of the Ming and had its own *Da Qing Hui Dian* 《大清會典》, *The Collected Statutes of the Qing Dynasty.* Our reference is a copy of the woodblock copy published during the reign of Emperor Wan Li (A.D. 1573 – 1620).

in particular, the prayer songs from the ceremony, thus serve as another important signpost that reveals to us what the ancients believed about Shang Di, the One True Creator God.

Preparations for the Ceremony

Selection of the Sacrificial Animals: Three months before the day of the Sacrifice, officials went to the outskirts of the city to select unblemished sacrificial animals, usually calves.

Emperor's Proclamation: Six days before the Sacrifice, the emperor and many officers went to the Altar Mound and proclaimed the coming sacrifice,

> The reigning son of Heaven [i.e., the emperor] of the Great Ming Dynasty has solemnly prepared a proclamation to inform:
> The spirit of the great light [i.e., the sun]; The spirit of the night light [i.e., the moon]; The spirits of the five planets, the constellations of the zodiac, and of all the stars in all the heaven; The spirits of the clouds, the rain, wind, and thunder; The spirits which have duties assigned them throughout the whole heaven; The spirits of the five mountains and five hills; The spirits of the five guardians and five hills; The spirits of the five hills: Ji Yun, Xiang Sheng, Shen Lie, Tian Shou, Chun De; The spirits of the four seas; The spirits of the four great rivers; The spirits which have duties assigned to them upon the earth; All the celestial spirits under heaven; All the terrestrial spirits under heaven; The spirit presiding over the present year; The spirit ruling the tenth month, and the spirits over everyday; And the spirit in charge of the ground around the altar mound:
>
> On the first day of the coming month, I [the emperor] shall reverently lead my officers and people to honor the great name Shang Di, dwelling in the sovereign heavens, looking up to that nine-storied lofty blue sky. Beforehand, I inform you, all you celestial and all you terrestrial spirits, and will trouble you, on our behalf, to exert your spiritual influences, and display your vigorous efficacy, communicating our poor desire to Shang Di, and praying Him mercifully to grant us His acceptance and regard, and to be pleased with the title which we shall reverently present.

For this purpose I have made this proclamation for your information. All you spirits should be well aware of it. You are solemnly informed.

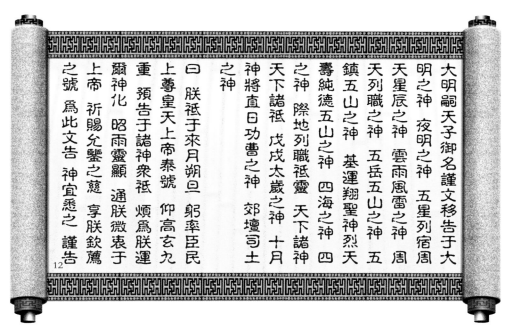

大明嗣天子御名謹文移告于大
明之神 夜明之神 五星列宿周
天星辰之神 雲雨風雷之神 周
天列職之神 五岳五山之神 五
鎮五山之神 基運翔聖神烈天
壽純德五山之神 四海之神 四
之神 際地列職祗靈 天下諸神
天下諸祗 戊戌太歲之神 十月
神將直日功曹之神 郊壇司土
之神
曰 朕祗于來月朔旦 躬率臣民
上尊皇天上帝泰號 仰高玄九
重 預告于諸神衆祗 煩爲朕運
爾神化 昭雨靈顯 通朕微衷于
上帝 祈賜允鑒之慈 享朕欽薦
之號 爲此文告 神宜悉之 謹告

It is important to note that in this proclamation, the emperor used the superlative "I," 朕 (Zhen), to refer to himself. This "I" (Zhen, which in the translation above we have indicated with a bold "**I**") was used by everyone as a first person reference before the 3rd century B.C. From the time of the first emperor of the Qin Dynasty (248–207 B.C.), however, it was reserved for use by the emperor alone; from then on, no one was allowed to refer to himself as "Zhen." The emperor, by using "Zhen," was addressing the spirits as their superior. In other words, the emperor did not consider these spirits worthy of his worship.[13] Notice, however, that when the emperor addressed Shang Di, he always used the inferior "Chen" 臣 to refer to himself. "Chen" literally means "a subject" and was used by a subject when referring to himself while in the presence of his emperor.

Just from this simple distinction in the choice of a pronoun, we see that even the

12. 《大清會典》 *The Collected Statutes of the Ming Dynasty*, Volume 82, pp. 22–23.
13. The tablets of these spirits and those of the ancestors were placed in secondary positions in various halls at the Altar complex and during the sacrifice ceremony; as this proclamation makes amply clear, they were not the objects of the emperor's worship.

emperor regarded Shang Di as his superior, the One and Only Sovereign. Equally important, his inclusion of the spirits in his proclamation was not so that he could worship them along with his worship of Shang Di. Rather, he called for all the spirits—not just one or even a few but all of them—to support him in his worship of Shang Di. In like manner, a psalmist of Israel summoned all creation and all spiritual beings to join in his worship of God,

> *Praise the LORD!*
> *Praise the LORD from the heavens;*
> *Praise Him in the heights!*
> *Praise Him, all His angels;*
> *Praise Him, all His hosts!*
> *Praise Him, sun and moon;*
> *Praise Him, all stars of light!*
> *Praise Him, highest heavens,*
> *And the waters that are above the heavens!*
> Psalm 148:1–4

Inspection of the Sacrificial Animals: Five days before the ceremony, a prince went to the location where the sacrificial animals were being held and inspected them to make sure each was without spot or blemish. This was such an important job that the emperor himself specifically appointed the prince who would undertake this responsibility, and the chosen prince was usually the emperor's brother.

The Hebrews were required to follow the same strict requirements in the selection of sacrificial animals. The Bible is very clear that God will accept only a clean, unblemished sacrifice. Consider, for example, this account of one of the very first sacrifices recorded in the Bible:

> *Then Noah built an altar to the LORD, and took of every clean animal and of every clean bird and offered burnt offerings on the altar.*
> Genesis 8:20

Later, God instructs the Hebrew nation,

> *Your lamb shall be an unblemished male a year old; you may take it from the sheep or from the goats. You shall keep it until the fourteenth day of the same*

month, then the whole assembly of the congregation of Israel is to kill it at twilight.
Exodus 12:5 – 6

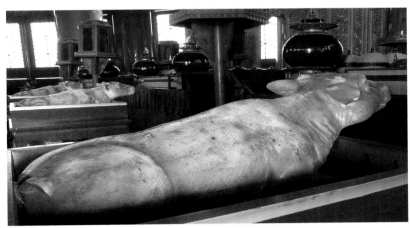

Replicas of unblemished sacrificial calves on display in the Prayer Hall for Good Harvest.   Credit: Dong Yali

Although these animals were unblemished, they were not the perfect sacrifice required by the Holy God to solve man's problem of sin once and for all. Such strict requirements were only a symbol for and a precursor of the ultimate sacrifice, Jesus Christ. It is unlikely that the Chinese emperors who carried out the ceremony understood that. What is clear, however, is that the Chinese shared with the Hebrews an understanding that God demanded propitiation for sin and required that it be a perfect and excellent sacrifice.

Emperor Begins Fast: Three days before the ceremony, the emperor began a fast. For two days, he fasted in his imperial palace, the Forbidden City, and on the final day at the Hall of Abstinence within the Altar of Heaven complex. This fast required the emperor to abstain from drinking wine and eating meat, to shun the company of women, and to refrain from enjoying any type of entertainment. To keep his mind pure, he did not handle any criminal cases. The objective was for him to be purified in body and soul, in thought and in deed. During this period of preparation, he wrote his prayers on wooden boards that would later be used during the sacrifice. Government officials joined him in this three-day fast at their official residences.

FINDING GOD IN ANCIENT CHINA

In ancient Chinese tradition, fasting was the most sacred of all religious behaviors. Of course, not all emperors took this seriously, but the faithful ones always did. Ming Emperor Hong Wu 洪武 was so conscientious that he had the Board of Rites cast a bronze statue of "the admonisher" to remind him of the gravity of his obligations. This bronze statue is displayed today in the Tower of the Bronze Fasting Figure 齋戒銅人亭 in the Fasting Palace 齋宮.

Bronze Fasting Figure

In the Bible, fasting is an important spiritual discipline that was modeled by Jesus as well as great men of faith such as Moses, David, Elijah, and Daniel. Fasting is very important in man's relationship with God because it is the outward expression of an inner attitude of repentance and of repudiation of physical desires. The Bible describes very clearly the kind of fast that God desires.

> *Is this not the fast which I choose,*
> *To loosen the bonds of wickedness,*
> *To undo the bands of the yoke,*
> *And to let the oppressed go free,*
> *And break every yoke?*

Painting showing an ancient Border Sacrifice Ceremony.

Is it not to divide your bread with the hungry.
And bring the homeless poor into the house;
When you see the naked, to cover him;
And not to hide yourself from your own flesh?
Isaiah 58:6 – 7

Emperor Inspects the Offerings: Two days before the Sacrifice, the emperor inspected the written prayers, jade offerings, and incense at the Hall of Great Harmony 太和殿 (Tai He Dian) within the Forbidden City. When the inspection was completed, the Royal Ceremony Guards transported these offerings to the Divine Treasure House at the Altar of Heaven complex, where they were stored in tents and on tables that had been set up the previous day.

Emperor's Procession to the Altar Complex: On the day before the Sacrifice, at 10 o'clock in the morning, the emperor left the Forbidden City by the Meridian Gate 午門 (Wu Men) with an impressive and colorful entourage—at times more than 5,000 strong—of cavalry, elephants, horses, guards, ministers, eunuchs, and attendants, all dressed in their regal attire. No women, not even the empress, were allowed to participate in this procession. Ordinary citizens were ordered to stay inside with their windows and doors shut—not allowed even a peek at this pageant. The procession was a very solemn event; no one and nothing was to profane it. Absolute silence was maintained along the entire 4.5-kilometer (3-mile) route to the Altar.

At the Imperial Vault of Heaven: The entourage entered the Altar of Heaven complex by the West Gate. All the princes, ministers, and officials who would assist in the Sacrifice moved to the Hall of Abstinence and waited respectfully outside the gate of the Hall. The emperor proceeded immediately to the Imperial Vault of Heaven 皇穹宇 (Huang Qiong Yu).[14]

Once inside the Imperial Vault, the emperor presented himself before a tablet inscribed with the Name Above All Names in China 皇天上帝 (Huang Tian Shang Di), meaning Supreme Lord of the Great Heaven.[15] With his face to the floor, China's emperor—the most powerful man in the most powerful nation of the world at

14. 皇 (Huang) means Great, 穹 (Qiong) means Sky or Heaven, and 宇 (Yu) means a Chamber or Hall. Literally Huang Qiong Yu means Hall of Great Heaven. It is 19.5 meters (64.5 feet) tall and 15.6 meters (51.5 feet) around at the base. Built entirely of wood, the building is supported by eight pillars.

15. In more ancient times, this supreme name was 昊天上帝 (Hao Tian Shang Di), which has the same literal meaning as 皇天上帝 (Huang Tian Shang Di). 昊 (Hao) means "bright" and 皇 (Huang) "great" or "imperial." In Chapter 8 we will relate how the first Great Emperor of the Qin Dynasty, Qin Shi Huang Di, usurped this title and this role.

FINDING GOD IN ANCIENT CHINA

Map of the Altar of Heaven Complex

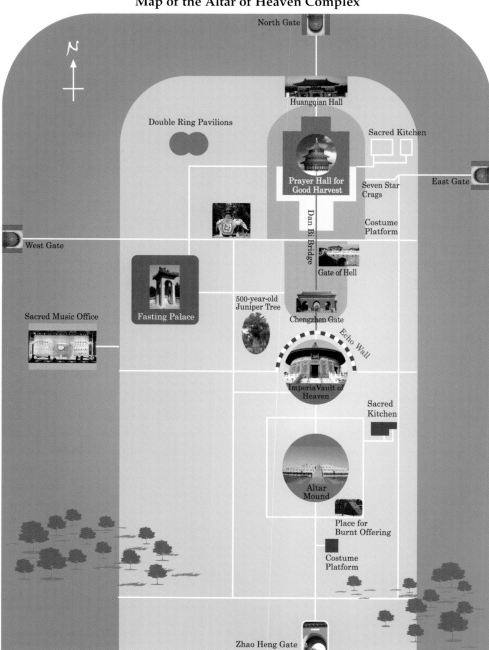

North Gate

N

Huangqian Hall

Double Ring Pavilions

Sacred Kitchen

Prayer Hall for Good Harvest

Seven Star Crags

East Gate

Costume Platform

West Gate

Dan Bi Bridge

Gate of Hell

500-year-old Juniper Tree

Fasting Palace

Chengzhen Gate

Sacred Music Office

Echo Wall

Imperial Vault of Heaven

Sacred Kitchen

Altar Mound

Place for Burnt Offering

Costume Platform

Zhao Heng Gate

The Imperial Vault of Heaven.

Inside the Imperial Vault, the tablet with the name of the Supreme of the Great Heaven is displayed in its place of honor in the middle of the hall.

that time—humbled himself to worship and burn incense to Shang Di. He accorded Shang Di the highest honor by kneeling three times and kowtowing three times with each kneeling, for a total of nine kowtows.[16] Kowtowing is but an outward expression of an inner attitude of humility, shown by the emperor only before Shang Di. The Bible also teaches that God requires humility in man's worship of Him.

> *He has told you, O man, what is good;*
> *And what does the Lord require of you But*
> *to do justice, to love kindness, And to walk*
> *humbly with your God?*
> Micah 6:8

The Chinese characters on the right side of this tablet read: *Huang Tian Shang Di*, which means Supreme Lord of the Great Heaven.
Credit: Dong Yali

Imperial Site Inspections: The emperor then proceeded to the Altar Mound 圓丘 (Yuan Qiu) to inspect the altar and the sacrificial paraphernalia already assembled and arranged there. It is at the Altar Mound that the rites of the Great Sacrifice were performed. The Altar Mound is 5 meters (16.5 feet) tall and made entirely of white marble; white marble balustrades adorn each of its three tiers. Three enormous lanterns were hung on poles of 9 zhang 丈, 9 chi 尺, 9 cun 寸,[17] on the west side of the mound. The number 9 symbolizes eternity or longevity because it is a homophone for the Chinese character for "eternity";[18] it is also considered the symbol of the "Most High" or the "Greatest" because it is the highest and greatest number.[19] The lanterns were 8 chi (or feet) tall, 6 chi wide; inside each was a huge candle, 1 chi wide and 4 chi tall, that could burn for 12 hours. They were lit at midnight and competed with the moon to illuminate the night sky. Large jade gongs were hung on a nearby stand entwined with a beautiful golden dragon.

From the Altar Mound, the emperor went to the Divine Treasure House and the Divine Kitchen to inspect the sacrificial vessels, offerings, and animals. Everything

---

16. This most humble form of worship consists of kneeling and prostrating three times, face down with forehead touching the ground; the prostrations were themselves repeated three times.

17. One zhang is about 1 yard; 1 chi is nearly 1 foot; 1 cun is about 1 inch.

18. The pronunciation in Chinese for both the number 9, which is written as 九, and the word for "eternal" 久 is "jiu."

19. Traditionally, on the 9th day of the 9th month, Chinese celebrated the holiday 重陽节 (Chong Yang Jie) by "ascending to the heights" 登高.

had to be done to perfection, because only a perfect sacrifice was good enough for Shang Di. The offerings had to be of one solid color, either white or red or black, because the solid color symbolized unity and purity. The animals, as already noted, had to be without blemish.

In the Old Testament, God also required the Hebrews to sacrifice only unblemished animals, a foreshadowing of the perfect sacrifice of Jesus Christ. Such sacrifices were intended to reflect an inner attitude of reverence and submission, as suggested in this psalm:

> *The sacrifices of God are a broken spirit;*
> *A broken and a contrite heart, O God, You will not despise ....*
> *Then You will delight in righteous sacrifices,*
> *In burnt offering and whole burnt offering;*
> *Then young bulls will be offered on Your altar.*
> Psalm 51:17, 19

In the Hall of Abstinence: After completing the inspections, the emperor went to the Hall of Abstinence. Once he had entered, the princes, ministers, and officials who had been waiting outside the gate of the Hall to assist in the sacrifice moved to their respective places of service to complete their preparations.

Inside the Hall of Abstinence, the emperor continued his fast and bathed himself with fragrant water; both were purification rites to demonstrate respect to Shang Di. These rituals suggest an awareness that man needed to be purified in body, mind, and soul in preparation for coming into the presence of Shang Di. The Bible has the same emphasis.

> *Who may ascend into the hill of the LORD?*
> *And who may stand in His holy place?*
> *He who has clean hands and a pure heart,*
> *Who has not lifted up his soul to falsehood*
> *And has not sworn deceitfully.*
> Psalm 24:3 – 4

At midnight, service officials lit the lamps throughout the Altar of Heaven complex and brought the sacrificial offerings from the Divine Kitchen to the Altar Mound.

The Day of the Sacrifice

The day began seven quarters — or an hour and 45 minutes — before sunrise; since the sun rises at about 6:00 a.m. at the winter solstice, the time would have been about 4:15. The Master of Ceremonies, a cabinet minister known officially as the Tai Chang Si 太常寺, came to the Hall of Abstinence to wake the emperor. The emperor changed into ceremonial robes of plum-colored silk, a black satin cap, and blue satin boots and left the Hall of Abstinence in a ceremonial sedan chair. The bell of the Hall of Abstinence rang continuously to announce the beginning of the Sacrifice and to summon all service personnel to readiness at their posts. The emperor was carried in his sedan chair to the south gate of the inner wall where, in the specially erected Great Tent, he changed into sacrificial robes used exclusively for this ceremony. The robes were made of "bo" 帛, a silk of the highest quality that was so precious that it was used for gift-giving purposes between nations, usually as a peace offering.[20] A parallel can be drawn between the emperor's donning of the sacrificial robes and the Old Testament Levitical priests' robes that set them apart as the high priests of their nation. The color and design of these robes worn during Hebrew religious ceremonies symbolized the presence of God with his people.

Before leaving the Great Tent, the emperor washed his face and hands in a golden basin and then proceeded to the Altar Mound. Here the tablet for 皇天上帝 (Huang Tian Shang Di), Supreme Lord of the Great Heaven, and tablets for the spirits and for

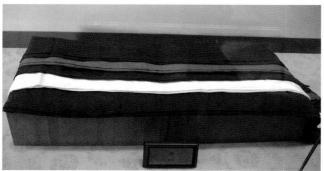

the imperial ancestors were arranged under blue tents. It is of vital importance to note that the tablets for the spirits and ancestors occupied positions secondary to the tablet for the Supreme Lord of the Great Heaven. This is the same subordinate rank the spirits received in the proclamation issued by the emperor six days earlier.

Bo silk, the highest-quality silk, was one of the many precious sacrifices offered to Shang Di during the Border Sacrifice ceremony.

20. This practice is behind the Chinese proverb, "Turning weapons into jade and bo 化干戈爲玉帛."

The three-tiered Altar Mound, the site of the Border Sacrifice each Winter Solstice.

The spirits and ancestors were invited to join in the worship of Shang Di; they were not in any way themselves the objects of worship.[21] This ceremony was clearly dedicated to worship of Shang Di alone.

The contemporary painting showing the Altar Mound at midnight of Winter Solstice.
Credit: Altar of Heaven Administration.

21. Emperor Kang Xi 康熙 of the Qing Dynasty defended the presence of these ancestral tablets by saying, "There was no idea, when an ancestral tablet was erected, that the soul of the ancestor dwelt in that tablet. And when sacrifices were offered to Heaven it was not the blue existent sky that was addressed, but the lord and creator of all things. If the ruler Shang-ti was sometimes called Heaven, T'ien, that had no more significance than giving honorific names to the emperor." Cited by Jonathan Spence, *Emperor of China, Self-Portrait of K'ang-Hsi* (New York: Random House, Vintage Books Edition, 1988), p. 79.

The Nine-Stage Great Sacrificial Ceremony

Stage 1: Welcoming Di 迎帝神

Based on his rank and function, each of the princes, ministers, musicians, and ceremony officials had a designated spot on or around the Altar Mound; all faced north, a reflection of their inferior position.[22] The emperor was led reverently by the Master of Ceremonies to the second-tier platform on the south side of the Mound, where he stood before a yellow canopy facing the shrine for Huang Tian Shang Di. This shrine was located on the top tier. (Position 1 of Altar Mound diagram on p. 133.) The emperor's position on the middle tier (Position 17) suggests that his role in this ceremony is that of a mediator between God and the people of the nation placed in his care. This was a foreshadowing of the role of Jesus Christ:

> For there is one God, and one mediator also between God and men, the man Christ Jesus, who gave Himself as a ransom for all, the testimony given at the proper time.
> 1 Timothy 2:5–6

The bell of the Hall of Abstinence stopped ringing, to signal the beginning of the first stage of the ceremony: the welcoming of Shang Di. Pine and cypress branches were burnt in a green-tiled furnace at the southeast side of the Mound to provide a fragrant greeting for Him. Officials in charge of the incense approached the emperor bearing their incense vessels. These nine incense handlers distributed fresh incense of cedar, sandalwood, and pine on the north, east, and west sides of the Mound. Fragrant smoke rose skyward throughout the ceremony. Musicians then began playing the music of the "Zhong He 中和之曲" (Song of Central Peace), and the singers started to sing the ancient lyrics that told of God's creating power:

> Of old in the beginning, there was the great chaos, without form and dark. The five planets had not begun to revolve, nor the two lights to shine. In the midst of it there existed neither form nor sound. You, O spiritual Sovereign, came forth in Your sovereignty, and first did separate the impure from the pure. You made heaven; You made earth; You made man. All things became alive with reproducing power.

22. Tradition held that the most favorable position was the one facing south. Therefore, this was where the emperor always stood, and all thrones in the palace faced south.

于昔洪荒之初兮， 混蒙， 五行未運兮， 雨曜未明， 其中挺立兮， 有無容聲， 神皇出御兮， 始判濁清， 立天立地人兮，群物生生。[23]

This song is strikingly similar to the opening verses of the Bible:

In the beginning, God created the heavens and the earth. The earth was formless and void, and darkness was over the surface of the deep, and the Spirit of God was moving over the surface of the waters. Then God said, "Let there be light"; and there was light. God saw that the light was good; and God separated the light from the darkness.
Genesis 1:1 – 4

Musical instruments like these, now on display in the Sacred Music Office of the Altar of Heaven complex, were used during the Border Sacrifice ceremony.

Next, the emperor was reverently guided from the middle tier of the Altar Mound to a position in front of the shrine of Shang Di on the highest-tier platform. The shrine faced south, the position normally held by the emperor himself, thus signifying Shang Di's supreme position. The incense official presented incense while kneeling, and the emperor was invited to kneel. In this posture of supplication, the

23. 《大明會典》 *Ming Statutes*, Volume 82, p. 28.

emperor offered incense and bowed deeply in worship before Huang Tian Shang Di. The emperor rose and moved to the shrines where the ancestral tablets to five emperors were placed (Position 2). Getting down on his knees again, he offered incense to these ancestors, whose tablets were set in inferior positions, facing east and west. Returning to his place on the second tier, the emperor again performed the "three kneelings and the nine kowtows 三跪九叩" towards Shang Di. All the princes, dukes, and officials followed the emperor's example in this most humble act of worship.

Now the second song, "Yuan He 元和之曲" (Song of Beginning Peace), began:

> Lord Di, when You separated the Yin and the Yang [i.e., the heavens and the earth], Your creative work had begun. You did produce, O Spirit, the seven elements [i.e., the sun and the moon and the five planets]. Their beautiful and brilliant lights lit up the circular sky and square earth. All things were good. I [臣, Chen], Your servant, thank You fearfully, and, while I worship, present this memorial to You, O Di, calling You Sovereign.

1. Shrine to Shang Di with table (facing south).
2. Shrines to the 5 emperors (facing east and west).
3. Prayer place with the table for the Written Prayer.
4. Wine Vessel.
5. Place for the Reciter of the Written Prayer.
6. Large censers for incense.
7. Imperial guards.
8. Officials in charge of incense.
9. Officials in charge of silk offerings.
10. Officials in charge of sacrificial vessels.
11. Place for the Reciter of the Prayer.
12. & 19. Officials in charge of kneeling cushions.
13. & 20. Officials of the Censorate.
14. Officials in charge of the meat and drinks.
15. Officials in charge of placing the shrine.
16. Officials of the Board of Rites.
17. The emperor's position.
18. Assistants of the emperor.
21. Shrine to the sun.
22. Shrine to the North Star.
23. Shrine to the 5 planets.
24. Shrine to the 28 constellations.
25. Shrine to the host of stars.
26. Shrine to the moon.
27. Shrine to the clouds.
28. Shrine to the rain.
29. Shrine to the wind.
30. Shrine to the thunder.
31. Place for the Princes.
32. Place for the Censors.
33. Officials of the Board of Rites.
34. Place for the Ushers.
35. Place for the Master of Ceremonies.
36. Place for the subordinate attendants.
37. Place for the Dukes.
38. Place for the musicians and dancers.
39. Place for minor officials.
40. Place for the singers.
41. Furnaces for burning the silks, etc.
42. Place for officials in charge of this burning.
43. The great furnace for the whole - burnt bull.
44. Place to witness this sacrifice.
45. Assistants.
46. Place for minor officials to witness this sacrifice.

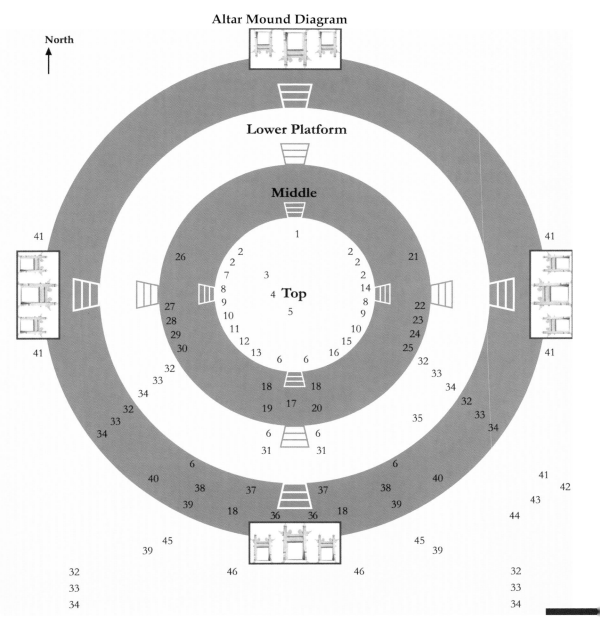

Altar Mound Diagram

North

Lower Platform

Middle

1

Top

Source: *The Original Religion of China*, by John Ross; copied from the *"Manchu Directory of Ritual."*

帝辟陰陽兮，造化張，神生其政兮，精華光，圓覆方戴兮，
兆物康，臣敢祇报兮，拜薦帝曰皇。[24]

Compare the words of this song with the Bible again:

> *God made the two great lights, the greater light to govern the day, and the lesser light to govern the night; He made the stars also. God placed them in the expanse of the heavens to give light on the earth, and to govern the day and the night, and to separate the light from the darkness; and God saw that it was good.*
> Genesis 1:16–18

Throughout these songs and acts of worship, the emperor of China—considered by his millions of subjects to be the most powerful man on earth—prostrated himself on the ground in sub-zero temperatures before Shang Di! Once again, note that he addressed himself as Chen 臣, that is, as a servant before Shang Di. Contrast this with the superlative Zhen 朕 he uses in addressing the spirits in the proclamation before the Sacrifice. These very deliberate distinctions in the language again clearly indicate that the emperor was worshipping Shang Di and only Shang Di, and that the spirits were not considered objects of worship.

Stage 2: Offering of Gems & Silk 奠玉帛

The second stage of the ceremony was the offering of jade tablets and bolts of silk. Officials in charge of the jade and silks approached the altar, each carrying a basket, while the musicians played the third song "Xiu He 休和之曲," a song of thanksgiving for God's great name and His abundant love.

> *You have promised, O Di, to hear us, for You are our Father. I, Your child, dull and unenlightened, am unable to show forth my dutiful feelings. I thank You, that You have accepted our pronouncement. Honorable is Your great name. With reverence we spread out these gems and silks, and, as swallows rejoicing in the spring, praise Your abundant love.*

帝垂聽兮，義若親，子職庸昧兮，無由申，册表荷鑒兮，泰
嘷式尊，敬陳玉帛兮，燕贺洪仁. [25]

24. Ibid.
25. Ibid., p. 29.

Chapter Four The Great Sacrifice

This concept of God as our Father is not a common notion in other Chinese religions. In Christianity, however, it is one of the most basic elements of God's relationship to man. Even in the Old Testament, God is frequently referred to as "Father," as in this example where God himself speaks of this relationship:

> *I will be a father to him and he will be a son to Me; when he commits iniquity,*
> *I will correct him with the rod of men and the strokes of the sons of men, but*
> *My loving kindness shall not depart from him.*
> 2 Samuel 7:14–15

During the playing of this song of thanksgiving, the emperor ascended to the top platform again, to stand before the shrine of Shang Di. The officials bearing the jade and silks knelt and presented their baskets, which the emperor received kneeling. The silks were covered with prayers that had been written on them. After these prayers were formally presented and read before Shang Di, the silk was taken away to be burned in the furnace.

Stage 3: Offering of the Zu 进俎

A large Zu 俎, a lacquer wooden platter used to hold the sacrificial meat of a roasted calf, was brought to the emperor. An official poured a thick, boiling hot broth with no added seasonings into a vessel and into the Zu, over the roasted meat, filling the air with a rich, fragrant aroma. The original intent of offering sacrifices to heaven was to give back to God what He had bestowed. Food, a very important gift from God, was to be offered as much as possible in its original state, hence the lack of seasonings in the broth.

The instructions God gave to the Hebrew people about their sacrifices to Him were the same; they also had to meet these three specific requirements: to be simple, unblemished, and aromatic.

> *Your lamb shall be an unblemished male a year old; you may take it from the*
> *sheep or from the goats.*
> Exodus 12:5

> *The other lamb you shall offer at twilight, and shall offer with it the same grain*
> *offering and the same drink offering as in the morning, for a soothing aroma,*

FINDING GOD IN ANCIENT CHINA

an offering by fire to the LORD.
Exodus 29:41

The emperor, bearing the vessel that contained the broth, ascended the platform from the south and approached the shrine of Shang Di and the shrines of his ancestors. He knelt once before Shang Di, and then knelt once in front of each of two groups of ancestors, presenting the broth by raising it reverently. Walking down the west steps, he returned to his place on the second tier while the musicians played the fourth song "Yu He 豫和之曲" (Song of Comforting Peace):

> *The great feast has been set forth, and the sound of celebration is like thunder. The Sovereign Spirit promises to enjoy our offering, and Your servant's heart feels like a particle of dust. The meat has been boiled in the large caldrons, and the fragrant provisions have been prepared. Enjoy the offering, O Di, then shall all the people be blessed. I [臣, Chen], Your servant, am filled with thanksgiving. How blessed I am!*

大筵弘開，備聲如雷，皇神賜享，臣衷涓埃，大鼎炮烹，肴饈馨饈裁，帝歆兮，兆民之福，臣感恩兮，何如幸哉。[26]

The emperor ascended the platform for the fourth time to present the sacrificial animal. He knelt humbly in front of Shang Di and presented the Zu with the meat on it, then did the same before his ancestors. This sacrificial animal that he presented was the specially selected calf of pure color. As mentioned earlier, its selection by a prince was very strict: it had to be a year-old firstborn without blemish. In Old Testament times, God also required firstborn animals as sacrifices because they foreshadowed the preeminence of Jesus.

> *However, a firstborn among animals, which as a firstborn belongs to the LORD, no man may consecrate it; whether ox or sheep, it is the LORD's.*
> Leviticus 27:26

Stage 4: First Presentation of Wine — Martial Dance 初獻

The Border Sacrifice ceremony continued with three toasts and a grand prayer during the second toast. Then dancers with shields and hatchets entered from the south gate to perform the Wu 武, a martial dance, a tribute to the dynasty's military

136

26. Ibid.

might. The dance was accompanied by the music and singing of the song, "Shou He 嘉和之曲" (Song of a Peaceful Longevity), which included these lyrics:

A reenactment of the Martial Dance.　　　　　　　Credit: Altar of Heaven Administration

> *The great and lofty One pours out His grace and love; how unworthy are we to receive it. I, His foolish servant, while I worship, hold this precious cup, and praise Him, whose years have no end.*
> 大高降思微情何以承，臣愚端拜捧瑶觚积堅壽無極并。[27]

The Old Testament prophet Isaiah also speaks of the high and lofty God who is eternal.

> *For thus says the high and exalted One/Who lives forever, whose name is Holy.*
> Isaiah 57:15

While the dance was being performed, the wine official approached the emperor and knelt to present the ceremonial wine[28] to him; the emperor, also kneeling,

27. Ibid.
28. The ancients thought that their offerings should be as pure and natural as possible, so, although they were able to brew fine wine for consumption, they offered pure water to God and called it Xuan Wine, 玄酒. Centuries later, however, the water was replaced by a special wine that had to be brewed by a designated department and could not be used for any other purpose.

received the wine vessel, the Jue 珏. Still kneeling, the emperor lifted the vessel over his head to present to Shang Di. Then he rose and moved to the table, where he again knelt worshipfully and placed the vessel in the center of the table of the shrine. Afterwards, he rose and went to the prayer table (Position 3).

The official designated as the Reciter approached the prayer table, knelt, and prostrated himself three times. He remained kneeling before the table, until the music stopped. The emperor joined him on his knees and all the officials knelt as well, while the Reciter read the written prayer called the Zhu Wen 祝文 from a prayer board (Zhu Ban 祝版). This prayer of thanksgiving was what the emperor himself wrote during his three-day fast, and it was a lengthy acknowledgement of the goodness of God throughout the previous year. It expressed gratitude to God for His multitude of blessings, including favorable weather, fruitful seasons, and protection of the people. Everyone remained kneeling until the Reciter had completed his reading. Below is an excerpt of a ceremonial prayer used by Emperor Jia Jing 嘉靖, who reigned from A.D. 1522 to 1566:

O awesome Creator, I look up to You. How imperial is the expansive heavens. Now is the time when the masculine energies of nature begin to be displayed, and with the great ceremonies I reverently honor You. Your servant, I am but a reed or willow; my heart is but as that of an ant; yet have I received Your favoring Mandate, appointing me to the government of the empire. I deeply cherish a sense of my ignorance and foolishness, and am afraid lest I prove unworthy of Your abundant grace. Therefore will I observe all the rules and statutes, striving, insignificant as I am, to be faithful. Far distant here, I look up to Your heavenly palace. Come in Your precious chariot to the altar. Your servant, I bow my head to the earth, reverently expecting Your abundant grace. All my officers are here arranged along with me, dancing and worshipping before You. All the spirits accompany You as guards, from the east to the west. Your servant, I prostrate myself to meet You, and reverently look up for Your coming, O Di. O that You would promise to accept our offerings, and regard us, while we worship You because Your goodness is inexhaustible!

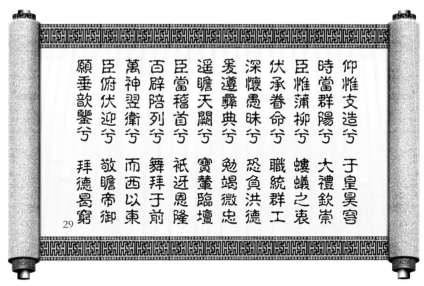

仰惟支造兮　于皇昊穹

When the Reciter finished, all stood as he approached the shrine to Shang Di. Kneeling, he laid the written prayer on the table, and kowtowed three times before retiring. The musicians resumed playing; this time, it was a song of thanksgiving called "Jing He 景和之曲" (Song of Brilliant Peace):

> *When Di, the Almighty, had so decreed, He called into existence heaven, earth, and man. Between [heaven and earth] He separately appointed men and things. But Heaven has given me the Mandate. So, I, a servant of Di, pray for His enlightenment — so may I, a simple person, forever appear before Him who is in the highest heaven.*

帝皇立命兮，群三才，中分民物兮，惟天該，小臣请命，用光帝陪，永配于皇穹哉。[30]

A psalmist of Israel expressed similar sentiments,

> *May you be blessed of the LORD,*
> *Maker of heaven and earth.*
> *The heavens are the heavens of the LORD,*
> *But the earth He has given to the sons of men.*
> Psalm 115:15–16

29. 《大明會典》 *Ming Statutes*, Volume 82, p. 29.
30. Ibid.

Tablet bearing the name of the Supreme Lord of the Great Heaven (Huang Tian Shang Di) inside the Prayer Hall for Good Ha

As the tempo of the music quickened, the emperor and his officials knelt three times, kowtowing thrice each time. The emperor then offered the wine vessels to the secondary tablets to the east and west, and returned to his position on the second tier (Position 17). The martial dance ended and a second group of dancers moved to the performance site.

Stage 5: Second Presentation of Wine — Civil Dance 亞獻

This second presentation of wine was similar to the first. At the second offering of wine, the song "Tai He 太和之曲" (Song of Excellent Peace) was performed:

All the numerous species of living things are indebted to Your grace for their beginning. Men and things are all enveloped in Your benevolence, O Di. All living things are indebted to Your goodness, but who knows from Whom his blessings come to him. It is You alone, O Lord, who are the true Ancestor of billions and trillions of things.

群生總總兮，悉蒙始恩。 人物盡囿兮，于帝仁。 群生荷德兮，誰識所從來。 于惟皇兮，德兆物之祖真。[31]

The Bible also speaks of God's goodness to His creatures.

You shed abroad a plentiful rain, O God;
You confirmed Your inheritance when it was parched.
Your creatures settled in it;
You provided in Your goodness for the poor, O God.
Psalm 68:9–10

As the music of "Tai He" was played, eight civilian dancers entered from the east and performed the "Feather and Bamboo Dance 羽竹之舞," a dance of peace.

Stage 6: Final Presentation of Wine 终獻

The emperor approached Shang Di with his third and final toast as the musicians played and the singers sang "Yong He 永和之曲" (Song of Everlasting Peace):

The precious feast is wide displayed; the gem-filled benches are arranged; the pearly wine is presented, with music and dances. The spirit of harmony is present; men and beasts are happy. The breast of His servant is troubled, that he is unable to repay his debts.

寶宴弘，玉幾憑，瓔浚升，樂舞翻，協氣凝，民物仍，臣衷蹇蹇，報無能。[32]

A Hebrew songwriter expressed similar joy over God's presence and the harmony between people and beast.

Your righteousness is like the mountains of God;
Your judgments are like a great deep.
O Lord, You preserve man and beast.

---

31. Ibid., pp. 29–30.
32. Ibid., p. 30.

FINDING GOD IN ANCIENT CHINA

How precious is Your loving kindness, O God!
And the children of men take refuge in the shadow of Your wings.
They drink their fill of the abundance of Your house;
And You give them to drink of the river of Your delights.
Psalm 36:6–8

A reenactment of the Civil Dance.   Credit: Altar of Heaven Administation

The Feather and Bamboo Dance, the same civil dance as in the Second Presentation of Wine, continued to the music of "Yong He."

After the music stopped and the civil dancers departed, the Master of Ceremonies presented the wine and meat to two officials who then brought the wine and meat before the shrine to Shang Di, raising them reverently. As silence filled the dawn, the emperor ascended the platform to taste the wine and meat with Shang Di. Two officer-guards approached and stood at the emperor's left. Those bearing the wine and meat joined him at his right. The emperor knelt, as did all the officials to his left and right. Those on his right presented the wine to the emperor who took the vessel and, raising it reverently, presented it to Shang Di. The official with the meat brought the platter forward, and the emperor took it and presented it in a similar manner. He then knelt three times before returning to his position and leading all his officials in kneeling three times and kowtowing nine times.

Stage 7: Removal of the Offerings 撤饌

The last three stages of the ceremony began with the removal of the offerings, which was done to the music of "Xian He 咸和之曲" (Song of Splendid Peace):

> *The service of song is completed, but our poor sincerity cannot be expressed. Your sovereign goodness is infinite. As a potter, You have made all living things. Great and small are sheltered [by Your love]. Imprinted on the heart of Your poor servant is the sense of Your goodness, so that my feeling cannot be fully displayed. With great kindness You do bear with us, and, notwithstanding our demerits, do grant us life and prosperity.*

> 太秦既成，微誠莫傾，皇德無京，陶此群生，巨細馔饼，刻小臣之感衷兮，罔罄愚情，實弘涵而容纳兮，賜曲生成。[33]

It is interesting that this analogy of God as the Potter is used many times throughout the Bible. For example,

> *But now, O LORD, You are our Father, We are the clay, and You our potter; And all of us are the work of Your hand.*
> Isaiah 64:8

Stage 8: Sending Off Di 送帝神

The appointed official approached Shang Di's shrine to remove a magnificent round ceremonial ashen jade that had been placed there in preparation for the ceremony.

This gem, a symbol of Heaven, was later carried back to the Treasure House. As this jade was being removed, the musicians performed the "Qing He 清和之曲" (Song of Pure Peace):

> With reverent ceremonies the record has been presented, and You, O sovereign Spirit, have accepted our service. The dances have all been performed, and nine times the music has responded. Grant, O Di, Your great blessing to increase the happiness of my house. The instruments of metal and precious stones have given out their melody. The jeweled girdles of the officers have emitted their tinkling sound. Spirits and men rejoice together, praising Di, the Lord. While we celebrate His great name, what limit can there be, or what measure? Forever He sets fast the high heavens, and establishes the solid earth. His government is everlasting. His unworthy servant, I bow my head; I lay it in the dust, bathed in His grace and glory.

> 禮詆册薦亏，皇神垂享，萬舞畢舉亏，九成已行，帝賜洪庥亏，大我家慶，金鳴玉振亏，聲鎧鎧，群潦環佩亏，響叮當，神人交賀^，醫帝皇，贅稱泰號亏，曷有窮量，永固富厚亏，宰御久常，微臣頓首卬首亏，攸沐恩光。 34

The Bible also speaks of the everlasting government of God, but goes one step further, looking forward to the day when this government will rest on the shoulders of the Savior of the world, Jesus Christ.

> For a child will be born to us, a son will be given to us;
> And the government will rest on His shoulders;
> And His name will be called Wonderful Counselor, Mighty God,
> Eternal Father, Prince of Peace.
> There will be no end to the increase of His government or of peace,
> On the throne of David and over his kingdom,
> To establish it and to uphold it with justice and righteousness
> From then on and forevermore.
> The zeal of the LORD of hosts will accomplish this.
> Isaiah 9:6–7

34. Ibid.

As the "Qing He" was performed, the emperor led all the officials in a final prostration, once again kneeling three times and kowtowing nine times as they sent off Shang Di. This send-off suggests an understanding that God does not live as a physical presence on earth, a view similar to that of the Hebrews.

Stage 9: The Burnt Offering 奉燎

After this final prostration, the appointed officials took up the bull, the written prayer scroll, the silks, the incense, and other offerings and reverently placed them in the roaring flames of the furnaces at the sides of the Altar Mound. The emperor stood at his position on the top tier facing east to watch this burnt offering as the sun rose in the distance. He then went to his position on the second tier as the incense and silks were removed from the secondary shrines—shrines to the sun and moon, for instance—and burnt in their appointed furnaces. At this time, the musicians played the "Xi He 熙和之曲" (Song of Glorious Peace):

> We have worshipped and written the Great Name on this gem-like sheet. Now we display it before Di, and place it in the fire. These valuable offerings of silks and fine meats we burn also, with these sincere prayers, that they may ascend in volumes of flames up to the distant sky. All the ends of the earth look up to Him. All human beings, all things on the earth, rejoice together in the Great Name.

瑤簡拜書亏，泰號成，奉揚帝前亏，資離明，珍幣嘉肴，于祝誠，均登巨燧亏，達立清，九域四表ˆ，莫不昂，膜庶類品匯亏，楚麇洪名。[35]

When all the offerings were half burnt, the Emperor was invited to go to the viewing place (Position 44) to watch the rest of the offerings being completely consumed by the flames.

Finally, the song "Ritual Completed" was played. The emperor was then respectfully guided out southwards by the left gate of the Altar's outer wall, where he entered the Costume Platform (see Map of the Altar of Heaven Complex, p. 124) to change his robes. Then, with the musicians leading the way and playing the music of the "Hu He 護和之曲" (Song of Protecting Peace), the emperor left the Altar of Heaven complex riding in his ritual chariot and escorted by his guards. He exited

35. Ibid.

This contemporary painting shows the burnt offerings to Shang Di going up in flames at the end of the Border Sacrifice ceremony.

Credit: Altar of Heaven Administration

This contemporary painting shows the emperor leaving the Altar of Heaven from the south gate, called the Zhao Heng Gate, to return to the Imperial Palace.

Credit: Altar of Heaven Administration

This section of a 60-meter-long (197-foot-long) painting shows the emperor's procession to the Border Sacrifice ceremony. The emperor's sedan is shown above, in purple. This entire painting, which is on display at the Ji Tian Museum at the Altar of Heaven Complex, is a modern reproduction of a 1748 original.
Credit: Altar of Heaven Administration

through the southern Zhao Heng Gate 昭亨門 and retraced the three-mile route to the Imperial Palace, arriving—to the sound of a ringing bell—at the Meridian Gate, where the princes, dukes, and officials who did not go to the sacrifice ceremony waited on their knees for his return.

THE MEANING BEHIND THE SACRIFICE

Like the nation of Israel, which has forgotten the significance of God's appointed sacrificial system, the emperors of China carried out this great Border Sacrifice for thousands of years without understanding its full meaning. Like many people today who simply go through the motions of liturgical services in churches all over the world, the ancient Chinese rulers performed these ceremonies motivated more by tradition than by a heart-felt desire to worship the true God. Yet, Shang Di's character and His plan for rescuing a fallen and flawed human race shine through the rote practices and the intervening millennia of the Border Sacrifice. Through the rituals associated with this sacrifice, God has shown us, as He did the China of the emperors, certain truths.

God Has Strict Requirements

The Border Sacrifice reflects the way that God wants us to approach Him. Although it is politically correct today to say that there are many ways to reach God, the Bible clearly teaches that this is not true. The meticulous steps, the painstaking preparations, and the careful attention to required details suggest that those participating in the Border Sacrifice understood that the holy and majestic Sovereign of the Universe had indeed designated a specific and precise way for people to come into His presence. The emperor was in a unique position to understand these strict demands. As a supreme ruler, he would similarly have expected his subordinates and subjects to show their respect to him by following his prescribed protocol.

One important element of both the Chinese and Hebrew worship of God was the sacrifice of an animal that was perfect, without blemish and of one solid color. Only the blood of a perfect sacrifice could satisfy a holy God and be deemed acceptable to cover the sins of the one offering the sacrifice. God does not and cannot accept any lesser sacrifice. These strict requirements for an animal without blemish were to foreshadow the sacrifice of God's own sinless Son, Jesus Christ, to take away the sins of all mankind. As Jesus Himself said,

> *I am the way, and the truth, and the life; no one comes to the Father but through Me.*
> John 14:6

The Principle of Substitution

On the way to the Slaying Pavilion, the animals chosen for the Border Sacrifice passed through a gate underneath the Danbi Bridge 月陛橋 that connects the Imperial Vault and the Prayer Hall for Good Harvest. This gate was called the "Gate of Hell 鬼門翻." This name suggests an understanding that, in the upcoming ritual, the penalty of death that rightly should be paid by the worshippers was being borne instead by the sacrificial animal. In Biblical terms, the sacrificed was taking the penalty of hell so that those performing the rite could be forgiven of their sins and come before the living God.

There are historical events in China's far past that suggest this profound understanding of the concept of substitution in sacrifice. Perhaps the most dramatic is this story recorded in the *Historical Records*. In the waning days of the Shang Dynasty, as war raged with the forces of the ascendant King Wu 武王, the elder brother of the last emperor of the Shang, Di Xin 帝辛, went into hiding. When King Wu defeated Di Xin and established the Zhou Dynasty, this elder brother of Di Xin, the Prince of Wei 徽子, emerged from hiding and literally offered himself as a living sacrifice to the new king. He approached King Wu's camp with his upper body stripped, his wrists bound together, dragging a lamb and accompanied by an attendant carrying sacrificial vessels. This was to show that he was ready and willing to be used as a sacrifice, like a lamb, at the conqueror's whim.[36]

In the Bible, God promises to send a perfect sacrifice to take the punishment of sinful man upon itself. Jesus Christ is the fulfillment of that promise first made to the Hebrew people; His sacrifice negated the need for any further blood sacrifices to be made in either the Jewish temples or the Chinese Altar of Heaven. The Apostle Peter explains Jesus' substitution for us:

---

36. 《史記卷三十八–世家八–宋微子世家》 *Historical Records*, Volume 38, Genealogy of Song Wei Zi. King Wu himself untied the prince's wrists and restored him to all the honors he had enjoyed in the Shang court.

For Christ also died for sins once for all, the just for the unjust, so that He might bring us to God, having been put to death in the flesh, but made alive in the spirit.
1 Peter 3:18

Worship with a Pure Heart

Fasting, staying away from profane thoughts, and ceremonial purification rites were meant to prepare the emperor to meet His God in a state of cleanliness. Similarly, we can only approach God with a pure heart, as described in this psalm,

Who may ascend into the hill of the LORD?
And who may stand in His holy place?
He who has clean hands and a pure heart,
Who has not lifted up his soul to falsehood And has not sworn deceitfully.
Psalm 24:3 – 4

Worship with Joy

The ringing bell, the dances, the music and songs all speak of joyous worship. Relationship with God brings a joy that bubbles from within and leads to a state of blessedness that the world cannot destroy. When we know the true God, He gives us joy in our hearts, just as Jesus promised,

These things I have spoken to you so that My joy may be in you, and that your joy may be made full.
John 15:11

Conclusion

In the ancient Chinese ritual of the Border Sacrifice, the emperor welcomed Shang Di's presence and worshipped Him joyously, but then the emperor had to send Him off again. Under the old covenant, interaction between God and man was brief and prescribed. Centuries of Chinese emperors painstakingly performed these elaborate sacrifices year after year to seek forgiveness for new sins that had been committed by the nation. Today, however, that final sacrifice has been made once for all — for all time and for all mankind — by Jesus Christ, through His death on the Cross and His resurrection. Therefore, we can enjoy a new covenant relationship with God in which we have the privilege of His presence with us at all times. When we accept His gift of this new covenant relationship, we have the assurance that He will never leave us; Jesus himself promised it:

> *Go therefore and make disciples of all the nations, baptizing them in the name*
> *of the Father and the Son and the Holy Spirit, teaching them to observe all that*
> *I commanded you; and lo, I am with you always, even to the end of the age.*
> Matthew 28:19–20

The sacred texts of religions around the world share many common teachings, such as doing good and avoiding evil, but only the Bible teaches that the One True Creator God has sacrificed His Son to pay for the sins of all mankind. At this signpost marked "Border Sacrifice," I found striking similarities in the ceremonies associated with the sacrifices performed by the ancient Chinese and the ancient Hebrews. These very discoveries, though, raised further questions. Where did these concepts of substitutionary death — that is, an innocent dying for the guilty — and of atoning death — the requirement of death to pay for sin — originate? Are they part of my Chinese heritage or were they borrowed from a foreign culture? Even more surprises about my ancient roots awaited me at the next signpost: the Blood Covenant.

REFLECT and RESPOND

The rituals of the Border Sacrifice may seem complex and elaborate, but the essence of the ceremony was simple. The utensils used and the site where the sacrifice was conducted were all designed to reflect utmost simplicity, the highest form of tribute to a Mighty God. The Cross upon which the ultimate sacrifice was made also was a simple structure. It was there that God sent His Son Jesus Christ to die a gruesome death. That is how far God was willing to go to show His love for us, and the magnitude of that love and that desire to redeem us from eternal damnation is beyond words. Look to the Cross and accept His love for you. Knowing God is a simple exercise in faith.

伍

Blood Covenant

That which is most important in performing the rites is to understand the meaning intended in it. The Son of Heaven who understands the meaning and practices it, he will be able to rule the nation.

~ Record of Rites

血盟

5

Blood Covenant

The centuries-old pattern of China's dynastic cycles was set at the very beginning of the nation's history. China's first dynasty, the Xia 夏, fell in 1766 B.C., about the same time that the first king of Babylonia set forth history's first detailed code of laws, the Code of Hammurabi. The Xia Dynasty's cruel and tyrannical Emperor Jie 桀 was deposed and his ruling house overthrown by a man named Tang 湯, who was described as possessing "valor and prudence." Ever after, this was how the ruling houses of China rose and fell: successive reigns by bad emperors ultimately culminated in the overthrow of the ruling dynasty by a righteous man who inaugurated a new dynasty. At the outset, the new dynasty was characterized by clean government and service to the people, but over many generations it would itself become corrupt and ultimately would either collapse or be overthrown.

Tang, founder of the Shang Dynasty, was the archetype for all future challengers to the throne. Although his reign, from 1766 to 1753 B.C., was distinguished by successful military exploits and well-managed domestic affairs, it was Emperor Tang's singular devotion to his subjects that sets him apart as a truly exemplary ruler. The grave sense of responsibility with which he regarded the duties of his office is exemplified in this touching story recorded by various Chinese historical sources.[1]

A great drought began two years before Tang's reign. As the drought continued, it caused a devastating famine that lasted a total of seven years. All through those long years, Tang and the entire nation sacrificed to Shang Di, to lesser gods, and

1. See 《吕氏春秋–季秋纪–顺民篇》 *Lü's Chronicles*, 《墨子》 *Mo Zi*, 《荀子》 *Shun Zi*, 《國語》 *Guo Yu*, and 《説苑》 *Shuo Yuan.*

Photo at left shows the Zhao Heng Gate at the south entrance to the Altar of Heaven complex.

to their ancestors, praying desperately for rain. Yet, it was all to no avail. The drought continued to ravage the nation. Finally, a suggestion was made that a human victim should be offered in sacrifice to Shang Di, and then a prayer made for rain. Tang appointed a day for this to be done, and a great multitude gathered for the unprecedented event. To the amazement of all, the emperor, clad in rushes, presented himself prepared as the sacrificial victim. Having fasted, cut his hair, and trimmed his nails, he arrived in a plain carriage drawn by white horses at the designated site in the Mulberry Woods 桑林, near the capital city of Bo 亳.[2] There he fell to the ground and prayed:

> *I myself have sinned; the ten thousand people [i.e. all my subjects] have no part [in my sins]. If, however, the ten thousand people have sinned, the offenses must also rest upon me. So, pray, Shang Di, and pray, you spirits, do not let the fact that I am without virtue be a cause for the destruction of so many lives!*

余一人有罪，無及萬夫。萬夫有罪，在余一入。無以一人之不敏，使上帝鬼神爆民之命。[3]

According to the historical records, when he finished praying, a heavy rain fell and the drought was relieved, rendering the sacrifice unnecessary.

This remarkable prayer reveals an understanding that the sins of an entire people can be imputed or placed on a single person. Emperor Tang sought to spare his people further tragedy by taking upon himself the full brunt of the consequences of their sins: he was willing to die for his people because he loved them so much.

The Bible recounts a similar demonstration of a leader's great sacrificial love, that of Moses in the 13th-century B.C., for the people of Israel. When Moses ascended Mt. Sinai, where he conversed with God and received the Ten Commandments, his long absence worried the people. Fearing that he might not return, the people decided to make an idol to guide them in Moses' stead. After melting down all their gold, they fashioned a golden calf to worship, and when Moses descended from the mountain, he found the people dancing and singing around this powerless, heathen idol. Moses was enraged by the faithlessness of his people, yet he pleaded on their behalf before God, offering to die in their stead if God would forgive them their great sin.

2. Located in modern-day Cao County, Shandong Province, 山東曹縣.

3. 《呂氏春秋-第九卷季秋紀-順民》 *Lü's Chronicles*, Volume 9, Ji Qiu Ji, Shunmin, paragraph 2. Interestingly, this famine happened around the time of the seven-year famine recorded in Genesis 41–45.

*Then Moses returned to the L*ORD*, and said, "Alas, this people has committed a great sin, and they have made a god of gold for themselves. But now, if You will, forgive their sin — and if not, please blot me out from Your book which You have written!"*
Exodus 32:31 – 32

Neither Tang in China nor Moses in Israel, however, was an acceptable sacrifice for the sins of his people. As we discovered at the Altar of Heaven, God requires a perfect sacrifice to satisfy the justice of His perfect law. At best, the desire of Tang and Moses to sacrifice themselves for their people was but a foreshadowing of the Son of God, who came to earth as Jesus of Nazareth to be that perfect sacrifice for the sins of the whole world. Only Jesus Christ could be this perfect sacrifice because He was God manifest in the flesh. He is the only person to draw breath on this earth who lived a perfect life, never once sinning in thought or word or deed! As foreshadowed in the sacrificial animals demanded by Shang Di, Jesus was without spot or blemish:

Therefore He is able also to save forever those who draw near to God through Him, since He always lives to make intercession for them. For it was fitting for us to have such a high priest, holy, innocent, undefiled, separated from sinners and exalted above the heavens.
Hebrew 7:25 – 26

God, however, did grant the heartfelt prayers of Tang and Moses, clearly demonstrating that it was not a human sacrifice that He desired. He has always been merciful toward those who approach him with humility and sincerity.

The sacrifices of God are a broken spirit;
A broken and a contrite heart,
O God, You will not despise.
Psalm 51:17

Both the Hebrew and Chinese historical records reveal a belief in the necessity of the death of a perfect sacrifice to cover the sins of the nation. This then presents another question on our journey of discovery: Why is such a sacrifice involving the shedding of blood necessary? Why did Jesus have to go through the Passion, or Suffering, an event that has been captured in art and remembered in religious

ceremonies ever since His death and resurrection?[4] Unlike the beautiful music that accompanies many religious rites, there is nothing esthetically pleasing about the shedding of blood; and unlike gold or gems, blood is not regarded as a valuable commodity. Why then this requirement for shed blood where forgiveness of sins was involved? At "The Blood Covenant" signpost on my journey of discovery, I learned more about both the Chinese and Hebrew cultures that helped to shed light on the answers to these questions.

The Origin of Covenants

The word "covenant" carries a variety of meanings, but it essentially refers to a binding of two or more parties into a new relationship or agreement. The Holy Bible, God's specific revelation to mankind, is comprised of the Old Testament and the New Testament, but these would be more accurately called the Old Covenant and the New Covenant. Understanding the importance of covenants is foundational to understanding the way God relates to mankind.

Ancient form of the character for "covenant"

The first covenant recorded in the Bible was the one between God and Adam, in which God pledged eternal fellowship with and blessing upon Adam and Eve so long as they obeyed one rule. If they disobeyed, the penalty was death. As we saw in Chapter 2, the rule was to refrain from eating the fruit of the Tree of Knowledge of Good and Evil. Adam and Eve, however, failed the test, thus breaking this covenant. Immediately, the first physical death occurred. God killed some of the animals that Adam had named and presumably befriended. He did this to clothe Adam and Eve, who in their loss of innocence had become ashamed of their nakedness. God had warned Adam and Eve of death, but they had never before encountered it. To see the first dead animals—animals that were killed so that they could be clothed (and then later to have to kill animals themselves, to shed blood to cover the shame revealed by their sins)—undoubtedly brought home to them the gravity and the eternal consequences of breaking this covenant and disobeying God.

This first covenant in the Bible provides us with the best explanation for the

---

4. This event was vividly retold in Mel Gibson's 2004 blockbuster film, *The Passion of the Christ*. Though it is a graphic portrayal of the twelve hours leading up to the crucifixion of Jesus, it only captures to a small degree the real sufferings of Christ on behalf of mankind. His greatest suffering was the three days before His resurrection when He was separated from and forsaken by God.

origin of the blood covenant. Death was the just penalty for breaking a covenant, and death involved the shedding of blood. This interpretation is supported by the derivation and usage of the term itself. In Hebrew, the word translated as "covenant" actually means "cutting." The word "covenant" frequently appears in the Bible with the verb "to cut." A blood covenant was literally cut as an animal was killed with a sword or knife. In English, this act is translated in the Bible as "to make a covenant," but it literally means "to cut a covenant."[5]

In no single passage of the Bible is the whole ceremony of blood covenants described or fully explained. One likely reason for this is that blood covenants were so common and so universally known at the time that they did not need to be explained: Everyone in those days knew the procedure and its significance. Today, it is possible to piece together a full picture by studying the different covenants recorded in Hebrew and Chinese history.

First, we will look at examples from the Old Testament and from ancient China to learn the procedures for cutting a blood covenant; these examples will show the striking parallels between the two cultures. Then we will look at how the symbolism and ceremonial details in these procedures find their ultimate and final fulfillment in God's last covenant with mankind, made through Jesus Christ. The Bible tells us that God gave Jesus to mankind for a covenant of the people,[6] but it is up to each individual himself to decide if he will accept the salvation offered by that covenant or be forever cut off from God.

CUTTING A BLOOD COVENANT
An Innocent Victim Had to Be Killed

Old Testament: Blood covenants always involved the sacrifice of an innocent animal. Sometimes the animal was split in half and the two halves were laid side-by-side on the ground. The covenanting parties then would walk together in a figure-8 pattern between the two halves. This appears to be the case in Genesis 15:10 and 17 when God made a covenant with Abram (later called Abraham), and in Jeremiah 34:18 where God refers to His covenant with the Israelites when he brought them out of slavery in Egypt.

The Bible makes it clear that the blood represents life.

5. See Genesis 21:27; 26:28; 1 Samuel 18:3.
6. See Isaiah 49:8–12 which foretold what Jesus would do for mankind.

> *For the life of the flesh is in the blood.*
> Leviticus 17:11

As all sacrifices had to be perfect (without blemish) both internally and externally, we can conclude that the blood symbolized a perfect life.[7]

Chinese: The Chinese word translated as "covenant" is 血盟 (xue meng), which literally means "blood covenant." Historian and Sinologist James Legge explains that no other term would be adequate in English: "On all occasions there was the death of the victim, over which the contracting parties appealed to superior powers, wishing that, if they violated the terms of their covenant, they might meet with a fate like that of the slain animal." He goes on to explain, "The offering of the blood was because of the breath which is contained in it. The (examination of the) hair and the (taking of the) blood was an announcement that the victim was complete within and without. This announcement showed the value set on its being perfect."[8] Other Sinologists have made the same point.[9] For the ancient Chinese, the blood — the breath of a complete animal — also represented a perfect life!

New Testament Fulfillment: The vital importance of the blood in sealing a covenant is ultimately revealed in the shedding of the blood of Jesus to restore the covenant relationship between God and all mankind that was broken in the Garden of Eden. The blood of Jesus was sacred because it was the blood of God in human form, and thus the most precious thing in the world; it alone was sufficient to redeem us from all our sins and make us fit for fellowship with God and to spend eternity in His presence.[10] The shed blood of Jesus represented His perfect life offered up to God on our behalf, once and for all.

> *How much more will the blood of Christ, who through the eternal Spirit offered*
> *Himself without blemish to God, cleanse your conscience from dead works to*
> *serve the living God?*
> Hebrews 9:14

The fact that the Border Sacrifice had to be repeated annually clearly demonstrates that the shed blood of an innocent and seemingly perfect animal

7. See Leviticus 1:3, 6 – 10; Numbers 6:14; Exodus 12:5.
8. James Legge, *The Ch'un Ts'ew with The Tso Chuen* (Taipei: SMC Publishing Inc., 2000), p. 5 commentary section. "Ch'un Ts'ew" was an earlier English transliteration for Spring and Autumn, a reference to the specific historical period from 770 to 476 B.C. It is also the title of the Annals of this period. We will refer to the Chinese source as *Spring and Autumn Annals* 《春秋》; *Tso Chuen* 《左傳》, or *Zuo Zhuan* in modern usage, is the commentary that accompanied the Annals.
9. Ibid. See also John Ross, *The Original Religion of China* (London: Oliphant Anderson & Ferrier, 1909), p. 289.
10. See 1 Peter 1:18 – 19; Acts 20:28; Hebrews 10:29 – 30; Ephesians 1:7.

provided only temporary reconciliation with Shang Di. The same was true of the Old Testament sacrifices: they provided only temporary absolution of sins for the Israelites, who had to repeatedly and regularly perform these sacrifices. The blood of Jesus Christ, however, makes permanent reconciliation with God possible. Jesus died on the cross to redeem us,

> *with precious blood, as of a lamb unblemished and spotless, the blood of Christ. For He was foreknown before the foundation of the world, but has appeared in these last times for the sake of you.*
> 1 Peter 1:19 – 20

An Oath Was Sworn

Old Testament: The covenanting parties would meet between the two halves of the parted sacrifice and raise their hands to heaven. Clasping their hands together, they proclaimed the covenant oath, which could include a curse or a blessing proclaiming the benefits and purpose of the covenant.[11] Sometimes the covenanting parties would make an imprecatory oath with reference to the slain animals as if to say, "Let happen to me what has happened to these animals if I ever break our covenant."[12] If one party failed in his covenant obligations, he would suffer just as the slain animals had suffered. Similarly, two long passages in the Book of Deuteronomy describe in detail the misfortunes that would befall the nation of Israel if she broke her blood covenant with God. Correspondingly, great blessings were promised if Israel faithfully kept her covenant.[13]

The idea that a person's handshake binds him to his word may have originated from the binding power of blood covenant oaths. One of the words translated "swear" in the Bible means literally "to lift up (the hand)."[14] God uses this same metaphor to express the binding power of His covenant with Israel.

> *The Lord has sworn by His right hand and by His strong arm.*
> Isaiah 62:8

Chinese: Imprecatory prayers or oaths were a common feature of blood covenant ceremonies around the world,[15] and the Chinese were no exception. We find clear examples of this in the words of some of the covenants recorded in the Chinese *Classics*. For example,

11. See Genesis 15:6 – 18; 21:23-27; 22:16 – 18.
12. See Genesis 26:28; Deuteronomy 29:11 – 20; 2 Samuel 3:35, etc.
13. See Deuteronomy 27:5 – 26 and 28:15 – 45; 28:1 – 14.
14. Hebrew = nasa. This term is used of God in Exodus 6:8; Numbers 14:30; Nehemiah 9:15; and of man in Isaiah 3:7.
15. H. Clay Trumbull, *The Blood Covenant* (Minneapolis, Minn.: James Family Christian Publishers, n.d. Original: Philadelphia, 1893), p. 154.

May he who breaks this covenant lose his nation.
渝盟無亨國。[16]

We will all assist the royal house, and do no harm to one another. If anyone transgresses this covenant, may the intelligent spirits destroy him, so that he shall lose his people and not be able to possess his state, and, to the remotest posterity, let him have no descendant old or young.
皆獎王室，無相害也，有渝此盟，明神殛之，婢隊其師，無克祚國，及其玄孫，無有老幼。[17]

New Testament Fulfillment: Blessing and curse both are clearly part of the New Covenant that God made with mankind when Christ died on the cross for our sins. One of the most familiar passages of the Bible says,

> *For God so loved the world that He gave His only begotten Son, that whoever believes in Him shall not perish, but have eternal life. For God did not send the Son into the world to judge the world, but that the world might be saved through Him. He who believes in Him is not judged; he who does not believe has been judged already, because he has not believed in the name of the only begotten Son of God.*
> John 3:16–18

Only Jesus can save us from the curse of breaking or ignoring God's blood covenant with mankind.[18]

Gifts Were Exchanged

Old Testament: The covenanting parties often exchanged clothes, armor, or other gifts.[19] In exchanging military attire, the parties were pledging their armies or military strength to each other. If an enemy attacked one party of the covenant, the other would come to his defense. This would have been Abraham's understanding when God told him,

> *Do not fear, Abram, I am a shield to you; Your reward shall be very great.*
> Genesis 15:1

What great peace a man can have when he has entered into a blood covenant

16. 《左傳–桓公》 *Zuo Zhuan*, Duke Huan, Year 1, paragraph 2.
17. 《左傳–僖公》 Ibid., Duke Xi, Year 28, paragraph 17.
18. See Galatians 3:13; see also Matthew 27:45; Ephesians 1:3.
19. See Genesis 21:27; 24:42–58; Isaiah 49:18; 61:10.

relationship with the One True Almighty God! God Himself became Abraham's "exceeding great reward."

Chinese: In China, the giving of gifts was an established practice in covenant making. When the army of Chu 楚 threatened the State of Lu 魯 in 538 B.C., Meng Sun 孟孫, one of the three senior ministers,[20] volunteered to be the envoy to negotiate peace with the advancing enemy. He took with him one hundred craftsmen, one hundred female embroiderers, and as many weavers, along with Duke Cheng's son Gong Heng 公衡 as a hostage, and with them requested a covenant. Then the Chu army agreed to make peace.[21]

According to the *Record of Rites,*

> *What is done at sacrifices afforded the greatest example of the dispensation of favors. Hence when the superior possessed the greatest blessing, acts of favor were sure to descend from him to those below.*

祭港澤之大港也。是故上有大澤，則惠必及下。[22]

> *Anciently[sic] at the Di Sacrifice they conferred rank, and bestowed robes. At the Chang Sacrifice they gave out fields and homesteads.*

古港干裫也發爵賜服，順陽義也；干營也，出田邑，發秋政，順陰義也。[23]

New Testament Fulfillment: The Bible tells us that after Jesus cut the new covenant in His death and resurrection, He gave the gift of the Holy Spirit and other spiritual gifts to enable man to live an obedient life.

> *When He ascended on high, ... He gave gifts to men.*
> Ephesians 4:8

God's gifts are all encompassing.

> *Every good thing given and every perfect gift is from above, coming down from the Father of lights, with whom there is no variation or shifting shadow.*
> James 1:17

We know that God intends to shower us with all kinds of gifts because He has already given us the Ultimate Gift when He cut the covenant with us.

---

20. Meng Sun held the post of 司空 (Si Kong) of the State of Lu. The other two ministerial positions were 司徒 (Si Tu) and 司馬 (Si Ma).
21. See 《左傳-成公》 *Zuo Zhuan*, Duke Cheng, Year 2, paragraphs 8–10, Winter.
22. 《禮記-祭統》 *Rites*, Ji Tong (Summary of Sacrifices), end of paragraph 11.
23. Ibid., middle of paragraph 23.

He who did not spare His own Son, but delivered Him over for us all, how will
He not also with Him freely give us all things?
Romans 8:32

A Meal Was Shared

Old Testament: The covenants in Scripture all seem to have included a covenant meal together. When God and the people of Israel established the covenant of Sinai, in which God gave the Ten Commandments, Moses and the elders went up the mountain and had a covenant meal in the presence of God![24] After the Hebrew patriarch Jacob and his kinsman Laban entered into a covenant delineating the boundaries of their territory, they also shared a feast.[25] Jacob's father, Isaac, and Abimelech, a Philistine king, made a covenant pledging to live peaceably with each other and then had a feast.[26]

God has worked out his redemptive plan with mankind using this universal knowledge of the meal associated with the blood covenant. When He gave the people of Israel His instructions for appropriate and acceptable worship on the occasion of the covenant of Sinai, He ordained a unity between the brass Altar of Sacrifice, which represents access and reconciliation to God through the blood of a perfect sacrifice, and the Table of Showbread, which represents communion with God. According to Levitical law, eating the bread on the Table of Showbread was done as an act of worship.[27] Just as two parties celebrated their covenant with a meal, so God wanted to feast with His people.[28]

Chinese: From the *Zuo Zhuan Commentary* to the *Spring and Autumn Annals* 春秋左傳, it is clear that in China, those who entered into a covenant had a feast together after making the covenant. They might also sing "odes," songs from the *Classic of Poetry*, at the feast.[29] At the emperor's annual sacrifice at the Altar of Heaven, the altar for sacrifice and the tables for meals are placed in close proximity. In fact, so prominent a feature was the feasting at the yearly sacrifices that one foreign scholar said, "The Chinese idea of a sacrifice to the supreme ruler of Heaven and Earth is that of a banquet."[30] Access to God is obtained by the shedding of blood (at the altar), after which the emperor can enjoy communion with God at the meal (the table).

24. See Exodus 24, especially verse 11.
25. See Genesis 31:54.
26. Genesis 26:26 – 31; 31:44 – 54; Exodus 24:1 – 11 especially verses 8 – 11.
27. See Exodus 25:23 – 30; 27:1 – 8; 37:10 – 16; 38:1 – 7.
28. See Leviticus 24:9; Deuteronomy 14:23; Isaiah 25:6; 1 Corinthians 10:17 – 18.
29. See 《左傳–文公》 *Zuo Zhuan*, Duke Wen, Year 4, paragraph 4.
30. Joseph Edkins, *Religion in China, Containing a Brief Account of the Three Religions of the Chinese* (London: Trübner & Co., 1884), pp. 23, 32.

New Testament Fulfillment: We know from God's special revelation in Scripture that Jesus Christ is the spiritual fulfillment of the sacrifice and the fulfillment of the bread and wine of the covenant meal.

> *Jesus said to them, "I am the bread of life; he who comes to Me will not hunger, and he who believes in Me will never thirst."*
> John 6:35

That is why Jesus instituted the Lord's Supper, often called Communion, in which the bread is the symbol of His body and the cup is the symbol of His blood.[31] Now we can regularly feast at the Lord's Table, in fellowship with Him, without having to repeat the sacrifice ever again![32]

A New Name Was Given

Old Testament: Sometimes people were given a new covenant name after making a blood covenant. This is quite common in marriage covenants, which were considered in the Bible to be blood covenants because blood is shed when a marriage is consummated.

> *The Lord has been a witness between you and the wife of your youth, against whom you have dealt treacherously, though she is your companion and your wife by covenant.*
> Malachi 2:14

The wife takes a new name from the husband with whom she has entered into a marriage (blood) covenant. God gave both Abram and Sarai new covenant names when He entered into a blood covenant relationship with them. Abram, meaning "exalted father," became Abraham, meaning "father of many nations," while Sarai's new name was Sarah.[33]

Chinese: In the past, Chinese had different names at different stages of their lives as their responsibilities and relationships changed. An infant would be given a "milk name 乳名" (ru ming). When he was of school age, he would have a "school name 學名" (xue ming). When he came of age at 20 years old, he was given a "hat name 冠名" (guan ming), which comes from the idea that only adults wore hats. An emperor would be given a reign title 年號 (nian hao) when he assumed the throne and a posthumous name 謚號 (shi hao) upon his death.

31. Hebrews 10:5–14; John 6:32–35; Matthew 26:26–29; Mark 14:22–25; Luke 22:17–20; 1 Corinthians 11:23–29.
32. Hebrews 10:10–14.
33. Genesis 17:5 and 15.

New Testament Fulfillment: After Saul of Tarsus, an impassioned persecutor of Christians, was confronted by Jesus on the road to Damascus and converted, his name was changed to Paul, to indicate his new life as a Christian. Likewise, many people adopt a "Christian name" after their conversion.

When Jesus returns and sets up His eternal kingdom, He will give each believer a new name.

> *He who overcomes, I will make him a pillar in the temple of My God, and he will not go out from it anymore; and I will write on him the name of My God, and the name of the city of My God, the new Jerusalem, which comes down out of heaven from My God, and My new name.*
> Revelation 3:12[34]

The Covenant Was Memorialized

Old Testament: Often, after a covenant was cut, a special sign would be designated to serve as a constant reminder of the special covenant relationship. Sometimes the covenanting parties would plant a tree or trees as a memorial of their covenant. In the case of Jacob and Laban, a pile of stones was designated the "heap of witness" to their covenant, which we will look at in more detail below. In one of Abraham's covenants, seven ewe lambs were set apart as "a witness" to the covenant transaction.[35] In Abraham's covenant with God, the sign was circumcision.[36]

Chinese: Whether or not the Chinese understood its blood covenant significance, the planting of trees in the Altar of Heaven complex has been an important feature of this most significant religious site in Beijing. Some of the cypress trees there are 500 years old. Also interesting to note are the special "Seven-Star rocks" that the Ming emperor Jia Jing 嘉靖 ordered placed to the southeast of the Prayer Hall for Good Harvest.[37] Although he did it on the advice of Taoist priests,[38] it is possible there was some connection unknown to them with the ancient rites of using stones to memorialize blood covenants, as in the case of Jacob and Laban.

New Testament Fulfillment: The memorial ceremony of the New Covenant is water baptism, the ritual by which a Christian publicly demonstrates that he is now

34. See also Revelation 2:17.

35. See Genesis 21:30

36. See Genesis 17:11.

37. There are now eight rocks at this site because the Qing emperor Qian Long, 乾隆, later ordered another rock to be placed to symbolize the North Star.

38. See Heyi Chen, editor, *Tiantan* (Beijing: Pictorial Publishing House, 1992), p. 20.

"immersed in Christ" and that he has a new relationship with and a new identity in Christ. Water baptism parallels the Old Covenant practice of circumcision. It signifies that the Christian is now a totally new person because of Christ's death on the cross. By correlation, the cross has become the universally recognized visible sign of the Christian's blood covenant relationship with God.[39]

The Covenant Must Be Renewed

Old Testament: Once a covenant was established, each successive generation of the two covenanting parties had to decide for themselves whether they would also enter into the covenant made by their forefathers. For the nation of Israel, every male entered into the Abrahamic covenant with God through the act of circumcision.[40]

Chinese: Many of the covenants cited in the *Zuo Zhuan* were actually "renewals" of earlier covenants, a practice that was common in biblical history as well.[41] Various reasons are given in the *Zuo Zhuan* for renewing covenants by the shedding of new blood, but the fact that this had to be done reveals a major underlying principle. This is the same principle that required the emperor to sacrifice yearly at the Altar of Heaven, and required the Israelites to repeat the sacrifices on the annual Day of Atonement at the Tabernacle of God.[42]

The reason these sacrifices had to be repeated year after year and the covenants renewed was because they were just shadows of good things to come; they were not themselves perfect. Being imperfect, they could not make perfect those who offered the sacrifices and entered into the covenants; hence, they had to be repeated annually, again and again. If they had been able to accomplish reconciliation with God once for all, the practice of covenants and sacrifices would have ceased.[43]

New Testament Fulfillment: The sacrifices that were made before Jesus' arrival were no more than

> *a symbol for the present time. Accordingly both gifts and sacrifices are offered which cannot make the worshipper perfect in conscience, since they relate only to food and drink and various washings, regulations for the body imposed until a time of reformation.*
> Hebrews 9:9–10

39. Colossians 2:11–12; Romans 2:29; Galatians 6:12–14.
40. Genesis 17:7–14.
41. Abimelech, Ahuzzath, and Phichol cut a covenant with Isaac in Genesis 26:26–31. This was a renewal of a covenant that had previously been made between Abraham and another man named Abimelech, in Genesis 21:22–33.
42. See Leviticus 16 and 23:26–32.
43. Hebrews 10:1–2.

When He was crucified, the Lord Jesus Christ ushered in the "time of reformation" through His ultimate sacrifice on the cross of Calvary. For Jesus,

> *having offered one sacrifice for sins for all time, sat down at the right hand of God, waiting from that time onward until His enemies be made a footstool for His feet. For by one offering He has perfected for all time those who are sanctified.*
> Hebrews 10:12 – 14

Now, each person in each new generation has to decide for himself whether to enter into this perfect covenant relationship. Those who choose not to enter into a blood covenant relationship with God through Jesus Christ will be cut off from the covenant promises of glory and will spend eternity in hell.

USES OF THE BLOOD COVENANT IN THE ANCIENT WORLD

The large numbers of international treaties preserved in texts that survive to this day, particularly those from the ancient Near East, provide ample evidence of the importance of covenants across the ancient world. Henry Clay Trumbull, the noted 19th-century scholar and evangelist, in his seminal work *The Blood Covenant*, documents the fact that blood covenants were common to virtually all peoples the world over.[44] Evidence of covenant-making rites are found among primitive peoples from all corners of the world, dating back long before the days of Abraham, which was c. 2000 B.C.[45] Though some of the specific details of these ceremonies differed from one society to another, Trumbull finds basic underlying principles common to almost all of them. Proof of the independent existence of this rite of blood covenants in Asia, Africa, Europe, America, the islands of the Pacific, and among the five major divisions of the human family—Caucasian, Mongolian, African, Malay, and American—suggests a common origin.[46]

It should not be at all surprising, therefore, to find striking similarities between rituals recorded in the Old Testament and those of ancient China, and to discover that blood covenants were employed in much the same way in both cultures. Again, we will first look at examples as they occurred in Hebrew culture and in ancient China. Then we will look at how the symbolism and ceremonial details in these

44. Trumbull, *The Blood Covenant*, pp. 219–20.
45. Ibid., p. 206.
46. Ibid., p. 57.

covenants find their ultimate and final fulfillment in God's final covenant with mankind through Jesus Christ.

To Establish Peace

"So now come, let us make a covenant, you and I, and let it be a witness between you and me." Then Jacob took a stone and set it up as a pillar. Jacob said to his kinsmen, "Gather stones." So they took stones and made a heap, and they ate there by the heap. Now Laban called it Jegar-sahadutha, but Jacob called it Galeed. Laban said, "This heap is a witness between you and me this day." Therefore it was named Galeed, and Mizpah, for he said, "May the LORD watch between you and me when we are absent one from the other. If you mistreat my daughters, or if you take wives besides my daughters, although no man is with us, see, God is witness between you and me." Laban said to Jacob, "Behold this heap and behold the pillar which I have set between you and me. This heap is a witness, and the pillar is a witness, that I will not pass by this heap to you for harm, and you will not pass by this heap and this pillar to me, for harm. The God of Abraham and the God of Nahor, the God of their father, judge between us." So Jacob swore by the fear of his father Isaac. Then Jacob offered a sacrifice on the mountain, and called his kinsmen to the meal; and they ate the meal and spent the night on the mountain.
Genesis 31:44–54

Old Testament: This covenant between Jacob and Laban was a mutual non-aggression pact. A sacrifice was made, an oath or the words of the covenant were spoken, a covenant meal was eaten, and God was called on as witness to the covenant.

Chinese: Covenants in China were made to establish peace between two or more feuding parties, such as the covenant cut at Ai 艾 in 716 B.C. between the state of Lu 魯國 and the state of Qi 齊國.[47] They were also a means of bringing about reconciliation, such as the renewal in 668 B.C. of an earlier covenant between Duke Huan of Qi 齊桓公 (685–43 B.C.), and Zhu Zi Ke 邾子克 the ruler of Zhu 邾.[48] Thus, a covenant brings with it a commitment to banish everything contrary to good relations between the covenanting parties.[49]

47. See 《左傳–隱公》 *Zuo Zhuan*, Duke Yin, Year 6, paragraph 2.
48. See 《左傳–桓公》 Ibid., Duke Huan, Year 17, paragraphs 1–2.
49. See 《左傳–僖公》 Ibid., Duke Xi, Year 9, paragraph 4.

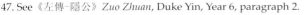

Finding God in Ancient China

New Testament Fulfillment: The Bible teaches that, through the new and everlasting covenant cut on the cross, the enmity between God and man that resulted from man's disobedience has been removed, covered over by the blood of Jesus. God wants everyone to worship Him and fellowship with Him now through the eternal Son of Heaven, Jesus Christ.

> But God demonstrates His own love toward us, in that while we were yet sinners, Christ died for us. Much more then, having now been justified by His blood, we shall be saved from the wrath of God through Him. For if while we were enemies we were reconciled to God through the death of His Son, much more, having been reconciled, we shall be saved by His life.
> Romans 5:8–10

> But now in Christ Jesus you who formerly were far off have been brought near by the blood of Christ. For He Himself is our peace, who made both groups into one and broke down the barrier of the dividing wall.
> Ephesians 2:13–14

To Unite Armies

Old Testament: After making a covenant with Israel, the Gibeonites came under military attack from a coalition of five kings. Because Israel had already cut a blood covenant with the Gibeonites, the Israelites were obligated to come to the Gibeonites' defense.[50]

Covenant friends would come to each other's defense when one of them was attacked. This is what Jonathan, son of King Saul, was symbolically saying to David by giving David his sword and bow when making their blood covenant in 1 Samuel 18:3–4.

This is one of the encouraging aspects of entering into a blood covenant relationship with God: He promises to be our protector.[51] In the Old Testament, when Israel lived up to her blood covenant responsibilities with God, He himself would come to Israel's defense when she was attacked by powerful enemies.[52] On the other hand, when a king of Israel worshipped idols, God would deliver him into the hands of his enemies.[53]

170

50. See Joshua 9:1–20 and 10:1–10.
51. See Genesis 15:1.
52. Jehoshaphat in 2 Chronicles 20; Uzziah in 2 Chronicles 26:5–8; Hezekiah in 2 Chronicles 32:15–22.
53. For example, Ahaz in 2 Chronicles 28:1–5.

Chinese: Many of the covenants mentioned in the *Classic of History* were for the purpose of uniting armies for war and defense. The ruler of the state in which a covenant was made was expected to supply the provisions for all the covenanting parties.[54] Covenants also were made to establish a person in political office.[55] They also conferred upon the covenanting parties the right to make requests for supplies or help from the other party or parties.[56]

New Testament Fulfillment: In Christ, God has made all His spiritual weapons available to Christians, enabling us to win our battles against Satan and demons.[57] Now "the weapons of our warfare are not of the flesh, but divinely powerful for the destruction of fortresses."[58] We now can overcome Satan "through the blood of the Lamb," that is, through the blood of the everlasting covenant that guarantees our eternal life in heaven.[59]

To Protect the Weaker Party

Old Testament: When the Gibeonites came to make a covenant with Joshua, they did so because they were the weaker nation and wanted the Israelites to protect them from being destroyed.[60]

Chinese: A covenant was often made between a superior and a politically or socially inferior party. This was done for the protection or benefit of the inferior.[61] The inferior or weaker party sometimes would acknowledge their humility and dependence by prostrating and touching their heads to the ground.[62] Thus, covenants were a strong bond of submission to "the greater." The accepted protocol in making covenants was that the larger, stronger state was considered the initiator of covenant relationships. The *Zuo Zhuan*, says, "A small state is sure to bring trouble on itself when it seeks to dominate a covenant. The state of Song will surely perish, they would be fortunate if this is delayed."[63]

New Testament Fulfillment: Jesus cut the new covenant with the Heavenly Father by His sacrifice on the cross, and in so doing, He protects us from all our spiritual enemies. In making a blood covenant with mankind, it is God, as sovereign, who initiates the covenant. This is because

54. See 《左傳-僖公》 *Zuo Zhuan*, Duke Xi, Year 19, paragraph 2–4.
55. See 《左傳-薛公》 Ibid., Duke Zhuang, Year 9, paragraphs 2–3, and Year 16, paragraph 4.
56. See 《左傳-簡公》 Ibid., Duke Wen, Year 1, paragraph 4.
57. See Ephesians 6:11-13.
58. Second Corinthians 10:4.
59. See Revelation 12:9–12; Hebrews 13:20.
60. See Joshua 9.
61. See 《左傳-文公》 *Zuo Zhuan*, Duke Wen, Year 3, paragraph 6.
62. Example: Duke of Xiang 襄公 kowtowing to the Duke of Jin 晋侯公 as recorded in 《左傳-襄公》 Ibid., Duke Xiang, Year 3, paragraph 3.
63. "小國爭盟，禍也，宋其亡乎，幸而后敗" in 《左傳-僖公》 Ibid., Duke Xi, Year 21, paragraph 1.

without any dispute the lesser is blessed by the greater.
Hebrews 7:7

As human beings, we all have many weaknesses. It is to our present and eternal advantage to enter into a blood covenant relationship with Shang Di. We can then "be strong in the Lord and in the strength of His might."[64] We can be protected from powerful evil spirits because Shang Di will eventually destroy all these lesser gods.[65] If we enter into a blood covenant relationship with Shang Di, it is absolutely necessary that we break off all our relationships with lesser gods and idols. One need not fear the spirits of angry idols or anything else once Almighty God is the protector! We can say confidently, as the psalmist did,

> *The LORD is my light and my salvation;*
> *Whom shall I fear?*
> *The LORD is the defense of my life;*
> *Whom shall I dread?*
> Psalm 27:1

To Strengthen Friendship

Old Testament: The covenant of David with Jonathan in 1 Samuel 18:1–4 was a friendship covenant that was to extend to their descendants forever.[66]

The highest use of blood covenant is to establish an eternal friendship with Almighty God. Abraham entered into such a blood covenant relationship with God through the sacrifice of animals,

> *a three-year-old heifer, and a three-year-old female goat, and a three-year-old*
> *ram, and a turtledove, and a young pigeon.*
> Genesis 15:9

Later, circumcision became the sign of that covenant. Once the covenant was established, Abraham was called the friend of God![67] The Bible mentions others who also entered into covenants of friendship with God; for instance, King Hezekiah in 2 Chronicles 29:10.

Chinese: In China, a covenant was a way to publicly declare or confirm one's strong friendship with the other party.[68] A covenant could also be a strong commitment to

64. Ephesians 6:10.
65. See Psalm 82:6–8.
66. See 1 Samuel 20:15.
67. See Genesis 15:1–18; 17:10–13; and James 2:23.
68. See 《左傳-定公》 *Zuo Zhuan*, Duke Ding, Year 3, paragraph 5.

carry out a plan of action to secure common goals.[69] Covenant friends would come to each other's defense if an enemy attacked. The *Zuo Zhuan* says,

> *Qi and Chu are bound by a covenant, and we have lately made a covenant with Jin. Jin and Chu are striving for the supremacy over all the states. The army of Qi is sure to come [against us]; and though the people of Jin invade Qi, Chu will go to its relief: thus both Chu and Qi will together attack us.*

齊楚結好，我新與晋盟，晋楚争盟，齊飾必至，雖晋人伐齊，楚必救之，是齊楚同我也，知難而有烯，乃可以逞。[70]

Such blood covenants are found all over the world. "It is a peculiarity of the primitive compact of blood-friendship, that he who would enter into it must be ready to make a complete surrender of himself, in loving trust to him with whom he covenants," observes Trumbull in *The Blood Covenant*.[71]

New Testament Fulfillment: When we enter into a blood covenant relationship with God, to become His friend, we must trust and obey Him by giving up all our associations with idols and false gods. When the priest Jehoiada made a covenant between the Lord and the king and his people, that they should be the Lord's people, they went and destroyed the altars to idols and the images of idols.[72] We have to do the same when we accept Jesus' gift of salvation and eternal life.

THE SERIOUS CONSEQUENCES OF A BROKEN COVENANT

Historical texts reveal one more very important characteristic of blood covenants that is evident in both the Chinese and Hebrew cultures. The relationships that were forged through the dramatic experience of a blood covenant were held together by an unusually strong bonding power. Consequently, these covenants could not be broken without serious consequences.

Old Testament: When Joshua and the Israelites agreed to a covenant with a nearby peoples, the Gibeonites, it was the result of intentional deception on the part of the Gibeonites. Even so, Joshua and the Israelites could not break or violate the oath of the covenant once it was made. The leaders of Israel said, "We have sworn to them

69. See 《左傳－僖公》 Ibid., Duke Xi, Year 5, paragraph 5.
70. 《左傳－成公》 Ibid., Duke Cheng, Year 1, paragraph 5.
71. Trumbull, *The Blood Covenant*, pp. 219–20.
72. See 2 Kings 11:17–18.

FINDING GOD IN ANCIENT CHINA

by the Lord, the God of Israel, and now we cannot touch them. This we will do to them, even let them live, so that wrath will not be upon us for the oath which we swore to them."[73] When King Saul violated this covenant with the Gibeonites and killed them, a deadly curse came upon his entire family.[74]

Just as Shang Di required a proper heart attitude on the part of those offering sacrifices to Him in China, so the Bible tells us a proper heart attitude and righteous living are required to offer an acceptable sacrifice to God. Shang Di and the God of the Bible are one and the same, and He will hold every one of us accountable for keeping our word.[75]

Chinese: In every place where blood covenants were practiced, they were regarded as the most intimate, holiest, and most indissoluble compact conceivable.[76] Covenants were meant to give security to an established relationship by guaranteeing that it would never be broken. This guarantee reflects an understanding that the spirit world, specifically Shang Di, was somehow involved in holding people accountable to keep their blood covenant oaths. Blood covenants in China were cut with this solemn understanding.

In one account in the *Zuo Zhuan*, the state of Jin calls for a renewal of a covenant with other states. At the meeting, Ji Wen Zi 範文子, a minister of the state of Lu, told the Jin general Fan Wen Zi 季文子, "Since your virtue is not strong, of what use is the renewal of covenants?" Fan Wen Zi responded in part by saying, "by appealing to the intelligent spirits to bind [our agreements, covenants], by gently dealing with those who submit, and by punishing the disaffected, we exhibit an influence only second to that of virtue."[77] This clearly shows that the early Chinese believed the spirit world observed and held the people accountable for their oaths and covenants.

In another account recorded in the *Zuo Zhuan*, many officials of the state of Chu arrived to negotiate a covenant with several other states while wearing armor inside their clothing. Seeing this, Chu's Chief Minister, Bo Zhou Li 州犁, said, "We have called the States to this covenant, and we are acting without integrity; how can this be? ... If we do not maintain integrity, we are throwing away the very thing that will make the other States submit to us." Zi Mu 子木, another Chu official, replied, "Jin and Chu have never really trusted one another; let's

174

73. See Joshua 9:3–9, 14–20, especially verses 19 and 20.
74. See 2 Samuel 21:1–7.
75. See Numbers 30:2; Isaiah 1:11-17; Jeremiah 7:21–23; Hosea 6:4–7; and Matthew 12:36–37.
76. Trumbull, *The Blood Covenant*, pp. 204, 206.
77. "德則不效。尋盟何爲" and "範文子曰，勤以撫之，寬以待之，堅疆以禦之，明神以要之，柔服而伐貳，德之次也，是行也，將始會吳，吳人不至" in 《左傳–成公》 *Zuo Zhuan*, Duke Cheng, Year 9, paragraph 2.

do whatever gives us an advantage. As long as we can accomplish our goals we will not care about integrity." When Bo Zhou Li heard this, he said, "Zi Mu will certainly not escape an evil end. Good faith is seen in the maintenance of propriety, and propriety is a protection to the person. If a man puts away both good faith and propriety, though he wishes to avoid an evil end, can he do so?" He predicted that Zi Mu would die within three years.[78]

The binding power of these agreements can be seen in the fact that Duke Huan of Qi did not break a covenant by entering into a new covenant even though he had been forced into the original covenant at sword point at an altar in the Qi capital of Ke.[79] His commitment to the covenant earned him the respect of other rulers during this tumultuous time in China, and he later rose to become the leader of all the warring states because of his integrity. One ancient Chinese commentator said the "good faith of Duke Huan began from this covenant at Ke to be acknowledged throughout the Kingdom."[80] Duke Huan understood the binding power of an established covenant. Of course, not everyone was similarly faithful, but those who broke their covenants were believed to be risking the wrath of the spirit world which held people accountable for keeping covenants.

Thus, the high moral character of the covenanting parties combined with the solemnity of shedding the blood of an innocent sacrifice resulted in the establishment of the strongest relationship possible between two parties.

New Testament Fulfillment: The writer of the New Testament Book of Hebrews warns,

> *Anyone who has set aside the Law of Moses dies without mercy on the testimony of two or three witnesses. How much severer punishment do you think he will deserve who has trampled under foot the Son of God, and has regarded as unclean the blood of the covenant by which he was sanctified, and has insulted the Spirit of grace? . . . It is a terrifying thing to fall into the hands of the living God.*
> Hebrews 10:28-29, 31

WHEN CHINA LOST SIGHT OF THE BLOOD

As in the previous chapters, we have discovered here many similarities between ancient China and ancient Israel in their understanding of the One True God.

---

78. ″合諸侯之師，以爲不信，無乃不可乎，夫諸侯望信于楚，是以來服，若不信，是棄其所以服諸侯也″，″晋楚無信久矣，事利而已，苟得志焉，焉用有信″and ″令尹將死矣，不及三年，求逞志而弃信， 志將逞乎，志以發言，言以出信，信以立志，參以定之，信亡<可以及三″ in《左傳−襄公》Ibid., Duke Xiang, Year 27, paragraph 6.
79. See《左傳−莊公》Ibid., Duke Zhuang, Year 13, paragraph 2.
80. As quoted by Legge, *The Ch'un Ts'ew*, pp. 90–91.

FINDING GOD IN ANCIENT CHINA

China's centuries-old written language even today reflects knowledge of God's earliest relationship with man. Ancient writings show that the Shang Di who was worshipped of old had the same attributes as the Hebrew God of the Old Testament. The sacrificial rites that China's emperors all through the centuries were careful to observe were based on reverence for the Name Above All Names. At some point in China's long history, however, this intimate, widespread knowledge of the One True God faded and became confused with other beliefs and rituals in Chinese culture. This occurred when China lost sight of the blood and its significance in the blood covenant.

In the ceremony of the Border Sacrifice described in the previous chapter, the sacrificial animal was prepared for the ritual by someone other than the emperor, thus sparing the emperor the bloody and unpleasant task of cutting the live animal and killing it. This, however, was not always the case. In the earliest religious rites, the emperor was required to perform this distasteful task himself. The *Record of Rites* makes it clear that this act of offering the sacrifice was a most unpleasant job, and the emperor and other worshippers would get blood all over their hands.[81] This changed in the Eastern Zhou Dynasty 東周 (770–249 B.C.), marking a major departure from earlier practices and stripping the ceremony of its most profound meaning. "Thus, the shedding of the victim's blood was no longer a significant aspect of the rites. Some of the immediacy and deep meaning of the sacrificial performance were dispensed with in favor of maintaining the dignity of the imperial position," one historian observed.[82]

Before this departure from the ancient rites, the Chinese people had observed a unified religion in which these sacrificial rites carried out by the emperor were of primary importance. A serious breakdown in the observation and preservation of these ceremonies occurred when many new theories of religion came into play. The *Record of Rites* pinpoints the first symptoms of decline as occurring during the reign of Yi 夷, the ninth emperor of the Zhou Dynasty (894–879 B.C.).[83] Confucius mentions the kings Li 厲 (reigned 878–828 B.C.) and You 幽 (reigned 781–771 B.C.) as also corrupting the ways of Zhou.[84] This period was roughly about the time of the prophet Isaiah in the Old Testament, the legendary reign of seven kings in Rome, and the first Olympic games in Greece. It was during this period of 2,138 years—from the beginning of the Eastern Zhou in 770 B.C. to the beginning of

81. 《禮記-禮器》 *Rites*, Li Qi (Ritual Articles), beginning of paragraph 10.
82. Lester James Bilsky, *The State Religion of Ancient China*, Asian Folklore and Social Life Monographs: Volume 70-71 (Taipei: Oriental Cultural Service for the Chinese Association for Folklore, 1975), p. 269.
83. 《禮記-郊特牲》 *Rites*, Jiao Te Sheng (Border Sacrifice Animal), Section 1, end of paragraph 4.
84. 《禮記-禮運》 Ibid., Li Yun (Ritual Usages), beginning of paragraph 8.

the Ming Dynasty in A.D. 1368 — that most of the corruption of the original faith in Shang Di took place. It was also during this time that Confucianism, Taoism, and Buddhism, which were to become the three main religions of China, grew to dominate the Chinese people and to fill them with fears of evil spirits and false teachings about the One True God. Emperors of the earliest dynasties had carefully observed the Border Sacrifice that was a cornerstone of China's covenant relationship with Shang Di, but during this long period of more than two millennia, the ceremony was corrupted.

As recounted in the previous chapter, the Border Sacrifice or Sacrifice to Heaven was revived when the first Ming emperor, Hong Wu 洪武 (reigned A.D. 1368 – 1398), commissioned an investigation into ancient rites and practices. As a result of this investigation, the Ming Dynasty returned to the pure worship that was taught in the *Classics*:

The border sacrifice is the illustration of the way of Heaven.

郊所以明天道也。[85]

Hence we have the saying that the first and greatest teaching is to be found in sacrifice.

故曰：祭渚，教之本也已。[86]

That which is most important in performing the rites is to understand the meaning intended in it. If the meaning is lost, then the sacrifices are simply presented as a national celebration. Then subsequent generations will present the sacrifice but not understand its significance. The Son of Heaven [i.e., the Emperor] who understands the meaning [of the sacrifice] and practices it, he will be able to rule the nation.

禮之所尊，尊其義也。失其義，陳其數，祝史之事也。故其數可陳也，其義難知也；知其義而敬守之，天子之所以治天下也。[87]

Sacrifices to false gods were abolished from the ceremony, and Ming Emperor Jia Jing (reigned A.D. 1522 – 1566) subsequently repaired and expanded the Altar of Heaven complex in Beijing. This ceremony acknowledging the preeminence of

85. 《禮記–郊特牲》 Ibid., Jiao Te Sheng (Border Sacrifice Animal), Section 2, end of paragraph 9.
86. 《禮記–祭統》 Ibid., Ji Tong (Summary of Sacrifices), end of paragraph 12.
87. 《禮記–郊特牲》 Ibid., Jiao Te Sheng (Border Sacrifice Animal), Section 2, beginning of paragraph 3.

Shang Di and restoring the blood covenant continued until the founding of the Republic in 1911.

When Jesus celebrated what is now called the Last Supper the night before His crucifixion, He passed around a cup of wine to his disciples and instructed them,

> *Drink from it, all of you; for this is My blood of the covenant, which is poured out for many for forgiveness of sins.*
> Matthew 26:27–28

This was a foreshadowing of the new and everlasting covenant between Almighty God and mankind that Jesus, the Lamb of God, cut when He shed his blood and died on the cross for the sins of all men. The Bible makes it very clear why this was necessary:

> *Without shedding of blood there is no forgiveness [of sins].*
> Hebrews 9:22

THE NEW COVENANT

Henry Clay Trumbull in his seminal work on blood covenants observed:

> *The prevailing idea in the ancient world and the Bible was that the blood represents life (Leviticus 17:10–14); that the giving of blood represents the giving of life; that the receiving of blood represents the receiving of life; that inter-comingling of blood represents the inter-comingling of natures; and that a divine-human inter-union through blood is the basis of a divine-human inter-communion in the sharing of the flesh of the sacrificial offering as sacred food.*[88]

In China, as in the Mosaic law of the Hebrew people, the symbols and symbolic ceremonies of the blood covenant pointed to the possibility of a union of man's spiritual nature with God. These symbols and symbolic acts, however, did not in themselves either assure that such a union could be established or indicate that it already had been accomplished. They were merely a "shadow of things to come." Man can be united to God only through Jesus Christ and that only because of the blood of the new covenant shed on the cross. As the Bible puts it, "the one who joins himself to the Lord is one spirit with Him."[89] This intimate union with God

88. Trumbull, *The Blood Covenant*, p. 209.
89. First Corinthians 6:17.

is a glorious mystery that is divinely foreshadowed in the marriage relationship:

> *For this reason a man shall leave his father and mother and shall be joined to*
> *his wife, and the two shall become one flesh. This mystery is great; but I am*
> *speaking with reference to Christ and the church.*
> Ephesians 5:31 – 32

Since the very beginning of China's history, Shang Di has been revealing the truth of blood covenants to the Chinese people. The parallels between China's practice of covenants and God's perfect revelation of covenants in the Holy Scriptures are vivid and eloquent. God used these dramatic ceremonies to teach eternal principles that were finally fulfilled in Jesus Christ. When we correctly understand that the divine intent was for these ceremonies to be a "tutor to lead us to Christ,"[90] we should never have any desire to go back to the Old Law, which was meant to pass away, giving way to the New Covenant!

> *When He said, "A new covenant," He has made the first obsolete. But whatever*
> *is becoming obsolete and growing old is ready to disappear.*
> Hebrews 8:13

Why did the offering of sacrifice continue unbroken for 4,000 years of history in China? Because those sacrifices could never make the one who offered them perfect. If they had been able to do so, it would not have been necessary to keep offering these sacrifices over and over, and the ceremonies would have ceased long before the revolution of 1911 that marked the end of dynastic rule in China. That was not the case, however, because the blood of bulls, sheep, pigs, and goats can never take away sin, and so the sacrifices were offered year after year as a remembrance of sin. Shang Di, however, has supplied another sacrifice, one that was perfect to take away all sin for all time: Jesus Christ, the Lamb of God, sacrificed on the cross of Calvary, for the sins of the whole world.

> *For by one offering He has perfected for all time those who are sanctified.*
> Hebrews 10:14

This sacrifice was made for all time for all people, including the Chinese people. The use of blood covenants by peoples and civilizations the world over is well-documented. The Chinese were no exception. Our comparative examination of blood

90. Galatians 3:24 – 25.

A reenactment of the emperor offering sacrifices to renew China's covenant with Shang Di annually.   Credit: CBN

covenants in the Chinese and Hebrew cultures showed us that the symbolism of these ancient rites was divinely ordained to prepare mankind for the final blood covenant: that which God cut with all mankind through the shed blood of Jesus Christ on the cross. From the very beginning of China's long history, Shang Di has been revealing the truth of blood covenants to the Chinese people in order to prepare them to receive life's greatest blessing: salvation through the eternal Tian Zi 天子, Son of God, who is Jesus Christ. Rather than being the founder of a foreign Western religion, Jesus Christ is the fulfillment of the longing expressed annually through the shedding of blood at the Border Sacrifice for an unbroken, unblemished relationship with Shang Di. The same Creator God that China knew dimly through many millennia can now be known intimately and clearly through His special revelation in Jesus Christ.

We have seen in the Chinese and Hebrew cultures many examples of a similar understanding of the One True God and His ways. I wondered why no one had pointed out these points of commonality to me earlier. Surely I was not among the first to recognize Shang Di as the same God worshipped by the Hebrews and the Christians! When I arrived at the signpost marked "Magi from the West," I found that I had been preceded in this journey of discovery by brilliant men from ages past.

REFLECT and RESPOND

Not only has China lost sight of the blood, but also our modern world in general has lost a genuine understanding of covenant relationships. In fact, this word "covenant" is now rarely used, and covenant-based relationships have become almost obsolete. In its place are highly technical legal relationships that are not founded on the intimate bonds of a blood covenant. When God is taken out of the equation, ancient covenants with their self-policing nature are reduced to modern relationships whose strength is based solely on the caliber of lawyers one can afford. The fragile state of the institution of marriage is but the most vivid example of what happens when covenant relationships are discarded. Human beings, however, were not made to live as isolated and self-focused individuals; we were made to enter into extended blood relationships with others, forming dynamic covenant-keeping communities.

Are you a member of such a community? If not, take the first step by entering into a covenant relationship with Jesus. The second step is to join others who are a party to this covenant in the regular corporate worship of God.

陸

Magi from the West

He who is called Lord of Heaven in my humble country is He who is called Shang Di in Chinese.

~ Matteo Ricci, eminent Italian sinologist, Jesuit priest, and advisor to Chinese emperor

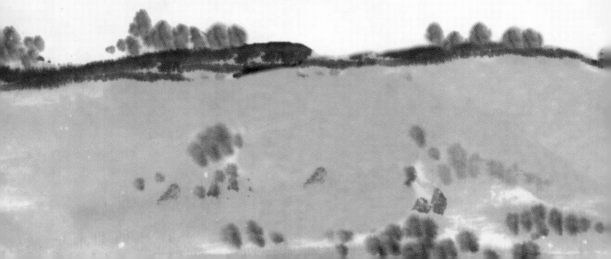

博士

6

Magi from the West

To usher in the 21st century, the Chinese government rushed to completion a Millennium Monument in Beijing and unveiled it on December 31, 1999, as part of the worldwide celebrations marking the turn of the century. The centerpiece of this monument is a circular wall relief entitled "Tribute to Chinese History 中華千秋頌."

Measuring 117 meters (386 feet) long by 5 meters (16.5 feet) high and made with 15 types of colored stones, the relief proudly depicts China's historical achievements and developments over 5,000 years. Surprisingly, among the parade of Chinese heroes—everyone from ancient philosopher Confucius to modern statesman Sun Yat-sen—is a Western face. It is that of Catholic priest and scholar Matteo Ricci, artfully superimposed on the "Map of the World 萬國全圖." This was the very map that Ricci himself drew, carved, and had printed in Beijing in 1602. Given China's disdain in the preceding centuries for Westerners in general and missionaries in particular, the inclusion of this Italian Jesuit missionary in a tribute to the glories of Chinese history and civilization is nothing short of astounding. The mystery, however, goes even deeper.

My journey of discovery took me to the west side of Beijing, to a site about 700 meters (0.4 mile) west of the city's Second Ring Road, which was built over the site of the old imperial city wall. There, tucked away within the secluded campus of the Communist Party School of Beijing 北京市委紫校, is a cemetery for foreigners, the only burial ground for non-Chinese that still exists in the Chinese capital.

Photo at left shows Matteo Ricci (upper left) with a medical doctor who made great contributions in herbology (foreground), as depicted by the "Tribute to Chinese History" mural at the Millennium Monument in Beijing.

FINDING GOD IN ANCIENT CHINA

Behind locked gates are some 60 headstones memorializing the lives of foreigners from many European nations. The cemetery's old facade still has this inscription: "欽賜" (qin ci), meaning "granted by the Emperor." Such an inscription signifies a high honor bestowed by the supreme ruler of the empire. Many of these headstones are adorned with dragons, another sign that the deceased were held in the highest esteem because, from the Zhou Dynasty (11th century B.C. – 221 B.C.) on, the symbol of the dragon was used exclusively by Chinese emperors. The image of the dragon, the Chinese character for "dragon," and even the inclusion of the word "dragon" in a person's name were permitted for use by the emperor alone; anyone who appropriated its use was subject to death. In the long history of China, there has never been another instance of emperors bestowing such honors so freely to a single group of people, not even to high-ranking Chinese officials.

Headstones of foreign missionaries, most of them Jesuit priests, buried in an imperial cemetary in Beijing.

Who then were these foreigners and what did they do to warrant such esteem? They could be called "magi" or, more simply, wise men from the West. Most were Jesuit missionaries who came to China in the 16th to 18th centuries. At the head of the list was Matteo Ricci (A.D. 1552 – 1610), the scholar memorialized on the Millennium Monument. His headstone occupies the most prominent position in the cemetery and is the largest. Flanking Ricci's marker are the headstones of his fellow Jesuits, Johann Adam Schall von Bell (A.D. 1591 – 1666) on the left and Ferdinand Verbiest (A.D. 1623 – 1688) on the right.

Beijing's Millennium Monument

As I explored the wealth of information at this signpost for "Magi from the West," I learned how Shang Di had revealed himself through the lives of these devout scholars in China. More significantly, I learned that they had been on a similar journey hundreds of years ago and had come to the same conclusion that was taking root in my mind: that Shang Di, whom they discovered being worshipped in China, was the same God of the Bible, whom they revered, served, and had dedicated their lives to. These men were considered the most brilliant minds of their day; they were sober-minded men of great scholarship. I wanted to know how men who had consecrated their lives to serving the One True God could have arrived at such a startling conclusion: that a far-off pagan nation to which they wanted to bring the Good News of salvation already knew and worshipped the same God.

A partial view of the 117-meter (386-foot) "Tribute to Chinese History" mural.

THE SOCIETY OF JESUS

The story of these great men begins with the Society of Jesus (Societas Jesu) and its founder, Ignatius of Loyola. More commonly referred to as the Jesuits, this monastic order, which received papal approval in 1540,[1] is widely considered the principal agent of the Catholic Reformation.

This was the Catholic Church's response to the 16th-century schism that resulted in the Protestant Reformation led by the German theologian Martin Luther. Luther and those who followed him in quitting the Catholic Church were protesting its general corruption and certain specific unscriptural doctrines that fostered such corruption. Not every Catholic priest who disagreed with church practices left, however, and those who remained sought to change the church from within. This self-renewal brought about an internal reformation during which the clerical hierarchy renounced worldly attitudes and practices and corrected many of the earlier abuses.

The Spaniard Ignatius of Loyola was a soldier before his conversion. While recovering from a serious battle wound, he underwent an extended period of study and contemplation that led to his acceptance of Jesus as Lord and Savior. During an intense time of prayer, he wrote *Spiritual Exercises*, a guidebook to transform the heart and mind to more closely follow Christ.[2] The goal of these spiritual exercises was to bring a person to "a personal decision … to embark unconditionally on 'the imitation of Christ,' a decision that is expected to be accompanied by some sort of concrete change in the course of one's own life."[3]

Ignatius' purpose in founding the Society of Jesus was to "do battle in the Lord God's service under the banner of Christ."[4] He championed a return to a biblical faith in Christ alone. "Since we acknowledge no other leader than Our Lord Jesus Christ, it is fitting that we have come together as the compania Jesus Christus," he said.[5] Out of this internal Catholic reformation characterized by a return to biblical faith arose a wave of missionaries to China in the waning years of the Ming Dynasty.

1. "Jesuit," Encyclopædia Britannica, from *Encyclopaedia Britannica Ultimate Reference Suite 2004 DVD*. Copyright © 1994–2003 Encyclopaedia Britannica, Inc., May 30, 2003.
2. Ibid.
3. Manfred Barthel, translated and adapted by Mark Howson, *The Jesuits: History and Legend of the Society of Jesus* (New York: William Morrow, 1984), p. 73.
4. Ibid., p. 39.
5. Ibid.

A Generation of Giants

Matteo Ricci 利瑪竇 (1552–1610)

Matteo Ricci was not the first Jesuit missionary to enter China, but his humility, patience, scholarship, and novel contributions made him the most recognized name among Jesuit missions in the nation. Ricci earned this high honor and esteem by first demonstrating his respect for the Chinese people and their culture. As a result, he discovered in China not a barbaric people but a nation with a rich, enduring history and a complex system of ethical standards and mores. Ricci's strategy was to strive for winsome introduction, cultural adaptation, and the avoidance of needless conflict with

Seventeenth-century portrait of Matteo Ricci in the Italian School style.   Credit: The Bridgeman Art Library

Chinese prejudices and suspicions. His goal was far-sighted: he was aiming for a deeply rooted indigenous church of sincere Christians rather than a multitude of half-hearted candidates for baptism.

Ricci was born October 6, 1552, to a noble family in Macerata, central Italy. At the age of 16, he went to Rome to study law. It was there that he joined the Jesuits in 1571. The order was already distinguishing itself in the scientific and spiritual disciplines; Ricci excelled in both, studying under the tutelage of the noted mathematician Christopher Clavius. The Jesuits' missionary ventures to the

FINDING GOD IN ANCIENT CHINA

New World were also well established, and Ricci decided to volunteer for work in the Far East. In 1577, he went to Portugal to await passage on the next Asia-bound ship. His journey took him first to Goa, on the west coast of India, where he continued his studies for the priesthood. In 1580, he was ordained in Cochin on the Malabar Coast of western India, and in April 1582, he was sent to China. When he died in 1610 at the age of 58, he had lived in China for 28 years. According to imperial rules of the time, foreigners who died in China had to be buried on the nearby Portuguese island of Macao. But Emperor Wan Li 萬曆 (reign 1573–1620) made an exception for Ricci in view of his immense contributions to China.

When Ricci arrived, the Chinese mainland was still closed to Westerners. The Western missionaries working on the nearby Portuguese island of Macao, like their merchant counterparts, held a superior attitude toward the Chinese. Hence, all Chinese converts were made to adopt European ways and customs, such as learning Latin and taking European names. Shortly before Ricci's arrival in Macao, however, Alessandro Valignano, who had jurisdiction over Jesuit missions in the Far East, initiated a significant change that was to have dramatic consequences: he strongly encouraged every Jesuit to study the Chinese language and acquire a knowledge of the culture, endeavors previously considered neither possible nor profitable.

Ricci, who had a prodigious memory and an unflagging spirit, was the right man for the time. He adopted Valignano's approach wholeheartedly and in every manner then possible. At first, he dressed as a Buddhist monk, which he mistakenly thought would accord him respect in Chinese society. When, through his new friendships with Chinese intellectuals, he learned that Confucian scholars rather than Buddhist monks were the most highly respected, Ricci immediately changed his approach. His embracing of Chinese ways, however, did not stop at outward appearances of attire. Armed with memorization techniques acquired as a student in Rome, Ricci set upon the formidable task of mastering the Chinese language with eagerness and remarkable perseverance. Not only was he not cowed by the enormous difficulty of learning the language, even today recognized as one of the hardest to master, but he was also invigorated and excited by the challenge. His amazing skills, most notably the practice of using "memory palaces" as a mnemonic tool, enabled him to memorize long lists of 400–500 characters at a time.

Chapter Six  Magi from the West

After just five months of study, Ricci was confident enough to say that he could write correctly any character he was shown. In three years' time, he had mastered enough of the language to start preaching and hearing confessions in Chinese without an interpreter; two years after that, he was able to read "almost everything"[6] with the help of a Chinese assistant. A decade after his first attempts at the language, the 41-year-old Ricci embarked on a "crash course" study of the *Four Books* that formed the core of the classical Chinese education: *The Analects* or *Lun Yu* 論語, the *Great Learning* or *Da Xue* 大學, *The Doctrine of Mean* or *Zhong Yong* 中庸, and *Mencius* 孟子. After 10 months of lengthy twice-daily lessons, Ricci felt that he was finally ready to start writing in Chinese on his own. Indeed, the next year, Ricci published the first of more than 20 books that included translations of the first six books of the 3rd-century Greek mathematician Euclid. He also translated the major Chinese *Classics* into Latin. In learning, he was equal to some of the best Chinese scholars of his time.

Ricci used his incredible memory skills to gain entrée into the highest levels of Chinese society. The priest himself relates with enthusiasm the first of these occasions at which he astounded his Chinese audience, earning a reputation that eventually took him within the vermilion walls of the imperial court. In a 1595 letter to his superior, which the eminent China scholar Jonathan Spence says "bubbles with the joy of achievement," Ricci describes an evening party to which he had been invited "by some holders of the first-level literary degree [where] something happened that gave me a great reputation among them and among all the other literati in the city."

> *I told them that they should write down a large number of Chinese characters in any manner they chose on a sheet of paper, without there being any order among them, because after reading them only once, I would be able to say them all by heart in the same way and order in which they had been written. They did so, writing many letters without any order, all of which I, after reading them once, was able to repeat by memory in the manner in which they were written: such that they were all astonished, it seeming to them a great matter. And I, in order to increase their wonder, began to recite them all by memory backward in the same manner, beginning with the very last until reaching the first. By which they all became utterly astounded and as if beside themselves.*

6. Jonathan D. Spence, *The Memory Palace of Matteo Ricci* (New York: Penguin Books USA, Inc., 1984), p. 138.

FINDING GOD IN ANCIENT CHINA

Ricci went on to say, "Immediately my fame began to spread so swiftly among the literati that I couldn't keep a counting of all the degree holders and other important people who came ... and paid me the courtesies as they would to a master.... "[7]

Ricci, however, regarded his memory skills as something akin to a "parlor trick," a tool that was simply useful for gaining the attention and interest of the intelligentsia. In fact, Ricci's body of knowledge was so vast that in his nearly three decades in China, he made contributions in all of these areas of learning: observational astronomy, optics, horology, music, geography, geometry, and surveying. His achievements in geography are particularly notable; Jonathan Spence writes that Ricci "performed the major feat of constructing an accurate world map with all the place names

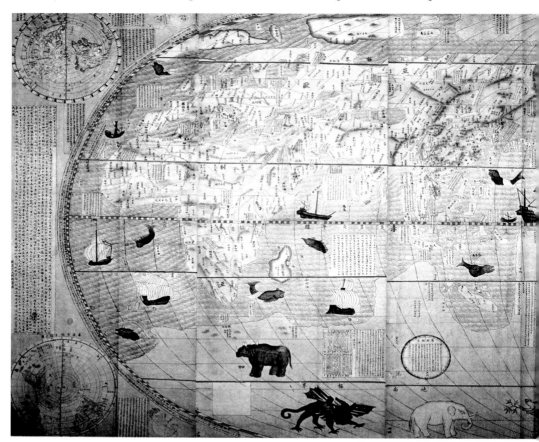

Full view of Matteo Ricci's famed "Map of the World." The original was made up of six panels and spread over six feet wide. Ricci presented it to Emperor Wan Li, who hung it in the inner chambers of the Imperial Palace.

Credit: Cultural Relics Publishing House

transcribed into Chinese — a map that went through scores of unauthorized printings, and ended up in a giant version of six separate panels over six feet wide in the inner chambers of the Peking palace of Emperor Wan Li."[8] It is this same map that has been reproduced in modern Beijing's Millennium Monument.

Some of the top scholars of the day sought out this Jesuit missionary to learn the Western sciences. Even today, the Chinese Communist Party mouthpiece, *People's Daily* 人民日報, credits Ricci with introducing the world map, Western mathematics, and astronomy to China.[9]

In order to translate into Chinese the first six of Euclid's 13 books, *The Elements*, Ricci devoted every morning for an entire year to going over the original Latin work

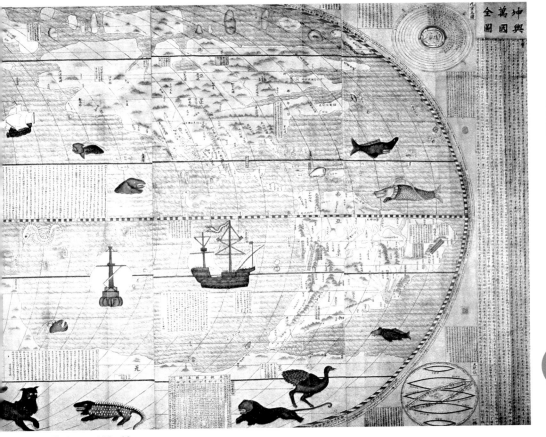

7. Ibid., pp. 138–39.

8. Ibid., p. 135.

9. "Scholars, Clergy Study Christian Impact on Chinese Culture," *People's Daily*, August 6, 2002. Available online at http://english.peopledaily.com.cn./200208/06/eng20020806_100962.shtml# (Cited September 2006).

line-by-line. He was assisted in this monumental task by one Chinese student, who later became a convert. Ricci published works in Chinese on geometry, explaining the astrolabe, the sphere, measures, and isoperimetrics. His scholarship in this area was so widely acclaimed that when he finally gained entry to the Chinese capital, he was appointed court mathematician. Ricci also introduced trigonometric and astronomical instruments to China. In astronomy, Ricci was able to do what the court astronomers consistently failed to do: accurately predict eclipses. When he precisely calculated the date of a 1592 solar eclipse in the southern Chinese city of Nanchang 南葛, Ricci sealed his reputation and drew the notice of the emperor, to whom eclipses were of the utmost importance. One of the most important duties of an emperor of China was to perform certain rites and rituals in conjunction with these rare heavenly events. Though there may not be an obvious correlation, Ricci's accomplishments in these fields were all part of his higher calling of bringing Christ to the Chinese. As Spence astutely points out,

> ... the important aim for Ricci in all this was to involve the Chinese in his scientific achievements so they would prove more receptive to the Christian faith.[10]

Ricci's matchless knowledge and talents were not confined to the sciences; he also excelled as a philosopher and theologian. A small book on the subject of friendship, published in 1595, brought him "more prestige and admiration among the Chinese elite than anything else he wrote, a view that is reinforced by comments made about the book by leading Ming scholars."[11] In it, he used quotations from some of the greatest Western thinkers—Seneca, Martial, Cicero, and Plutarch—to promote his view of friendship as something more than a relationship for financial gain or other material considerations; he described it rather as a heart bond that unites two bodies.

His brilliant ability to present Christian theology in a manner accessible and understandable to Chinese literati is evident in his seminal tome, *The True Meaning of the Lord of Heaven* 天主窗義, as well as in *Ten Discourses by a Paradoxical Man* 畸人十篇.

In all of these efforts, Ricci was working toward one goal: gaining access to the emperor and attaining a position in the court where he would be able to influence

10. Spence, *The Memory Palace*, p. 135.
11. Ibid., p. 149.

and evangelize the Son of Heaven. Catholics working in China at the time understood that if the emperor were a Christian, the conversion of the entire country would be possible. Without support from the elite, most crucially the emperor himself, their missionary endeavors would continue to be arduous and their impact limited in number and scope, being confined primarily to those on the fringes of Chinese society.

Matteo Ricci's efforts finally bore fruit in 1601, nearly two decades after he first set foot on Chinese soil, when he was invited by Emperor Wan Li to be an advisor in the imperial court, an honor never before bestowed upon a foreigner. Ricci served there for a decade until his death in 1610 at the age of 58. At the time of his death, there were 2,500 Chinese Catholics, including many of the educated class; of the 18 Jesuits working in missions in China, half were ethnic Chinese. A modern-day Jesuit scholar said of Ricci that he

> embodied the best goals of the Society of Jesus: spiritual depth, a love for learning and intellectual curiosity, finding of God in all things, a practical vision. He is a model for enculturation.[12]

Though he had failed in his lifetime to convert the emperor, Ricci had succeeded in winning the minds, as well as the hearts, of influential and powerful people in Chinese society with his integrity and learning. With the stellar example of his life, Ricci had personally breached and started to weaken some of the ingrained Chinese prejudices against "barbarians," including prejudicial views of Christianity. In the preface to a reprinting of one of his most popular books, *Ten Discourses by a Paradoxical Man* (also translated as *Ten Chapters of a Strange Man*), which describes the ways he appeared strange to the Chinese, a member of the Imperial Academy wrote of Ricci, "I know all his writings and am convinced that he is truly an extraordinary man …. His religion honors virtue, esteems the five social relations and serves heaven; in his words he never contradicts the teaching of Yao, Shun, the duke of Chou or Confucius."[13] Ricci's admittance into those nearly impenetrable imperial circles, where suspicion and intrigue ruled, was a testament to the trust and respect he had laboriously earned at the highest levels of government as well as among the most revered scholars of the day.

Although there may be those today, as there were in his day, who question

12. "Matteo Ricci, S.J.," from "About Us" page of website for University of Scranton, a Jesuit university. Available online at http://matrix.scranton.edu/about/ab_matteo_ricci.shtml (Cited September 2006).
13. Vincent Cronin, *The Wise Man from the West* (London: The Harvill Press, 1999), p. 259.

FINDING GOD IN ANCIENT CHINA

Ricci's scholarship and understanding of Chinese culture as well as his interpretations of Chinese scholarly works, these views contradict the most authoritative experts of the time—Ricci's own Chinese contemporaries. Questioning Ricci's conclusions is to presume an insight superior to that of a master of classical Chinese, who enjoyed unprecedented access in the culture for three decades and within the imperial court for nearly ten years.

Johann Adam Schall von Bell 湯若望 (1591–1666)

The foundation of goodwill painstakingly laid by Matteo Ricci was built upon by Johann Adam Schall von Bell, a German who arrived in the Chinese capital in 1623, thirteen years after Ricci's death. Sinologist Jonathan Spence describes Schall's approach to the work in China:

> Schall followed contemporary Jesuit theory and did as little as possible to upset the members of the Confucian elite or to disturb their existing beliefs. The quickest way to achieve conversion in China would be conversion from the top; to succeed, he must do the Emperor's bidding at all times and gain the respect of the Chinese who mattered. Schall therefore endeavored to live like a Confucian official. He worked hard at the Chinese language, studied the Confucian Classics, wore the long robes of the Chinese scholar, and lived in a considerable style .... By these methods, Schall and his fellow Jesuits were able to gain the confidence of influential Chinese, and had made several thousand converts in China by 1640, including fifty palace women, forty eunuchs and over one hundred others in the Emperor's entourage.[14]

Ricci, before he died, had urged the Catholic Church to send a trained astronomer, which it did in the person of John Terrentius (born Johann Schreck), a brilliant astronomer and mathematician. When Terrentius died unexpectedly in 1630, Schall, who had accurately predicted eclipses in 1623 and 1625, was designated his replacement in the court-appointed task of reforming the Chinese calendar. The establishment of the calendar each year by the court's 200-strong Calendar Bureau 曆局 was considered one of the most important affairs of state; virtually all aspects of daily life were dictated by this standard, which designated auspicious days for specific tasks. Mistakes in the calendar could portend a withdrawal of the Mandate

14. Jonathan D. Spence, *To Change China* (New York: Penguin Group, 1980), p. 14.

A 17th-century Dutch engraving of Jesuit priest Johann Adam Schall von Bell.
Credit: Private Collection, The Stapleton Collection, The Bridgeman Art Library

of Heaven, the right to rule bestowed on the emperor by Shang Di. Therefore, the astronomers' job was one of utmost consequence. Schall's appointment was an opportunity for the Jesuits to gain great prestige by proving mistakes in the Chinese calculations, which were based on empirical rules formulated without the benefit of scientific principles.

In examining the Chinese calendar, Schall discovered that the court astronomers were uncertain of their calculations for virtually every single day. To explain how their calculations had become so rife with error, Schall had to give the entire Calendar Bureau a complete course of instruction not just in astronomy but also in the basic sciences, such as arithmetic, geometry, and physics. By 1634, the Jesuits had composed 137 volumes on these subjects, of which 100 were published. By 1640, it appeared that Schall's attempts to reach and influence the emperor were close to bearing fruit. Then, in 1644, the Ming Dynasty was overthrown and it seemed that Schall's decades of labor were for naught.

Fortuitously, the invading Qing Dynasty 清朝 viewed Schall favorably, appointing him Director of the Bureau of Astronomy 欽天監. The first Qing emperor, Shun Zhi 順治 (reign 1644–1661), was religiously inclined and was for several years very much drawn to the missionaries. He was particularly fond of Schall, whom he appointed court astronomer and to whom he gave numerous favors and honors, even calling him "瑪法" (Ma Fa), which means "grandfather" in the Manchurian language. In 1653, Schall was awarded the title "Master of Universal Mysteries 通政大夫," and, in 1657, the title "President of the Imperial Chancery 太常寺卿" was added. In 1656 and 1657, the emperor visited Schall 24

times, often unannounced, and even celebrated his own birthday in Schall's home in 1657. The following year, Schall was made a mandarin of the first class with the title of "Imperial Chamberlain 光禄大夫."

This imperial favor, however, was short-lived. Shun Zhi died in 1661 of smallpox. Schall visited him on his deathbed and made one last attempt to convert the emperor, but the ruler put off further discussion until his recovery and died without making a decision. In part due to Schall's advice, Shun Zhi named the third of his eight sons as his successor, rather than the cousin the emperor himself preferred. As a result, China was blessed with one of its most enlightened and greatest rulers, Kang Xi 康熙. Unfortunately, Kang Xi was only seven years old when his father died, and the country suffered for seven years under the rule of regents, led by the ruthless General Oboi 黎拜, until the emperor came of age.

Because Oboi shared the native scholars' resentment of foreigners holding high posts in China, he began to move against Schall and the other missionaries once he had consolidated power. When Schall presented a 200-year calendar to the

Emperor Shun Zhi

Emperor Kang Xi

young Kang Xi, a Chinese calendar-maker named Yang Guangxian 楊光先 accused the German priest of implying by this act that the dynasty could last only 200 years. Using this pretext, Yang, who had been waging increasingly strong attacks against Christianity for five years, went on to charge Schall with errors in his astronomical calculations and with indoctrinating people with false ideas. In a treatise on the matter, called *Bu De Yi* 不港已, or "No Other Choice," Yang stated bluntly that he would "rather China have no good calendar than become friends with barbarian foreigners,"and that "it is exactly because of their excellent instruments and weapons that they are a potential enemy." Yang's ally, the dictatorial regent General Oboi, not only pronounced Schall's calendar "highly improper," but also sacked Schall, replacing him with Yang. In November 1664, Oboi threw Schall and three other Jesuits into prison for high treason, and a death sentence—to be cut in pieces and then beheaded—soon followed.

Enraged by the mistreatment of her son's great friend, the Empress Dowager, Xiao Zhuang 孝莊太皇太后, intervened on Schall's behalf. Her angry denunciation of the regents was the climax of rising popular support for the Jesuits, which fortuitously coincided with the convergence of several other dramatic events almost immediately after the pronouncement of the death sentence: a three-way test among Jesuit, Chinese, and Arab astronomers to accurately predict a solar eclipse, and an earthquake accompanied by a blanket of darkness over the capital and the appearance of a meteor. In the astronomy test, the Jesuits' calculations were correct to the minute, while the Arabs were off by 30 minutes, and the Chinese by 45 minutes.

This poor showing by the Chinese astronomers followed by the earthquake that caused a fire to break out in the

Empress Dowager Xiao Zhuang

imperial palace, as well as the meteor and unexplained darkness, led some members of the imperial grand council to conclude that heavenly forces were displeased with what was taking place. Schall was released and died peacefully the following year, 1666.

Ferdinand Verbiest 南懷仁 (1623–1688)

Although the anti-foreign, anti-Christian forces in the imperial court triumphed for a time, when 14-year-old Kang Xi began ruling without a regent, the Jesuits were given another opportunity to influence the imperial court, this time through Ferdinand Verbiest. Verbiest had served as assistant to Schall from 1660 until the older priest's death in 1666 and was one of the three Jesuits thrown into prison with Schall by the regent Oboi.

Verbiest had already been in China for almost ten years and had been held under house arrest for about half of that time by Yang and Oboi, when his fortunes suddenly changed. The scholarly Jesuit had spent those years on astronomical studies and so was prepared to make a ready reply when he was summoned by the emperor to work on the imperial calendars. Kang Xi, noticing that the calendars produced by Yang were increasingly inaccurate, asked Verbiest just days before the end of 1668 to check Yang's calculations. Verbiest submitted his response in just a month's time, pointing out several major errors. The young emperor dismissed Yang Guangxian, reinstated Johann Schall's honors posthumously, and appointed Ferdinand Verbiest court astronomer in Yang's stead. In February 1669, the Belgian Jesuit assumed the role of Director of the Bureau of Astronomy, the same post earlier held by his predecessor Schall under Kang Xi's father, Emperor Shun Zhi, and later the post of Vice President of the Board of Works 工部右侍郎 was added to Schall's imperial responsibilities. In addition to all the tasks involved in running these court bureaucracies, Verbiest also directed the construction of several large and complex instruments for the Imperial Observatory 觀象臺,[15] designed and made many ingenious "toys" requested by the emperor, such as sundials and a water clock, and oversaw the casting of 132 heavy cannons and 320 light cannons that were used successfully in civil war battles. Perhaps most significant of all was his personal relationship with the young emperor; Verbiest became a trusted aide and tutor of Kang Xi.

15. Some of these instruments can still be seen today on display at Beijing's Ancient Observatory not far from the center of town.

The Imperial Observatory

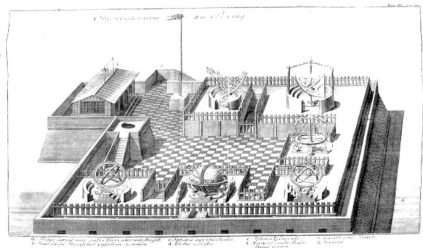

This sketch was drawn by Ferdinand Verbiest's own hand and shows the Imperial Observatory that was built according to his directions. The observatory still stands today and is open to the public. Visitors will quickly see that the observatory was built exactly to Verbiest's plan. The three photos show the instruments that are on display nowadays.

Finding God in Ancient China

The sharp-minded Kang Xi was keenly interested in Western science and mathematics, and it was Verbiest who personally taught him the principles of astronomy, tutored him on Euclid's *Elements*, introduced him to spherical trigonometry, and in time taught him astronomical observation and terrestrial measurement. As a trusted aide, Verbiest was expected to accompany the emperor on his imperial tours of the country. Verbiest recounts an evening on one such tour through Manchuria, when the emperor demonstrated for his teacher the skills he had learned years earlier.

> As it was a beautiful night, and the sky was clear, Kang Xi asked me to give him the Chinese and European names appearing on the horizon; he himself named first those that he had already learned. Then, taking out a little celestial map that I had given him some years before, he began to calculate from the start what hour of night it was, taking great pleasure in showing those around how much skill he had acquired in science.[16]

Like Ricci and Schall before him, Verbiest believed that "the Kang Xi Emperor, having been impressed by astronomy and delighted by mechanics, would swing to the faith behind the science."[17]

Upon Verbiest's untimely death in 1687 at the age of 64, from internal injuries after a fall from a horse, Kang Xi honored him with the posthumous title 遂號 (shi hao) of 勤敏 (Qin Min), meaning "Industrious and Intelligent." Since its inception in the Han Dynasty, this posthumous honor was betowed only upon emperors or high-ranking government officials. Verbiest was the first and only foreigner ever to receive this venerated title. This amply demonstrates the high value Kang Xi placed on Verbiest's enormous contributions to China.

SHINING LIKE STARS FOREVER

Just as the Hebrew prophet Daniel brought the knowledge of God through his knowledge of the stars to a pagan nation in the East—in his case, Babylon—the Jesuits also came to a nation in the East—China—to share the love of God through their expert knowledge of the skies. They were among the best minds of their time, but rather than seeking worldly accolades, they chose to live out their lives in a strange and unfriendly land. What they accomplished can easily be regarded as

16. Spence, *To Change China*, p. 30.
17. Ibid., p. 28.

the finest example of East-West relations, of transfer of technologies, and most of all, of Christian missions.

What the Chinese Millennium Monument does not depict, and what most Chinese fail to grasp, is that the greatest contribution made by these brave men was not the transfer of knowledge and technologies to China, but rather the eternally significant imparting of spiritual truths modeled by their lives of simple devotion and humility. These men loved the Chinese people so much that they gave them their lives and their expert knowledge for the sake of sharing God's love. In turn, they themselves were surprised and delighted to discover that God's eternal truths were embedded deep in Chinese culture. This enhanced their inclination to respect and honor Chinese culture and enabled them to defend their attitude to their superiors in Rome, who were suspicious of their ready adaptation of Chinese traditions and practices. The Jesuits in no way felt that they had compromised their faith to gain favor with the Chinese. They recognized that God had actually preceded them and prepared the way for them.

Their efforts bore much fruit. The Catholic Church in China experienced tremendous growth in the second half of the 17th century. In 1640, three decades after Ricci died, there were 60,000 to 70,000 Catholic converts; by 1651, their numbers had more than doubled to 150,000. By 1664, the figure had ballooned to at least 254,980.[18] In 1642, fifty of the high-ranking ladies in the palaces were Christians, and when Prince Gui 桂王 of the remnant Southern Ming Dynasty 南明 ascended the throne to continue the fight against the invading Manchus, his empress, as well as the crown prince, both dowagers, and several high officials all converted to Catholicism. One of the dowagers—christened Helena—even sent messages to Pope Innocent X in 1650 and to the general of the Society of Jesus asking for their prayers on behalf of the Ming cause.

Unfortunately, the tide was about to turn against the Jesuits again, and ironically the challenge to their hard-won successes was to come from a most unexpected quarter.

18. "Johann Adam Schall von Bell," *The Catholic Encyclopedia,* Volume XVIII (New York: Robert Appleton Company, 1912, Online edition 2003). Catholic Encyclopedia on CD-ROM, available online at http://www.newadvent.org/cathen/13520a.htm (Cited August 2006).

FINDING GOD IN ANCIENT CHINA

THE RITES CONTROVERSY

Matteo Ricci and the Jesuits who followed him were motivated by a passionate desire to bring the knowledge of God to China. What they discovered reflected in the written histories of China and embedded deep in Chinese culture was a belief in a Supreme Being with the same attributes as the One whom the Jesuits and the Catholic Church worshipped. This surprising discovery made it possible for Ricci and his associates to use established Chinese terms to express Christian ideas, to link Confucian moral concepts to Christian teachings, and to refrain from interfering with Chinese rites honoring sages and ancestors. It also allowed them to permit converts to continue to perform the kowtow as a form of civil obeisance. Among those who lacked the Jesuits' broad cultural experience and deep understanding of the Chinese *Classics*, however, there was much opposition to these views held by Ricci and his successors, and especially to their practice of using standard Chinese terms to express Christian concepts. Criticism of this practice continued long after the Jesuits' influence had waned in China.

Ricci, Schall, Verbiest, and the many other Jesuits who labored over their lifetimes in China had, through their perseverance and diligence, mastered the Chinese classical language and attained the highest levels of scholarship in the study of the Chinese *Classics*. Furthermore, their positions in the imperial palace meant they had access to ancient and imperial documents not normally available to ordinary scholars, much less to foreigners.

Hard as it might be to believe, their fluency in the classical language, which was abandoned in China for the vernacular beginning in the 1920s, gave these Jesuit scholars an advantage over any modern academician today in understanding and interpreting accurately those ancient manuscripts. No scholar today, even a Chinese scholar, can compare with the Jesuits in their fluency in the classical language. Nor can the modern-day scholar match Ricci and his associates in their degree of access to the ancient documents. That's because most of these cultural records were destroyed during the Boxer Rebellion in 1900 when the Hanlin Academy 翰林院, the elite scholarly institution founded in the 8th-century to establish the official interpretations of the Confucian *Classics* and perform secretarial, archival, and literary tasks for the court, was consumed by fire. Therefore, the conclusions

drawn by these scholarly and devout men on the correlation between Chinese terms and Christian concepts can be considered more authoritative than the view of any of their critics, whether contemporary or current. Ricci's *The True Meaning of the Lord of Heaven*,[19] in which he lays out the arguments and conclusions for accepting established Chinese terms already in use, is the definitive, representative work on this subject. We will look at *The True Meaning* in more detail later in this chapter.

The wisdom of the Jesuit approach of acculturation and evangelism bore its greatest fruit in 1692, when Emperor Kang Xi issued an edict granting all Christians throughout China the right to preach, teach, and convert. The only caveat was that those who held government offices had to accept Confucian principles and perform the rites and ceremonies connected with their offices. This imperial edict appeared to portend the eventual realization of the goal toward which the Jesuit missionaries had labored for more than 100 years: the conversion of all of China. The greatest blow to the realization of that dream was dealt, however, not by anti-Christian or anti-European elements in China but by elements within the Catholic Church itself. The final outcome of this dispute, known as the Rites Controversy, was the complete severing of relations at every level between China and the West.

Within the church, a faction arose made up of Franciscans, Dominicans, and a few Jesuits who were opposed to Ricci's approach to evangelization in China and who accused the Jesuits of condoning Chinese "pagan" practices and intentionally misinterpreting Chinese terms. Leading the opposition was the Franciscan Antonio de St. Marie, whose position on the matter he himself bluntly stated this way: "What does it matter to our mission whether the ancient Chinese knew God, or didn't know Him, whether they named Him in one way or another? The question is completely indifferent. We have come here to announce the Holy Gospel, and not to be apostles of Confucius."[20] The Franciscan and Dominican approach to evangelization lacked the Jesuits' cultural sensitivity. Often disdaining to learn the language, their missionaries condemned all the Chinese emperors to burning in hell and demanded that their converts give up the Confucian rites. For 70 years, through much of the 17th-century, this largely theological debate raged, but the Pope stayed out of it.

Shortly after Kang Xi's 1692 edict granting missionaries broad rights, however, the controversy intensified. So much so that the Jesuits appealed to the emperor

---

19. Ricci wrote the book in classical Chinese. Here, we are quoting from this Chinese-English edition: Edward J. Malatesta, ed., *The True Meaning of the Lord of Heaven (T'ien-chu Shih-i)* (St. Louis, Mo.: Institute of Jesuit Sources, February 1986).

20. Michael Billington, "Matteo Ricci, the Grand Design, and the Disaster of the 'Rites Controversy,'" November 9, 2001, *Executive Intelligence Review*. Available online at http://www.larouchepub.com/other/2001/2843m_ricci.html (Cited September 2006).

himself to issue another edict to clarify the Chinese view of the meaning of certain theological terms as well as the meaning of the rites honoring ancestors.

The emperor did so, stating without ambiguity that "there was, in Chinese philosophy, an omnipotent Deity who created and rules over the universe; and the rites of ancestor worship were signs of respect, without any superstitious beliefs in spirits existing in the stone tablets."[21] He said of the rites:

> *Honors are paid to Confucius not as a petition to favors, intelligence, or high office, but as to a Master, because of the magnificent moral teaching, which he has left to posterity. As for the ceremony in honor of the dead ancestors, it originates in the desire to show filial piety. According to the customs observed by Confucians, this ceremony contains no request for help; it is practiced only to show filial respect for the dead. Souls of ancestors are not held to reside in the tablets; these are only symbols, which serve to express gratitude and keep the dead in memory, as though they were actually present.[22]*

The effort, though, was for naught. On November 13, 1704, nine cardinals — all Italian and not one who had ever been to Asia — assembled in Rome, studied documents written only in Latin about the controversy, and ruled against Ricci's policy of tolerance, acceptance, and adaptation. Their guiding principle was that the missionary effort in China should be free of even the suspicion of harboring superstition. Pope Clement XI confirmed their decision by issuing a papal bull barring Christians from holding to Confucian beliefs or performing Confucian rites.

Rome sent a young Frenchman, Charles de Tournon, to enforce the papal order. De Tournon was described as one who "combined religious zeal with overbearing self-assertion and tactlessness."[23] Once in the capital, he enlisted as translator for his audience before Emperor Kang Xi the services of a French bishop, Charles Maigrot, who was vociferously outspoken in his antagonism to Chinese culture, its literati, and the Jesuits. The emperor was astonished by Maigrot's halting Chinese and his inability to identify three of the four characters on a scroll in the throne room. Maigrot, in his less-than-adequate Chinese vernacular, proceeded to insult Emperor Kang Xi by daring to challenge him on the precise meaning of classical Chinese terms. Upon reading the papal bull, Kang Xi wrote:

21. Ibid.
22. Cited in Cronin, *The Wise Man*, p. 280.
23. Ibid., p. 281.

I have concluded that the Westerners are petty indeed. It is impossible to reason with them because they do not understand larger issues as we understand them in China. There is not a single Westerner versed in Chinese works, and their remarks are often incredible and ridiculous. To judge from this proclamation, their religion is no different from other small, bigoted sects of Buddhism or Taoism. I have never seen a document, which contains so much nonsense. From now on, Westerners should not be allowed to preach in China, to avoid further trouble.[24]

Although Kang Xi banned Christianity after this meeting, he later relented and allowed those missionaries who agreed to follow Ricci's practices to stay in China. Meanwhile, he spent years trying to negotiate a solution and was dumbfounded when, in 1714, a new papal bull reconfirmed the position banning Confucian rites. Emperor Kang Xi, who had been tutored by the Jesuits, was sympathetic to Christianity, and may himself have secretly converted, seemed to demonstrate an understanding of the heart of the One True God as he lamented the Pope's decision:

You have corrupted your teachings and disrupted the efforts of the former Westerners. This is definitely not the will of your God, for He leads men to good deeds. I have often heard from you Westerners that the devil leads men astray — this must be it.[25]

By 1721, the emperor's former good will toward Christianity was dissolving, and his writings began to focus on the irreconcilable differences between East and West. In 1742, when yet another papal bull was issued, what remained of the good will established by Ricci and his successors was destroyed: in response to this bull, Christianity was banned, foreigners expelled, and scientific and technological exchanges with the West halted. The policies put in place during the Rites Controversy were not to change until 1939 when, after the Chinese government explicitly affirmed that the Confucian rites were civil rather than religious in nature, Rome finally lifted the papal bull.

24. Dan J. Li, trans., "The Chinese Rites Controversy, 1715," *China in Transition, 1517–1911* (New York: Van Nostrand Reinhold Company, 1969), p. 22. Available on website *Modern History Sourcebook* at http://www.fordham.edu/halsall/mod/1715chineserites.html (Cited September 2006).

25. Billington, "Matteo Ricci, the Grand Design, and the Disaster of the 'Rites Controversy.'"

FINDING GOD IN ANCIENT CHINA

THE TRUE MEANING OF THE LORD OF HEAVEN

At least as regrettable and equally as ill-founded as the papal bull that effectively negated a century of hard work and sacrifice by Ricci and his fellow Jesuits are the portrayals of their evangelization efforts as syncretistic. A reading of Ricci's brilliant work, *The True Meaning of the Lord of Heaven*, however, would suffice to refute such misguided views. It shows that there was no misunderstanding on Ricci's part of the Chinese people or their culture, nor was he trying to manipulate them into conversion, as some have charged.

The beginnings of the work on *True Meaning* can be traced back to 1591, when Ricci first translated the *Four Books* into Latin. During this process, Ricci discovered, to his great delight, a commonality that allowed him to present

天主實義重刻序

昔吾夫子語修身也先事親而推及乎
知天至孟氏存養事天之論而孟乃基
備蓋即知事事天事親同一事而天
其事之大原也說天莫辯乎易易為乎
字祖即言乾元統天為君為父又古
出乎震而紫陽氏解之以為帝者天之
主宰然則天主之義不自利先生刱矣

The introduction to a reprint of Matteo Ricci's definitive study, *The True Meaning of the Lord of Heaven.*

Christ to the Chinese not only in a manner that they could understand, but also in a practical way to a people who highly value pragmatism. He wrote,

> *Therefore, having leafed through a great number of ancient books, it is quite clear to me that the Sovereign on High and the Lord of Heaven are different only in name.*
>
> 歷觀古書，而知上帝與天主特異以名。[26]
>
> *He who is called Lord of Heaven in my humble country is He who is called Shang-ti [Sovereign on High] in Chinese.*
>
> 吾天主，即華言上帝。[27]

208

26. Ricci, *The True Meaning*, p. 125.
27. Ibid., p. 121.

Ricci also realized that an earlier colleague's evangelical work, *True Record of the Lord of Heaven*, was inadequate to explain Christianity to the Chinese because it failed to understand the Chinese way of thinking and therefore could not link these critical points of commonality.

Ricci started working on *The True Meaning of the Lord of Heaven* in 1595, but it was not until 1603 that it was finally published. That Ricci spent close to ten years working on the book before he was satisfied with it shows his dedication to fine scholarship and the high level of professionalism that he, and subsequent Jesuits in China, brought to their work in all areas. The many years Ricci spent observing Chinese society and life, his long years of dedicated study of the language, and the meticulous care he took in writing, rewriting, and editing *The True Meaning of the Lord of Heaven* and in seeking the input of both Chinese scholars and church leaders all vividly demonstrate the high level of scholarship that went into the book.

Like the apostle Paul who planted churches throughout his travels, Ricci was a master architect who sought to build an indigenous church with roots planted deep in the culture so that it could grow strong and stand steadfast. In order to do so, he knew that he had to address existing beliefs and philosophies that held sway among the Chinese people and refute those that conflicted with the Truth. The book, therefore, was a response to the teachings of Buddhism, as well as Daoism and Neo-Confucianism, because some adherents of those religions were increasingly antagonistic to Christianity and the Jesuits' efforts to win converts. Structured in the form of a dialogue between a Western scholar and a Chinese scholar, the book addresses the issues of incarnation and redemption, the nature and act of creation, proof of God, the question of intention and the goodness of human nature, and the differences between the souls of men and the souls of animals and birds, as well as the soul's immortality.

One translator described Ricci's book as "the first attempt by a Catholic scholar to use a Chinese way of thinking to introduce Christianity to Chinese intellectuals."[28] *The True Meaning of the Lord of Heaven* reveals not only a profound understanding on Ricci's part of China's cultural tradition, but a deep love and respect for the Chinese people.

28. Ibid., p. 47.

Matteo Ricci

Matteo Ricci and his disciple Paul Hsu

Some of Ricci's critics have charged that he and his fellow Jesuits had attempted to manipulate the Chinese into conversion and that they sought to "water down" or "sell out" Christianity through compromise with conflicting Chinese values and beliefs. That neither was the case and that Ricci held his faith in the highest regard is amply demonstrated in the way he, and fellow Jesuits after him, handled the problem of the Chinese practice of keeping concubines.

One of Ricci's most promising converts was Li Zhizao 李之藻, who at the time he met Ricci held a high-ranking government position in Nanjing 南京, and later served by imperial appointment on the Calendar Bureau. Li studied under Ricci and was considered one of his top two pupils. Despite their close relationship, Ricci refused for seven years to baptize Li because he would not give up his concubines. Only after Li embraced monogamy did Ricci agree to perform the ceremony. This occurred less than two months before Ricci's death, and it was Li who wrote the memorial to the emperor requesting permission for Ricci's burial on Chinese soil. When Li himself died in 1630, he was considered the second of the "three pillars of the Catholic Church in China."[29]

29. The three Chinese remembered in history as the "Three Pillars of the Catholic Church in China" were Paul Hsu 徐光启, Prime Minister and tutor of the Emperor, baptized on January 15, l603; Leo Lee 李之藻, baptized on March 3, 1610; and Michael Yang 楊廷筠, baptized Easter 1613. Outstanding among the many things that Lee did for the Church is his "First Collection of Celestial Science," edited in Peking, 1629. The collection contains 20 books, divided into two sections. From Matthias Lu, "Dialogue of Christianity with Cultures in China of Yesterday and Today," July 2000, on the International Saint Thomas of Aquinas Center website. Available online at http://www.everyonesaquinas.org/1dialogue.html (Cited September 2006).

A Man Who Loved the Chinese
James Legge 理雅各 (1815–1897)

Though James Legge shared nothing in common with the Jesuits in Christian affiliation or national origin, this brilliant Scotsman was a more-than-worthy successor to Ricci and his followers. Trailing them by some 300 years and a member of the Protestant non-Conformist Church, Legge devoted his life to the study of Chinese and spent a quarter-century translating the bulk of the most important Chinese *Classics* into English. His contribution to Chinese studies in the West cannot be overstated. One leading Chinese scholar and a contemporary of Legge, Wang T'ao 王韜, described the Scotsman's meticulous translations as having captured "the essence and nicety of the Chinese *Classics*."[30] Legge's works remain today the most authoritative English versions of these core texts of Chinese civilization and are, in fact, quoted extensively throughout this book.

Legge was born in Scotland on December 20, 1815. From the beginning, he excelled in his studies and showed early promise; at King's College, he was a prize-winning student many times over. It was at King's College that Legge first exhibited a strength of character that was to feature in his life again and again. He was offered a teaching assistantship that would have put him on track for significant academic promotions, but the job required that he join the Church of Scotland, the state church. Legge's father, however, had enthusiastically supported an independent church movement, and it was in this tradition that Legge had been raised. "I thought it would be a bad way of beginning life if I were, without conviction on the subject, to turn from the principles of my father merely because of the temporal advantages which such a step would bring me," Legge said of his decision.[31] Less than two years later, Legge felt called into the clergy and entered divinity school, a move that set the course for the rest of his life.

In 1838, at the age of 23, he joined the London Missionary Society. The following year, Legge and his bride set off on a nearly yearlong sea and overland journey, arriving in Malacca, Malaysia, in 1840. During their more than two years there, Legge considered his top priority to be the study of the Chinese language. His official post was serving as principal of the Anglo-Chinese College, established by

30. Lindsay Ride, Biographical Note, *The Chinese Classics: Volume 1*, by James Legge (Taipei, Taiwan: SMC Publishing Inc., 2000), p. 16. The quote is from a scroll hand-written by Wang T'ao in 1873 lauding Legge's scholarship. The scroll later was hung in the Chinese Department at Oxford University.
31. Ibid., p. 3.

FINDING GOD IN ANCIENT CHINA

FINDING GOD IN ANCIENT CHINA

Oil on canvas portrait of Professor James Legge, first Oxford University professor of Chinese. The painting is displayed in Corpus Christi College, Oxford.   Credit: The Bridgeman Art Library

the London Missionary Society to train missionaries for China. He also managed the college's press.

The press had been founded to further the vision of Robert Morrison, a pioneer in the missionary effort to China. Morrison's plan was to educate and train young Chinese believers so that they would preach to their own people. He envisioned the role of foreigners as one of establishing and operating schools, hospitals, and clinics, as well as organizing technical and intellectual societies that would benefit the Chinese people. To serve this two-pronged endeavor, the press produced Chinese Bibles and religious tracts as well as bilingual dictionaries and language textbooks.

212

When Legge arrived six years after Morrison's death, he assumed management of the press, which by then had been operating for a quarter-century. He ably carried on Morrison's vision and also adopted Morrison's ministry approach. The two men shared a passionate devotion to the call of missionary and preacher, as well as a recognition of the value of providing educational opportunities for Chinese believers.

In 1843, Legge and his family relocated to Hong Kong, where he founded the Union Church. He was its first minister and, after 30 years of service there, earned the title "Father of the Union Church." Though removed from its original site, the church still stands in Hong Kong today. Legge also helped lay the foundation for Hong Kong's Department of Education, which for decades after contributed greatly to Hong Kong society. He did this through his work in setting up schools for Chinese children and promoting education—in both English and Chinese. Legge's many civic contributions, including work in the field of education and every aspect of social services, were recognized by the Hong Kong government's presentation of a handsome testimonial on which was inscribed: "This salver, with tea and coffee service, presented to the Rev. James Legge, D.D., by the Government of Hong Kong for many public services readily and gratuitously rendered." More importantly though, it was in Hong Kong that he began in earnest his life's work, which he was later to describe as "more than twenty-five years of toilsome study."[32]

As one biographer put it, Legge recognized that "the key to China was a knowledge of the Chinese *Classics* which were responsible for the whole of the behavior pattern of the Chinese—their thinking, their beliefs, and their way of life, as well as their form of government."[33] Legge himself wrote that "he who would understand the Chinese nation, then, must know its classical literature" and would have had to have "mastered the *Classical Books* of the Chinese, and . . . investigated for himself the whole field of thought through which the Sages of China had ranged."[34] To that end, he began translating the Chinese *Classics* with the intent of explaining Chinese thought and learning to the West.

In his linguistic endeavors, he was—like Ricci many centuries before—blessed with a natural aptitude for learning languages and a prodigious memory, which was the envy of his colleagues. One colleague recalled, perhaps with some envy,

32. Ibid., p. 1.
33. Ibid., p. 10.
34. Ibid.

FINDING GOD IN ANCIENT CHINA

"He could store in his mind with ease the singular and complicated characters formed by the Chinese pencil in enormous variety. These same characters frighten many persons in their difficulty. To him they were attractive, because he could so readily remember them."[35] Even so, it would not be until 15 years after his arrival in Hong Kong, in 1858, that he was ready to start publishing his translations. Then it was a question of not only finding the money, but also arranging for such things as the ink and paper. Consequently, it was not until 1861 that the first edition of Volume 1 rolled off the presses.

Legge returned to England after three decades in Hong Kong and in 1876 was appointed the first Chair of Chinese at the University of Oxford. He continued his writing there and, in all, completed eight volumes of translations. These were four Confucian texts,

> Classic of History 書經 (Shu Jing),
> Book of Changes 易經 (Yi Jing),
> Book of Filial Piety 孝經 (Xiao Jing), and
> The Book of Rites 禮記 (Li Ji),

two Taoist texts,

> Dao De Jing 道德經 and
> The Thai Shang Tractate of Actions and Their
> Retributions 太上感應篇 (Tai Shang Gan
> Ying Pian),

and two literary texts,

> A Record of Buddhistic Kingdoms 佛都記錄
> (Fo Du Ji Lu) and
> Li Sao. 離騷

A page from James Legge's translation of the *Confucian Analects.*

He was working on a ninth—*Elegies of Chu* 楚辭 (Chu Ci)—when he died in London in 1897. A commentator observed that "his efforts in translating the 'sacred classics' of China into English can be judged as infinitely more successful than his missionary work."[36]

35. Ibid., p. 20. (These were the words of Dr. Joseph Edkins of Shanghai, in a sermon shortly after Legge's death.)
36. Bradley Winterton, "Victorian Britain comes to grips with the Chinese classics," *Taipei Times*, January 26, 2003, p.18. Available online at http://taipeitimes.com/News/feat/archives/2003/01/26/192543 (Cited September 2006).

Be that as it may, Legge's first passion, like that of his Jesuit predecessors, was to bring the knowledge of salvation through Jesus Christ to the Chinese people; he studied the Chinese classical works because he saw the benefit of such knowledge to his evangelistic endeavors. Upon completion of the translations, Legge wrote that he had embarked on the task so "that . . . our missionary labors among the people should be conducted with sufficient intelligence and so as to secure permanent results."[37]

Wang T'ao, the Chinese contemporary quoted earlier, observed that Legge's scholarly pursuit "was only subsidiary work done in his spare time. His main purpose was to preach the Gospel."[38] At a memorial service upon his death, Legge was eulogized for his love of the Chinese people:

> *He gained the affection and confidence of the Chinese as but few foreigners have ever done, for he loved them truly, and they knew the simple integrity of his love. It was characteristic of him that one of his very last acts was to rise from what was to be his death-bed to greet with his fine old-world courtesy a Chinese youth of humble origin and rank, whose only claim to such attention was the blood which ran in his veins.*[39]

Like the Jesuits nearly 300 years earlier, Legge's study of the Chinese *Classics* led him to the conclusion that the Chinese had worshipped a monotheistic Deity called Shang Di, who was clearly recognizable as the Christian God. Also like the Jesuits, Legge was forced to defend that unpopular view in a long, heated debate with critics. This controversy raged so fiercely that it was even mentioned in his memorial service eulogy:

> *And as he loved the people, he was jealous for all that was good and true in their faith. The longest and most embittered controversy in which he was ever engaged was one with certain missionaries who did not think of the root-ideas of the old Chinese religion as he did. Nominally, it related to the question, whether they had any word that could be used to translate the idea of God; really and substantially, it concerned whether they had any idea of God at all. And he maintained they had, for did he not judge with charity as well as knowledge?*[40]

In his thoroughly researched 1852 defense of his views, *The Notions of the Chinese*

37. Ride, Biographical Note, *The Chinese Classics*, p. 1.
38. Ibid., p. 18.
39. Ibid., pp. 23 – 24.
40. Ibid.

FINDING GOD IN ANCIENT CHINA

Concerning God and Spirits, Legge opened in the very first paragraph with the question, "Do the Chinese know the true God?" His answer was unequivocal:

> *I answer unhesitatingly in the affirmative. The evidence supplied by Chinese literature and history appears to me so strong that I find it difficult to conceive how anyone who has studied it can come to the opposite conclusion.*[41]

Like Ricci and the Jesuits, who had a profound understanding of Chinese history and the *Classics*, Legge also promoted the use of the ancient Chinese term Shang Di 上帝 for God. As the Jesuits before him, Legge faced vehement opposition from those less schooled in the ancient Chinese texts. The Catholics employed a completely new two-character combination in Chinese for the term, choosing 天 (tian) which means "heaven" and 主 (zhu) which means "lord" or "master" to form 天主 (tianzhu). Protestant missionaries of the time chose to use 神 (shen). Legge sparked a controversy with these other Western missionaries when he argued that 神 (shen) was equivalent to "god" or "spirits." Legge's 1852 *Notions* defense convincingly made the case that Shang Di had all along been used by the Chinese to refer exclusively to a supreme, monotheistic God, creator and ruler of all. "Shen," on the other hand, he likened to the use in English of the term "god" with a lower case "g" as distinguished from the term "God" with an uppercase "G." In marshalling evidence from Chinese literature and histories, he showed that "shen" referred to the plethora of spirits and smaller deities that populate Chinese folk religion and was not to be confused with the all-powerful Shang Di. Not everyone was convinced, however, and this continuing divergence of opinion resulted in there being printed in the early 20th-century two versions of the Chinese Bible. Shang Di was used in the southern edition of the Chinese Union Bible, while the northern edition used "shen."[42]

As the eulogist at Legge's memorial service astutely noted, the crux of the issue was not linguistic but theological. In choosing to use "Shang Di" for God, Legge joined ranks with Ricci and other Jesuits in their position that the ancient Chinese did have a knowledge of the One True God. Those who chose to use the new term "tianzhu" or the term "shen" had a theological predisposition that excluded the Chinese of ages past from being counted among those who knew and worshipped the same God as the one acknowledged in the Christian Bible. This view, however, is supported by little or no scholarship.

41. James Legge, *The Notions of the Chinese Concerning God and Spirits* (Hong Kong: Hong Kong Register Office, 1852; reprint, Taipei: Ch'eng Wen Publishing Company, 1971), p. 7.

42. "Shang Ti" entry on online encyclopedia *Wikipedia*. Available online at http://en.wikipedia.org/w/index.php?title=Shangdi&oldid=72377775 (Cited September 2006).

Those who argued for the use of Shang Di—Ricci, Schall, Verbiest, and Legge, to name the most prominent—were known for their scholarship, exactitude, and integrity. In fact, in Legge's case, one of the leading Chinese scholars of the day, Wang T'ao, regarded Legge as the only scholar—Chinese or otherwise—capable of succeeding him.[43] Though deeply committed to reaching the Chinese people with the Good News of salvation through Jesus Christ, the integrity of these men would not have permitted them to twist the truth in order to fulfill their evangelistic goal. Rather, they had clearly recognized the importance of cultural understanding and sensitivity in winning Chinese souls for Christ, and they had invested the time and energy to gain that understanding. These scholarly missionaries compromised neither faith nor professional integrity in pursuit of their lifelong mission to bring a saving knowledge of God to China.

It is perhaps most fitting to end this chapter with James Legge's own words:

> *I maintain that the Chinese do know the true God, and have a word in their language answering to our word God, to the Hebrew Elohim, and to the Greek Theos.*[44]

As I reflected on this, I wondered whether this knowledge of the True God, which for the Hebrews had been the foundation for their theocratic form of government, had had any similar impact in China. True, the emperors had been careful to observe the Border Sacrifices, but beyond these ritualistic and occasional ceremonial acts, did their worship of Shang Di have any influence over their lives and reigns? What I learned at the signpost for "God's Country," was a great encouragement.

REFLECT and RESPOND

The men in this chapter were giants of their generation. Few men left a more colossal and lasting legacy. These few men, by bridging Chinese and Western thought, nearly changed the course of history in China and the world. China has never had better friends, and the world has never had better guides to China! Most important of all, these men lived and died to help China return to God. They succeeded because God was their motivator and motivation, not China. To fully comprehend that strength and motivation, one needs to enter into an intimate relationship with God.

43. Ride, Biographical Note, *The Chinese Classics*, p. 15.
44. Legge, *Notions*, p. 2.

FINDING GOD IN ANCIENT CHINA

What motivates you? Do you know their God and the Shang Di of China? Ricci had to commit to the life described below before Chinese authorities granted him permission to live in China. Do you have the internal strength to make the same commitment for those you love?

> *You must not be joined by other barbarians; you must continue to wear our dress; you must promise to conform to our habits; you must obey our magistrate; if you marry, you must choose a woman of our country. You will become, in all save your physical appearance, men of the Middle Kingdom, subject to the Son of Heaven. Are you willing to make these promises?*[45]

45. Cronin, *The Wise Man*, p. 47.

The earliest extant terrestrial globe made in China, showing Asia and nearby areas, probably by two Jesuit missionaries in 1623. It was acquired by the British Museum in 1961.

Credit: Cultural Relics Publishing House

7

God's Country

Heaven, in order to protect the people below, has created for them rulers and teachers so that they will serve Shang Di in securing prosperity and peace for all the people.

~ King Wu, in the *Classic of History*

7

God's Country

The word "China" even today conjures up in the Western mind exotic scenes and a sense of extreme foreignness. In fact, the word is often used in English to express extremes, as in the most distant place ("you'd have to dig all the way to China"), the most radical change ("kind of like going to China"), and the most unimaginable numbers ("not for all the tea in China!"). What is called "China" in English, however, is not the name the Chinese themselves use for their country. The name "China" actually originated with Europeans who initially used the word to refer to the porcelain imported from a rich and mysterious country on the other side of the world. Eventually "china" came to be applied to the country that produced this beautiful and delicate tableware prized by the Europeans. The word "china" is, in fact, derived from the name of the Qin Dynasty 秦朝 (225 – 207 B.C.), which in an earlier transliteration system rendered the character 秦 into English as "Ch'in."

The Chinese, for whom names have great significance, have an altogether different name for their country: it is 中國 (Zhong Guo). This can be translated literally as "the Central Nation" or more poetically as "the Middle Kingdom." This name was first used during the joint reign of Emperor Yao 堯 (reigned 2357 - 2258 B.C.) and Emperor Shun 舜 (reigned 2257 – 208 B.C.), roughly the time that the Egyptians started building the pyramids and about 200 years before the time of the biblical patriarch Abraham. The first recorded use of the term is found in a document called "Yu's Tributes 禹貢" (Yu Gong). This was the report by Yu

Photo at left shows China's righteous emperors, Yao, Shun, and Yu, as depicted in the "Tribute to Chinese History" mural at the Millennium Monument in Beijing. Yu is shown at the top, taming the floodwaters.

submitted to the co-emperors at the end of his 13-year Herculean labors to control the Great Flood that had then raged for more than two decades.

Yu had traversed, by foot, the then-known territory of his country, which extended from the eastern coastline as far west as present-day Qinghai province, north to the border of present-day Inner Mongolia, and south to the border of present-day Guangdong province. As he traveled, Yu had surveyed the land and assigned grades to the fields under cultivation for the purposes of assessing tax collection, had climbed every mountain and hill to map the rivers and other waters and, at the same time, had cleared the mountainsides and driven out wild animals in preparation for human habitation. Then he had established a system of flood prevention by deepening riverbeds and providing drainage to nearby lakes, marshes, and swamplands. At the end of this incredible undertaking, Yu reported to the emperors that

> *The fields were all classified, and all revenues were established with reference to the three characters of the soil. The Central Nation then conferred lands and surnames so that all professed a foremost love of virtue and would not act in any way contradictory to imperial action.*
>
> 底慎財賦，咸則三壤，成賦中邦，錫土姓，抵蠢婕先，不距朕行。[1]

Prior to this, the mostly nomadic people of this region had neither lands nor surnames. As a result of Yu's single undertaking, however, they became a nation. They now acknowledged allegiance to a central ruler, accepted lands conferred by this ruler, began to adopt a settled, agrarian way of life in a fixed location, and were organized into people groups based on surnames. Years of flooding had wreaked havoc on their previous way of life, but Yu's accomplishments, performed at the behest of the co-emperors Yao and Shun, changed everything. Chinese historian K. C. Wu writes:

> *Hope was instilled anew in the entire population where there had been only despair, harmony where there had been only discord, and above all discipline where there had been only chaos .... Thus after the abatement of the inundation, the prestige of the Central Nation as represented by Yao, Shun, and Yu stood at its highest peak, never before reached by any government of man .... It is also*

1. 《尚書-夏書-禹貢》 *Classic of History*, Record of Xia, Yu Gong, and 《史記-卷二-夏本紀》 Historical Records, Volume 2, History of Xia. *Classic of History* uses 中邦 (Zhong Bang), but the *Historical Records* written during the Han Dynasty changed it to 中國 (Zhong Guo) because the first Han emperor's name was Liu Bang. Bang and Guo mean the same thing and are used interchangeably.

from this time, more especially from the document yugong, that the Chinese people derived the name for their country — zhongguo, "central Nation."[2]

This same name remains in use to this very day, forty-two centuries later!

The name Central or Middle Kingdom reflects China's political and administrative position in the ancient world. For the purposes of our journey of discovery, though, there is another name that appears in ancient historical documents that is even more significant. This is 神州 (Shen Zhou), which means "God's Country" or "Holy Country." *The Historical Records* 史記 (Shi Ji), the authoritative 2nd-century B.C. compilation by China's grand historian Sima Qian, suggests that *Shen Zhou* was probably more commonly used as the name for China at the time than *Zhong Guo*.

> *Zhong Guo is known as the red-earthed Shen Zhou. Red-earthed Shen Zhou has nine states, these are the nine states referred to by Yu.*
>
> 中國名曰赤縣神州。赤縣神州內自有九州，禹之序九州是也。[3]

Shen Zhou—God's Country—what an interesting name! At this signpost, I made the startling and gratifying discovery that China's early form of government was based on and informed by its ancient knowledge of Shang Di. Although the historical records available today do not explain the origins of this name *Shen Zhou*, the documents do show how appropriate this name was. They record a dynamic relationship between God and the Chinese people, in which leaders as well as dynasties were raised up or brought down depending on their attitude and behavior towards God. We are not suggesting that China was a nation specially chosen by God as Israel was, but God loves all His creation and consequently has been intimately involved with the affairs of this ancient nation from the start.

THE MANDATE OF HEAVEN

Closely related to the name Shen Zhou is the concept of the Mandate of Heaven 天命 (Tian Ming). This was the principle upon which the whole justification of imperial rule rested. It was a concept of utmost importance to the Chinese nation because it regulated the functions of government and, in turn, impacted the lives of millions of

2. K. C. Wu, *The Chinese Heritage: A New and Provocative View of the Origins of Chinese Society* (New York: Crown Publishers, Inc., 1982), p. 95.

3. 《史記-卷七十四-孟子荀卿列傳》 *Historical Records*, Volume 74, Meng Zi Xun Qing.

subjects. Though China was never a theocracy, the Chinese people have throughout their history always believed that only those selected by God could ascend to the throne. That is, God conferred directly upon each emperor the right to rule; therefore, the emperor's authority was derived from God. This divine election is called the Mandate of Heaven or the will of God, and the man thus selected was called the Son of Heaven 天子 (Tian Zi). It is important to understand that this Mandate did not deify the emperor. Unlike the Romans and the Japanese, the Chinese did not consider their rulers to be divine. Quite the contrary, although the Son of Heaven was the supreme ruler of the land, he was but a regent or viceroy chosen to rule China on God's behalf. This is obvious in the fact that the Mandate was not constant: What God gives, He can also take away.

Because of this, the allegiance that the people owed the emperor was conditional upon the ruler's ability to have and to hold the Mandate, and the emperor's ability to hold the Mandate was considered conditional as well. His personal virtues and wisdom in governing determined whether God continued to favor him with the Mandate. If the emperor became immoral or his rule tyrannical, the people would be justified in thinking that he had lost the right to rule and that he and his dynasty should be replaced, even by revolt. Refusal to obey the emperor out of a "higher" obedience to God or conscience could, of course, result in a death sentence; Chinese history celebrates many such martyrs. On the other hand, an emperor who was no longer ruling with benevolence could be overthrown—an interesting consequence of the conditional nature of obedience. Chinese history records many examples of these acts too.

This concept of the Mandate of Heaven gave rise to the cycles of dynastic rule that appeared throughout the millennia of Chinese history: a dynasty over time becomes corrupt and is replaced by a new dynasty that rules with some degree of virtue until it too becomes corrupt, thus repeating the cycle. Of course, not all new rulers were completely virtuous, but the opposite was always true: corrupt emperors did not hold on to the Mandate for long. Although most of China's emperors failed to live up to the standards prescribed in the Chinese *Classics*, all knew that if they failed to uphold the classical virtues, their vices would be their legacy; even worse, they might lose the Mandate of Heaven.

The doctrine of the Mandate of Heaven can be understood in several different ways. For those people who reject the notion that Heaven refers to an all-powerful Supreme Being personally involved in the affairs of mankind, the Mandate of Heaven could simply be understood as representing natural laws dictating the waxing and waning of dynastic cycles. The Chinese *Classics*, however, reveal that the ancient Chinese trusted in a Supreme Being who was actively involved in human affairs, as described in this passage from the *Classic of Poetry*:

> *Revere the anger of Heaven,*
> *And presume not to make sport or be idle.*
> *Revere the changing moods of Heaven,*
> *And presume not to be driven by your pleasures.*
> *Great Heaven is intelligent,*
> *And is with you in all your goings.*
> *Great Heaven is clear-seeing,*
> *And is with you in your wanderings and indulgences.*

This understanding that the Mandate of Heaven is predicated on a Supreme Being, then gives rise to at least the following four ways of explaining what the Mandate is.

The will of God: The ancient Chinese worshipped God as a moral Being; therefore, they believed that His decisions were consistent with His character. Because God is omniscient and humans are finite, His moral choices can be beyond our ability to understand. Accepting the decisions of God as the will of an intelligent Being is altogether different from the way Chinese today accept fate or the way the ancient Greeks and Romans accepted that their fate was determined by their capricious gods. Those who believe in fate believe that events on earth are ordered by impersonal beings or forces in the spiritual realm. The will of God is entirely different: it is always exercised for the good of those who love Him. Those who believe and trust in Him know His intentions and are confident that at the summation of all things all His ways will be clear. This is expressed in Romans 8:28: "And we know that God causes all things to work

4. 《詩經-大雅-生民之什-板》 *Classic of Poetry*, Da Ya, Anecdotes of Sheng Min, Ban, verse 8.

together for good to those who love God, to those who are called according to His purpose."

The moral order of the universe: Confucius said, "At fifty, I understood the Mandate of Heaven,"[5] meaning it was only after many years of study that he learned how to distinguish right from wrong. Clearly, the Mandate of Heaven was not a set of physical principles, but rather moral truths that have been established by an intelligent Creator for man. Man can, with study, comprehend these principles, and he has a free will to choose to obey or disobey them.

The right to rule: This has become the most important meaning of the Mandate of Heaven. Knowing the moral order of the universe and actually observing it make one a worthy ruler. Otherwise, one has neither the ability nor, indeed, the right to be in power. This idea is quite different from the mediaeval European concept of government, wherein the ruler — whether Pope, king, or emperor — derived authority directly from God and was answerable only to God. The ruled, therefore, had no right to rebel against an unjust or corrupt ruler.[6]

The judgment of history: This view is the combination of the idea of the "right to rule" with the idea of "the will of God" and resulted in the Chinese expectation that losing the Mandate of Heaven (that is, the right to rule) would inevitably and quickly be followed by the actual loss of power. The historical precedent for this view was the brief and cruel rule of the Qin Dynasty (221–207 B.C.), followed by the more benign and durable tenure of the Han emperors, who reigned for some 400 years (206 B.C.–A.D. 220). This was the concept of the Mandate that informed the writing of Chinese history: beginning with the Latter Han Dynasty 後漢 (A.D. 25–220), one of the first acts of each new dynasty was the commissioning of an official history of the previous dynasty.[7] The history became, in effect, a certificate of legitimacy for the new rulers. By showing how the previous dynasty was at first benevolent, but then lost the Mandate of Heaven, the history demonstrated that, in order to restore benevolent rule, the new dynasty was obligated to replace the former corrupt dynasty.

Each of these views of the Mandate of Heaven recognizes a moral requisite for the right to rule. Because the right to rule is derived from Heaven, the emperor is subject to Heaven and is expected to meet Heaven's requirements. Confucius in *The*

5. "五十而知天命" in 《論語-第二篇-爲政》 *The Analects,* Chapter 2, Wei Zheng, verse 4.

6. This was the case in Western thought until the Protestant Reformation, which challenged the absolute authority of Catholic rulers.

7. The first instance of this was the great *History of the Former Han Dynasty.*

Analects minces no words as to this point: "He who does not understand the Mandate [the will of God] cannot be a ruler!"[8] Should the emperor or a succession of emperors of a dynasty fail to rule virtuously and righteously, thereby causing the people to cry out over their oppression, Heaven would withdraw its Mandate from that dynasty and bestow it on a new emperor with attributes compatible with those of God. The *Commentary to The Analects* makes clear the need for a ruler to understand what the Mandate of Heaven requires of him: "He who understands the Mandate is worthy of trust. He who does not know the Mandate always [seeks to] dodge harm while pursuing [personal] gains. How can such a person become a ruler?"[9]

When Heaven transfers the Mandate to a new dynasty, it is called the "Change of Heaven's Mandate 天命變化." Such a transfer is described in the *Classic of Poetry* in the account of how the Shang Dynasty 商朝 ended and was succeeded, implausibly, by the Zhou Dynasty 周朝:

> *The descendants of Shang*
> *Numbered more than hundreds of thousands.*
> *But when God gave the command,*
> *They became subject to Zhou.*
> *They became subject to Zhou;*
> *The appointment of Heaven is provisional.*

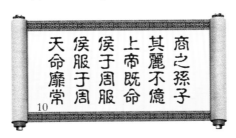

The *Classic of History* records the words of the founder of the Zhou Dynasty clearly articulating the concept of the Mandate of Heaven in his explanation of why the previous two dynasties, the Xia (2207–1766 B.C.) and Shang, also called Yin (1765–1122 B.C.), were replaced.

> *We rightly disposed of Yin's mandate to accomplish the will of Shang Di…. I have heard the saying, "Shang Di leads mankind to rest." The Xia emperors*

8. "不知命，無以爲君子也！in《論語-第二十篇-堯曰》 *The Analects*, Chapter 20, Yao Yue.

9. "知命者，知有命而信之也。人不知命，則見害必避，見利必趨，何以爲君子？" in《論語集注》 Attributed to Cheng Zi, 程子, by Zhu Xi, 朱熹 (1130–1200), in *Commentary to the Analects*, Volume 10, last paragraph.

10.《詩經-大雅-文王之什-文王》 *Classic of Poetry*, Da Ya, Anecdotes of Wen Wang, Wen Wang.

did not provide such rest, so Shang Di sent down corrections, revealing His will to Xia…. Whereupon He directed your founder, Cheng Tang, to overthrow the Xia Dynasty and to appoint able men to rule the empire. From Cheng Tang down to Emperor Yi, every emperor sought to rule by virtue and duly attended to the sacrifice…. But in these times, their successor showed himself ignorant of Heaven, and much less could it be expected of him that he would be mindful of the diligence of his fathers for the empire…. On this account, Shang Di no longer protected him, but sent down great ruin. Indeed, with regard to the overthrow of all States, great and small, throughout the four quarters of the empire, in every case there are reasons for their punishments.

敕殷命終于帝……我聞曰，上帝引逸，有夏不適逸，則
惟帝 降格，向于時夏，降致罰。……乃命爾先祖成湯革
夏，俊民甸四 方。自成湯至于帝乙，罔不明德恤祀。
……在今後嗣王，誕罔 顯于天，矧曰其有聽念于先王勤
家。……惟時上帝不保，降若 茲大喪。惟天不畀不明厥
德。凡四方小大邦喪，罔非有辭于罰。[11]

Though historians generally credit the doctrine of the Mandate of Heaven to the Zhou rulers or regard it as not being formalized until the time of the Zhou Dynasty 周朝 (1121–249 B.C.), the historical accounts of the early rulers, such as Huang Di 黄帝, which means "Yellow Emperor," Yao 堯, Shun 舜, Yu 禹, and Tang 湯, reveal that they subjected themselves, their rule, and their succession to the will of God. Particularly in the matter of succession, they took meticulous care in being sure to select as successors men of excellent moral standing.

Ancient Chinese history clearly shows that these early emperors saw the right to rule as a trust from God; hence, they believed that they had to rule in a manner consistent with the character of God. Therefore, the doctrine of the Mandate of Heaven

11. 《尚書-周書-多士》 *Classic of History*, Zhou History, Duo Shi (Numerous Officers).

gave not only a justification for the removal of corrupt rulers, but also provided positive performance indicators, such as benevolence 仁 (ren) and righteousness 義 (yi), which a ruler must possess and exhibit in order to hold on to the Mandate. Sadly, this form of virtuous leadership practiced early in China's recorded history became corrupted through time, with the result that the Zhou Dynasty was thrown into a state of anarchy leading to the period of the Warring States 戰國 (475–221 B.C.), which roughly spans the lifetimes of the Greek philosophers Socrates and Plato to the great scientist and thinker Archimedes of Syracuse. From then on, autocratic rule based on power and position rather than leadership by virtue has been the norm in China. Although there were some benevolent emperors who understood and adhered to the obligations of virtuous rule in the more than 2,000 years that followed, they were the exception. The authority of Shang Di's Mandate of Heaven was lost to the power of the Dragon, a development we will consider in the next chapter.

The significance of the Mandate of Heaven in Chinese history cannot be overstated. In contrast with Western civilization, where political order depended on a balance of power among multiple nation-states, Chinese order was achieved through the individual ruler's submission to the supreme will of God. This provided both accountability and balance of power. Note the emphasis on individual accountability in these excerpts from the *Classic of Poetry*, in which a wayward ruler is warned:

> *God has reversed his normal course;*
> *The commoners are full of distress.*
> *The words you utter are not right;*
> *The plans you form are not far-sighted.*
> *As there are no sages,*
> *you think you have no guidance —*
> *You have no real sincerity.*
> *Your plans are not far-sighted,*
> *therefore I admonish you.*
> *Heaven is now sending down calamities —*
> *Do not be so complacent.*
> *Heaven is now producing such movements —*
> *Do not be so indifferent.*

If your words were harmonious,
the people would be united.
If your words were gentle and kind,
the people would be settled.

上帝板板
下民卒癉
出話不然
為猶不遠
靡聖管管
不實于亶
猶之未遠
是用大諫
天之方難
無然憲憲
天之方蹶
無然泄泄
辭之輯矣
民之洽矣
辭之懌矣
民之莫矣

THE SON OF HEAVEN

From this understanding of the Mandate of Heaven, it is easy to see how the Chinese regarded their emperors as the Son of Heaven. This title reflects the enormity of the emperor's role, which—as the excerpt above suggests—extended well beyond just the worldly affairs of government. In addition to the heavy responsibility of ruling over the daily affairs of a vast empire with populations unrivalled in number, the Son of Heaven also had to ensure that his own character reflected and represented God, or Heaven, in word and deed. The concept of the Son of Heaven was established and continued to develop through more than three thousand years until the collapse of China's last dynasty, the Qing 清, in 1911. Despite the passage of such a long period of time, certain basic elements of the role of the Son of Heaven remained unchanged and unchallenged.

Foremost is the understanding that there was only one Son of Heaven. It was this one single man whom God held responsible for the welfare of the entire nation. As the Son of Heaven, this one man was the one who acted as mediator between God and his people, a role that was ultimately fulfilled in Jesus Christ.

> *For there is one God, and one mediator also between God and men, the man*
> *Christ Jesus, who gave Himself as a ransom for all, the testimony given at the*
> *proper time.*
> 1 Timothy 2:5–6

12. 《詩經-大雅-生民之什-板》 *Classic of Poetry*, Da Ya, Anecdotes of Sheng Min, Ban, verses 1–2.

The second principle is the right of the Son of Heaven to rule. As explained above, the Son of Heaven must have the Mandate of Heaven to reign, and the emperor and his dynasty must consistently reflect the virtuous character of God. By doing so, the emperor demonstrated that God had appointed him to rule, because God would not choose a representative who was contrary to Him in attributes. The Bible affirms the fact that all earthly governments are established by God.

> *Every person is to be in subjection to the governing authorities. For there is no*
> *authority except from God, and those which exist are established by God.*
> Romans 13:1

Finally, the Son of Heaven was responsible for providing spiritual leadership for the empire and for upholding God's standards. His personal spiritual condition determined the wellbeing of the entire empire: When God was pleased with the emperor, the nation prospered; when the emperor lacked virtue, the nation suffered calamities. The emperor's virtue was demonstrated in part through the observance of rituals and ceremonies, the most important of which was the Border Sacrifice, which we examined in Chapter 4. Though the original intent was that form (i.e., the rituals) follows function (i.e., upholding God's standards), in time only the form was left. This doctrine that the right to rule is linked to righteousness is also found in the Bible and in Hebrew culture.

> *By me kings reign, / And rulers decree justice. / By me princes rule, and nobles, /*
> *All who judge rightly.*
> Proverbs 8:15–16

The whole of China's more than 4,000 years of recorded history amply illustrates this truth that when a nation is governed by virtuous rulers, it prospers. By acknowledging the principle of the Mandate of Heaven, the ancient Chinese put their trust in the supreme will of God, to select and appoint rulers over them. Their trust was not unfounded, for they believed that God would do what was best for them and that His choice of ruler would be one who demonstrated virtues and character traits consistent with God Himself. The historical records show that this indeed was the case beginning with the very first emperor of China's long history, Huang Di.

Huang Di

Ancient records that have survived to the present begin the history of China with Huang Di, or the Yellow Emperor (reigned 2697–2599 B.C.), who lived some 2,000 years before Confucius and was roughly contemporary with the Sumerian king Gilgamesh. He was the first to unify China and the first to be called "Son of Heaven." His title 帝 (di as in Shang Di),[13] which means "Lord," indicates the high honor accorded him by the people. The length of his reign is traditionally rounded off to 100 years, and many major developments and Chinese inventions are either credited to him personally or believed to have come into being during his rule. These include the invention of Chinese writing, the creation of the calendar, the knowledge of collecting silk from mulberry silkworms, and the use of mass archery in warfare. Huang Di is personally credited with coining bronze money, practicing medicine, and inventing boats. He was probably the first to set up administrative government, dividing the nation into regions and appointing two senior supervisors.

Most significantly, according to the *Historical Records*, it was Huang Di who built an altar at Mount Tai 泰山[14] so that sacrifices could be made periodically to Shang Di. According to tradition, only the most worthy emperors, who also served as Shang Di's high priests, were permitted to perform the most important of these sacrifices, called 封禅 (feng shan). Surely it was no accident that a ruler whose reign yielded such a bounty of valuable discoveries and vital inventions was the emperor who gave due reverence to Shang Di and who institutionalized the practice of regular sacrifices to acknowledge that the emperor's role on earth was but that of a servant of the Most High. A commentary in the *Historical Records* identifies the Yellow Emperor as the emperor who performed "feng shan" more times than any other. Later, emperors who desired to project an image of a special relationship with God to protect their Mandate, such as the cruel and authoritarian Qin Shi Huang Di, also performed the "feng shan" at Mount Tai.

Emperor Yao and Emperor Shun

Huang Di was followed by a succession of three rulers whose reigns were rather lackluster. Then Emperor Yao (2357–2258 B.C.) ascended the throne.[15] The very first

13. 《史記-卷一 -五帝本紀》 *Historical Records*, Volume 1, Chronicles of the Five Emperors.
14. Located in modern-day Shandong province in eastern China.
15. For a more detailed account of the story of Yao, see Wu's *The Chinese Heritage*, pp. 65–77.

Chapter Seven   God's Country

A typical Chinese landscape painting of Mount Tai, where Huang Di made sacrifices to God.

document in the *Classic of History* is the Canon of Yao 堯典, which effusively praises this emperor:

> *According to antiquity, we find that Emperor Yao was called Fang Xun. He was responsible, intelligent, insightful, gentle, and gracious. His virtues reached to the four corners of the empire, from the greatest to the lowest. He promoted the capable and virtuous for the good of the nine branches of his kindred. When his kindred were harmonious, he distinguished and honored the virtues of the hundred clans. When the hundred clans knew what was right and wrong, he united and brought peace to all the states of the Empire. Thus all the black-haired people were transformed and lived in tranquility.*

曰若稽古，帝堯曰放勳，欽明文思安安，允恭克讓，光被四表，格于上下。克明俊德，以親九族，九族既睦，平章百姓，百姓昭明，協和萬邦，黎民于變時雍。[16]

16. 《尚書-唐書-堯典》 *Classic of History*, Book of Tang, Canon of Yao, paragraph 2.

FINDING GOD IN ANCIENT CHINA

Clearly, one so virtuous who could induce all people to live peacefully would be favored with the Mandate of Heaven, but this was just the beginning. Once he had brought peace to the land, Yao sent four ministers to the edges of his empire in four directions. They were to monitor astral movements so that Yao could fine-tune the imperial calendar. The accuracy of the imperial calendar played a crucial role in the increasingly agrarian society; it enabled farmers to know when to plant and sow, so as to reap the best yields from their crops. By improving the calendar, Emperor Yao was improving the lives of his subjects. He also continued to develop Huang Di's administrative government by establishing the office of the Four Dukes 四岳 (literally, Four Mountains). He then staffed the offices of the Four Dukes with four of his closest advisors, who were stationed at the outer edges of the empire in four different directions. From there they reported back to Yao on important events in their territories and supervised the activities of people in their area.

The most important event of Emperor Yao's reign occurred when a Great Flood swept over the empire. Obviously this was not the biblical flood of Noah, but it was a devastating natural catastrophe that was beyond the emperor's ability to handle; the devastation threatened to disintegrate his empire. In desperation, he scoured the land for someone who could curb the deluge. Yao even offered to abdicate the throne to give power to someone who knew what to do, or to share power with the Four Dukes in a joint effort to combat the inundation. The first man he tapped for the flood-control job struggled for nine years against the waters, but was unable to contain them. More desperate than ever, Yao offered to abdicate the throne to the Four Dukes, but they wanted none of the responsibility. Instead, they suggested another man, Shun (2257–2208 B.C.), who came from an extremely humble background, but who had become known in the land for his remarkable filial piety.[17] They described him to Yao this way: "… his father is stubborn; his [step-]mother is insincere; his [half-]brother Xiang is arrogant. But through his filial conduct he has maintained harmony in his family, influencing them for the better so that they no longer proceed to great wickedness."[18]

Both the *Classic of History* and the *Historical Records* provide a picture of Shun as a man of great virtue and integrity. In many ways, he was comparable to emperor Yao in his impeccable character. His father was called Gusou 瞽叟, which literally means "blind due to lack of a pupil," probably because he was unable to determine

17. For a more detailed account of the life of Shun, see Wu's *The Chinese Heritage*, pp. 70–87.
18. "嚚子，父頑，母嚚，象傲，克諧以孝，烝烝乂，不格奸 in 《尚書-唐書-堯典》 *Classic of History*, Book of Tang, Canon of Yao, last paragraph.

right from wrong. Gusou was a man without scruples, and he exploited Shun's filial devotion. Shun's mother died early, so Gusou married again, and the second wife bore him another son, Xiang 象. The three treated Shun worse than a slave, forcing upon him all the responsibilities for providing for the family, as well as all the other chores. Consequently, Shun had to master a variety of skills: he farmed; he fished; he made pottery, utensils, and implements; and he traded goods.

Despite his wretched family life, Shun was exceptionally intelligent and gifted, yet very humble. He had an insatiable desire to learn new things, and he became famous for his ability to improve on knowledge gained from others. Moreover, in the face of the rising flood, Shun seemed to have an instinct for knowing which places were safe to live. As his reputation for choosing secure locations grew and spread, more and more people began to follow him to avoid the floods. This is what is recorded about the last place to which he moved: "In one year it became a village; in two years, a hamlet; in three years, a town of considerable size."[19] Despite Shun's growing fame and abilities, he continued to be abused by his father, stepmother, and half-brother. This unjust treatment only increased people's admiration for him, and his determined filial piety became his hallmark. Because of the sacrifices he was forced to make for his family, he remained single until he was 30 years old.

For his virtuous character and abilities, Shun was recommended as a candidate to be Yao's successor. Shun's reputation notwithstanding, Yao put him through three rigorous tests that took three years to complete. Not only did Shun complete them, but he performed them exceedingly well. It was obvious after these tests that the Mandate of Heaven rested on Shun. Yao, now quite old, declared, "Come, you Shun. I have investigated into your deeds and compared them with your words. Three years have passed, and you have proved that you can in truth put your words into deeds. You do now ascend the imperial throne."[20] Shun, however, refused, and finally an arrangement was reached whereby the two reigned as co-emperors. Shun was commissioned to the throne in an elaborate ceremony that included the requisite sacrifice to Shang Di, performed in open country to the south of the capital.

Less than a month later, Shun went on an inspection tour of the entire empire.

19. "一年而所居成聚，二年成邑，三年成都，" in 《史記-卷一一五帝本記》 *Historical Records*, Volume 1, Chronicles of the Five Emperors. As translated by Wu, *Chinese Heritage*, p. 73.

20. "格，汝舜，詢事考言，乃言可績，三載，汝陟帝位" in 《尚書-唐書-舜典》 Ibid., Canon of Shun, paragraph 3.

FINDING GOD IN ANCIENT CHINA

The Great Flood was still raging, and Shun recognized that the best way to combat the raging waters was to mobilize the entire nation to work together in a systematic way. To coordinate such a grand project required discipline of the highest order, and that required the cooperation of all: the princes, the heads of clans, and the common people as well. Shun knew he could not bring about such compliance through force, but had to motivate the people from within. So he set off on his inspection tour to practice what in modern management is called "management by walking about." Shun spent nearly a year on the road, familiarizing himself with life in every corner of the empire. Upon his return to the capital, he created new administrative offices and systems and established a penal code that was surprisingly humane.

Before he could put his flood control plan into effect, however, Shun had to deal with an awkward situation: there already was a man in charge of flood control. A decade earlier, Emperor Yao had appointed Gun 薛 to the task. Shun concluded that Gun's approach, which was to build as many dikes as possible, was ineffective; as the floodwaters rose, the dikes all collapsed. Interestingly, Shun found in Gun's son, Yu, someone who was equally critical of Gun's methods. Yu had concluded that the widespread flooding could not be held back by dikes, so his solution was to deepen or widen all waterways to drain the floodwaters to the ocean as quickly as possible. Shun concurred with this approach and sought Gun's cooperation, but Gun responded by showing his disapproval of the installation of Shun, a commoner, to be co-emperor. Emperor Shun was forced to report the matter to Yao, who had Gun banished. In his place, Gun's son, Yu, was appointed to take over the flood control work. Yu performed this job with such great diligence and success, at incredible personal sacrifice, that when Yao and Shun died, the people could find no better person to rule them than Yu, who thus became the founder of the Xia Dynasty, China's first.[21]

Emperor Yu

Yu took on his flood control duties just four days after his wedding and did not return home for 13 years as he traversed the empire overseeing the flood-fighting efforts. A son was born during this time, but though his travels brought him near his home three times, he did not return to his family even once because of

21. For a more detailed account of Yu's life, see Wu's, *The Chinese Heritage*, pp. 86–95, 106–17.

the demands of his mission. Yu traveled throughout the empire time and again, climbing mountains to study the course of the waterways below and marking water levels to monitor the rising or receding flood levels. He traveled by cart over land, by boat over water, with sleds in miry areas, and with spikes on the mountains. Where no transport was available or possible, Yu walked, carrying his simple tools: a measuring rope, a pair of compasses, and a T-square. With these, he surveyed, charted, and superintended.

Yu came to the conclusion that because the floodwaters were not emptying into the seas fast enough, water levels were rising higher and higher, causing the deluge to inundate ever larger areas of land. This confirmed the validity of his initial assessment: the only feasible solution was to make the waters empty faster. He decided that since the area along the Yellow River had the highest concentration of inhabitants, it was necessary to start his work there. His efforts were not restricted to deepening the main waterway leading out to sea; altogether he deepened nine channels, vastly increasing their drainage capabilities. Finally, Yu was able to report that "the (rivers) are connected throughout the nine regions, the four frontiers are habitable, the nine mountains are accessible, the nine streams are nurturing the land, the nine flooded lands are now under control, and the nation is united."[22] The toil, however, had exacted a physical cost: his arms and legs had turned hairless from exposure to the elements, and his feet were maimed in such a way that they had to be dragged one after the other in a sort of limping, leaping gait.

Another challenge Yu faced was to ascertain the overall effects of his work and to make whatever adjustments might be necessary. Without the benefit of modern conveniences such as airplanes and helicopters, he had only one way to survey the results of his flood-control measures: climbing to the top of every hill or mountain. There he would perform his spiritual duty by offering sacrifices to God and then observe whether the flood had subsided and by how much. He would record which channels were flowing well and where any remaining large bodies of water could be diverted to drain. In this exhaustive survey work, Yu systematically divided up the mountains of China into west-to-east ranges in the north, central, and southern regions of the country. These three ranges spread over the entire empire except for the southernmost provinces. Yu ascended these mountains, range by range, peak by peak, again and again, until finally he could

22. "于是九州攸同，四奥既居，九山刊旅，九川滌原，九澤既陂，四海會同" in《史記-卷二-夏本紀》
Historical Records, Volume 2, History of Xia.

report with some satisfaction that "throughout the nine regions a similar order was effected: the grounds along the waters were everywhere made habitable, the hills and mountains were cleared of their superfluous wood and sacrificed to; the sources of the streams were cleared; the marshes were well banked; and access to the capital was secured for all within the four seas."[23]

Thus, Yu accomplished far more than just controlling and draining the floodwaters. He single-handedly mapped the entire empire, while at the same time preparing new territories for the rapidly expanding nation. It was also while performing these tasks that Yu accomplished the massive undertaking, referred to at the beginning of this chapter in the discussion of the origins of the term Central Nation, of assigning grades to the fields under cultivation for the purposes of assessing tax collection. At first glance, the system appears to be a simple nine-grade standard of soil quality linked to nine levels of taxes; in reality, the system Yu devised was far more complex and surprisingly flexible — taking into account such factors as density of population and extent of flood damage. In creating this taxation system, Yu made a major contribution to centralization of authority and brought a degree of unity to the vast empire that was unparalleled at that point in history.

When Emperor Yao died, the people mourned for him for three years. At the end of this period of mourning, co-emperor Shun left the capital, yielding the throne to Yao's son, Dan Zhu 丹朱. The people, however, would not accept Dan Zhu. According to the historical account, "All the princes, returning to the court to renew their allegiance, did not go to the son of Yao, but to Shun. Those who had disputes did not go to the son of Yao, but to Shun. And those who sang did not sing of the son of Yao, but of Shun. Therefore, we can say that this is [the will of] Heaven. It was after these things that Shun went back to the Central Nation and occupied the seat of the Son of Heaven."[24] Shun ruled alone for many more years, during which time he reorganized the government into a structure that is recognizable even today, with an office similar to that of the modern-day prime minister, and departments of the interior, education, justice, works, music, etc. He also instituted regular inspections of the empire and regular reviews of subordinate officials, whose promotion or demotion was decided by these performance reviews. Shun, at an exceedingly advanced age, died while on one of his regular inspection tours, when it took him to the southernmost reaches of the empire.

23. As translated by Wu, *Chinese Heritage*, p. 90.

24. "天下諸侯朝覲者，不之堯之子而之舜；訟獄者，不之堯之子而之舜；謳歌者，不謳歌堯之子而謳歌舜，故曰，天也。夫然后之中國，踐天子位焉" in《孟子－卷九萬章章句上－第五章》*Mencius*, Volume 9, Wan Zhang, Part 1, Chapter 5.

Upon his death, the people mourned for Shun as they had for Yao, for three years. Just as before, at the end of the mourning period, Yu, the remaining of the original flood-battling triumvirate, retreated from the capital so as to yield the throne to Shun's son. Again, however, the will of the people prevailed: "But the people under Heaven followed him [Yu], just as after the death of Yao, instead of following Yao's son they had followed Shun."[25]

MERITOCRACY

So it was that under the leadership of these three great men — Yao, Shun, and Yu — China flourished and enjoyed unparalleled peace and prosperity, such as has not been seen in the 4,000 years since. Throughout China's long history, its people — most notably Confucius — have longed for a return to the form of government modeled by Yao, Shun, and Yu. This form of government is referred to as 天下為公 (tian xia wei gong), which means "Righteousness Rules." The greatest legacy of these three men, to whom are credited achievements of near-mythical proportions, is probably the policy of 禪讓 (Shan Rang), that is, abdicating the throne to another person based on that person's merit.

Most dictionaries define the term "shan rang" simply as "to abdicate and hand over the crown to another person." Implicit in its meaning, however, is the idea that the transfer of power is to a person deserving of the position and equipped to rule. It is a policy of meritocracy, but one that specifically refers to the giving of authority to one who has virtue because of his devotion to God. Use of the word 禪 (shan) reveals that this policy reflects an awareness of God, because the character 禪 contains 示 (shi), the radical or modifier for "God." In each of the transfers of power — from Yao to Shun, from Shun to Yu, from Yu to Yi 益, and later from King Wu 武王 to the Duke of Zhou 周公 — the throne did not go to the emperor's son but rather to the most qualified person: he who most merited the honor and who would best serve the kingdom. In each case, the foremost consideration was not the perpetuation of a dynasty but rather what was best for the people. Underlying the concept of Shan Rang is the idea that the emperor was, above all else, a servant, albeit the servant-leader. The emphasis was on service rather than on leadership, and certainly not on power.

25. "天下之民從之，若堯崩之后不從堯之子而從舜也" in《孟子-卷九萬章章句上-第六章》Ibid., Chapter 6.

When Yao was looking for a successor, his ministers had suggested designating one of his sons, but Yao proceeded to list the vices of each of his sons and the manner in which the rule of each would not benefit the nation. When Shun was recommended to him, he tested Shun's suitability before offering the throne to him. Even when Yao did so, Shun did not accept right away; Shun himself had to be convinced that it was the will of God before he agreed to take up the reigns of power. Similarly, Shun determined that it was God's will that Yu should be his successor 17 years before his own death. Upon Shun's death, Yu was offered the throne but he did not immediately agree; he also waited until he was convinced that it was the will of God.

Though this form of peaceful transfer of power has not been practiced in China for several thousands of years, the Chinese people nonetheless continued to long for a return to this ideal. This kind of succession, however, is only possible when the one entrusted with the right to rule accepts that he is but a regent of God and that God alone has final authority. Similarly, the one accepting the rule should accept the Mandate only after careful consideration and with full understanding that he is only a "caretaker" and not a dictator with absolute power.

Shang Tang

Yu ruled as emperor for 15 years until his death at the age of 100. Just before he died, he abdicated the throne to Bo Yi 益, a very capable man. Unfortunately, before Bo Yi could establish his authority, the princes crowned one of Yu's sons, Qi 啓, as emperor, even though Qi was an inferior choice. Thereafter, imperial power in the Xia Dynasty was passed to the son or brother of the previous emperor. Thus, the Shan Rang policy was abandoned in favor of nepotism and with it came corruption in government. The right to rule was no longer dependent on character but rather on blood relationship. The Xia Dynasty lasted for more than 400 years, ending with the 17th emperor, Jie 桀, who is notorious in Chinese history as one of the nation's most evil and corrupt rulers. He ignored his duty to his people, cared nothing for their welfare, and lived only for his own pleasure and self-indulgence. As recounted in the opening of Chapter 5, Jie lost the Mandate of Heaven to Tang (reigned 1766–1754 B.C.), a prince of the house of Shang 商 and a man of integrity.[26]

26. For a more detailed account of the life of Tang, see Wu's *The Chinese Heritage*, pp. 129–143, 157–164.

The young Tang, observing the chaos into which the empire had fallen and the misery of the people under such oppressive misrule, was inspired by the examples of Yao, Shun, and Yu to rule his feudal state responsibly and wisely. In the face of attacks from roving nomads, he trained his farmers in military skills so that they could defend themselves. Such protection was supposed to be provided by the imperial court in return for the allegiance of princes such as Tang, but under Emperor Jie this duty was neglected. Tang also earned the devotion of his subjects by his practice of selecting and promoting officers based solely on merit rather than on family ties. As Confucius writes in *The Analects*, "If the people are governed by *dao* [moral principle], they will not resist."[27] In time, Tang's men developed into an excellent fighting force, while the empire and the well-being of the people declined further.

Under Tang's far-sighted and sensible leadership, his tiny territory flourished —and became a target of attack by neighboring feudal states. These attacks forced Tang to respond militarily, thus expanding his territory and winning him allegiance from the conquered people, who were eager to be put under Shang rule. After eleven such military expeditions, Tang had conquered all his enemies. In the process, however, he had aroused the suspicion of Emperor Jie, who became alarmed as he saw a growing number of states abandoning their allegiance to him and choosing to follow Tang instead. Tang sent an emissary five times to the capital to implore Jie to reform and pay heed to the growing discontent of his subjects, but the emperor scoffed at the warnings that his regime was faced with a fatal test. Leading forces far larger in number than those of the young prince, Emperor Jie marshaled his troops to attack Tang. Just before going into battle, Tang exhorted his men: "It is not I, this little person, who dare to cause trouble. But the Xia [emperor] has committed many sins. It is the will of Heaven to destroy him.... As I fear Shang Di, I dare not but correct this wrong."[28] As a fierce thunderstorm raged, a daylong battle ensued until Prince Tang emerged the victor, confirming that the Mandate of Heaven had passed from the corrupt Xia Dynasty.

This being the first time in Chinese history that the transfer of imperial power was not peaceful, Tang invoked the Mandate of Heaven more than any previous ruler. Upon his return home, Tang had one of his chief ministers issue a proclamation explaining what had happened. It read in part,

27. "天下有道，則庶人不議" in 《論語−季氏》 *The Analects*, Chapter 16, Ji Shi, paragraph 2.
28. "非臺小子，敢行稱亂，有夏多罪，天命殛之。……予畏上帝，不敢不正" in 《尚書−商書−湯誓》 *Classic of History*, The Book of Shang, Address of Tang, paragraph 2.

Listen: As Heaven has endowed people with passions, without a ruler, there will be chaos. So Heaven sees to it men of intelligence are born in order that the people may be well-governed. The Xia emperor corrupted himself; and the people were as if they had fallen into mire or burning charcoal. It is then that Heaven has graciously given you, our King, courage and wisdom to be an example and a leader for all the states and to continue the old ways of Yu. You are now only following the natural course, honoring and obeying the Mandate of Heaven. The Xia emperor was guilty of falsely appropriating Heaven's name to spread his own dictates far and wide. Shang Di has condemned him and handed His mandate to the house of Shang....O, to have a good end, one must begin well. Those who are proper will be established and those who are corrupt and unruly will be destroyed. Revere and honor the way of Heaven. This is the only way to preserve the Mandate of Heaven!

嗚 呼，惟天生民有欲，無主乃亂，惟天生聰明時乂，有夏昏德，民墜塗炭，天乃錫王勇智，表正萬邦，纘禹舊服，茲率厥典，奉 若天命，夏王有罪，矯誣上天，以布命于下，帝用不臧，式商受命。……嗚呼，慎厥終，惟其始，殖有禮，覆昏暴，欽崇天道，永保天命。[29]

In bringing down the Xia Dynasty, Tang earned for himself a place in Chinese history as the first revolutionary. In fact, the very term for "revolution" 草命 (ge ming) can be traced to Tang. The two characters literally mean "to overturn the mandate," and they first appeared in the *Classic of Changes* 易經 (Yi Jing), in reference to Tang and King Wu, whose story is told below. It said of these two men, they "overturned the Mandate in accord with Heaven and in response to the people."[30] Tang as emperor proved to be as virtuous and wise as he had been when he was merely a prince of the house of Shang. Recall the account in Chapter 5 of his response to the seven years of drought that devastated the land. When all other measures had failed and the suggestion was made that a human sacrifice

29. 《尚書-商書-仲虺之誥》 Ibid., Book of Shang, Proclamation of Zhong Hui.
30. "湯，武革命，順乎天而應乎人" in 《易經-傳文-彖辭-革卦》 *Classic of Changes*, Commentary, Tuan Notes, Ge Hexagram.

was required, Tang—the most powerful man in the nation—prepared himself to be that sacrifice.

The pattern of dynastic cycles, however, was already set. Just as Tang founded a dynasty in response to the oppression of a people ruled by a corrupt ruler who put his own selfish and evil desires above the good of his subjects, so with the passage of 600 years did the dynasty that Tang founded inexorably degenerate into the same state. A document in the *Classic of History* records the despair of the kingdom's "three good men," senior advisors to the last Shang emperor, as they described the situation:

> *The people ... small and great are given to theft, to robbery, to all sorts of depravity and wickedness. The officers, high and low, imitate and compete with one another in violating the law. Criminals are not apprehended. Consequently the common people all rise up to commit crime upon one another. The nation is now sinking into ruin like one crossing a river who cannot find its ford or bank. The nation is only hastening to its ruin at this present pace!*

殷罔不小大，好草竊奸宄，卿士師師非度，凡有辜罪，乃罔恒獲，小民方興，相爲敵讎，今殷其淪喪，若涉大水，其無津涯，殷遂喪，越至于今。[31]

Many of these troubles can be traced to Emperor Xin 帝辛, later known as Zhou 祭寸. He is regarded in Chinese history as one of the most evil monarchs who ever reigned. The condition of the Shang Dynasty during Zhou's reign was more or less anarchy with rampant and unrestrained wantonness and corruption. And Zhou himself was the worst offender. Alcoholism was pervasive throughout the land, and none was more given to drink than Zhou. A story from the historical record serves to illustrate the severity of the problem:

> *Zhou, having drunk day and night, suddenly awoke with the fear that he had lost count of time and did not know what day it was. He inquired to his left and to his right, and all did not know. So he sent a man to ask of Jizi, the senior tutor. Said*

31. 《尚書-商書-微子》 *Classic of History*, Book of Shang, Wei Zi (Viscount of Wei).

Jizi to his own people, "Being lord and master of the world, yet he and his court have all lost count of time; what a peril it is for the world! With the entire court not knowing what the day is, yet I alone know; what a peril it is for myself." He told the messenger that he did not know what the day was either.

紂爲長夜之飲，懼以失日，問其左右，盡不知也。乃使人問箕子。箕子謂其徒曰：　"爲天下主而一國皆失日，天下其危矣。一國皆不知而我獨知之，吾其危矣。"辭以醉而不知。[32]

Other stories tell of Zhou's bizarre cruelty. Upon seeing a poverty-stricken old man enduring the winter's cold wearing only a few rags, Zhou's favorite concubine wondered if perhaps the old man's bone marrow was different from that of ordinary people to enable him to withstand the frigid temperatures. Zhou obligingly had the man's thighs sliced open to satisfy her curiosity. Anther time she saw a pregnant woman and wondered whether the unborn child was male or female. Again the emperor indulged her curiosity: he ordered the mother's belly sliced open.

The *Classic of History* contains this lament penned by a trusted aide of Emperor Zhou:

O Son of Heaven! Heaven is about to bring an end to our Yin [Shang] Mandate .... It is not that the spirits of our former emperors do not try to aid us, their own descendants. But by your own indulgence and revelries, you yourself are bringing on the end! On this account, Heaven has abandoned us, so that there is not enough food. You do not consider the character of Heaven. You do not obey the statutes of the empire. Now all the people are wishing the dynasty to perish, saying, "Why is Heaven withholding His wrath?" Heaven's wrath has not arrived yet. What will the king do?

天子，天既訖我殷命。　...　非先王不相我後人，瞎王淫

32. 《韓非子-說林上》 *Han Fei Zi*, Shuo Lin, Part 1.

戲用自絕，故天棄我，不有康食，不虞天性，不迪率
典，今我民罔弗欲喪，曰，天曷不降威大命不摯，今王
其如臺。[33]

King Wen, King Wu, and Duke of Zhou

Once again, there was a just prince from among the vassal states whose character stood in stark contrast to that of the reigning emperor. He was known as King Wen 文王, which means King of Culture. Wen aspired to save his people from the tyranny and oppression of the disintegrating Shang Dynasty, and his wisdom and perseverance enabled him, along with his son King Wu 武王, to bring down the mighty empire.[34] Although it was the son, King Wu, who fought the decisive battles that ultimately toppled the Shang, when he consolidated power and proclaimed the Zhou Dynasty (1122–221 B.C.), King Wu said that "ge ming" (revolution), that is, the passing of the Mandate, had actually occurred eleven years earlier while his father, King Wen, was still ruling only the state of Zhou.

King Wen's fame and following as a wise, efficacious, honorable, and moral leader extended far beyond the borders of Zhou. Hundreds of years later, Confucius, whose lineage traced back to the very house of Shang that was deposed by Zhou and whose loyalties, therefore, ought to have been aligned with the Shang Dynasty, wrote instead of the virtues of Wen Wang: "In the *Classic of Poetry*, it is written, 'Profound was King Wen. Clearly and unceasingly, with reverence he conducted himself toward the goal.' For a ruler of men, the goal is humanity."[35]

King Wen's humanity was evident in the way he cared for the poor and for those with no family to rely on for help and in the rudimentary social security system he established for the aged. He is credited with setting up China's first educational system, which provided schooling for children from ages 8 to 15. At age 15, those who qualified could enter an academy for higher studies. His laws were the most humane of the time: it restricted punishment to the guilty party alone; family members were not punished, as was then the practice. Even in military conscription, King Wen developed a far more equitable and sophisticated system that sought to reduce the burden on each family. When he reorganized the military, King Wen based its new

---

33. 《尚書-商書-西伯戡黎》 *Classic of History*, Book of Shang, Duke of the West Defeated Li. Shang Dynasty was renamed Yin in its latter period.

34. For a more detailed account of the story of Wu Wang, Wen Wang, and the Duke of Zhou, see Wu's *The Chinese Heritage*, Chapters 7, 8, and 9.

35. "《詩》雲：'穆穆文王，于緝熙敬止！' 爲人君，止于仁'" in 《大學》 *Great Learning*, Chapter 42, paragraph 4, as translated by Wu, p. 247.

structure on his civil government structure. This meant that in times of war, local government leaders became military officers, leading into battle troops comprised of their own neighbors whom they had personally subjected to rigorous training in peacetime — an approach that promoted loyalty and obedience.

Indeed, King Wen's military was so effective and his reputation as a ruler so widespread that his influence eventually extended across two-thirds of the land. Such was his virtue, however, that King Wen still could not bring himself to war against his sovereign, much displeased though he was by the increasing degradation of the emperor. In fact, King Wen proved to be the force that kept the state together. As historian K. C. Wu explains, "... so thoroughly trusted by everyone for his integrity, for his compassion, and for his sense of justice and propriety, and so visibly and so vigorously supported by a military might that was feared by all, not only was peace and order firmly maintained within two-thirds of the empire, but a steadying influence could not but have been felt in the remaining one-third as well. Thus, in a manner of speaking ... it was [King Wen's] support of the imperial throne that prevented it from toppling."[36]

King Wen's son, however, was not hindered by the same sense of obligation and loyalty to the throne. King Wen had sworn allegiance to his sovereign, but when King Wu succeeded his father, he deliberately chose not to inform the imperial court of the transfer of power, thus avoiding any act of pledging loyalty to the emperor. Though he had 800 fellow princes on his side, King Wu did not immediately challenge the emperor. Wu was provoked into action, however, when he learned that the emperor had killed one of his three most trusted imperial advisors, arrested another, causing the third to flee into hiding. Speaking to his troops before the battle, King Wu invoked the Mandate of Heaven, just as Tang had done more than 600 years earlier:

> *Heaven, in order to protect the people below, has created for them rulers and teachers so that they will serve Shang Di in securing prosperity and peace for all people .... Heaven has compassion on the people. What the people need, Heaven will provide. Do you aid this one man, to cleanse the four seas? Now is the time — do not miss this opportunity!*

36. Wu, *Chinese Heritage*, p. 276.

天佑下民，作之君，作之師，惟其克相上帝，寵綏四
方。...天矜于民，民之所欲，天必從之，爾尚弼予一
人，永清四海，時哉 弗可失。[37]

In the ensuing battle, the use of 350 chariots, implements virtually unknown hitherto, sent the hastily mustered imperial troops into wild panic. The emperor himself fled to his palace, clothed himself in bejeweled garments and set the building on fire, burning himself to death.

Even with the emperor dead, King Wu took care to give due reverence to the Mandate of Heaven. In a simple ceremony at the imperial altar, he proclaimed: "The last descendant of the house of Yin [the Shang Dynasty], Ji Zhou, had violated and abandoned the brilliant virtues of former emperors, he was irreverent toward God and failed to offer the sacrifices, he was tyrannical and oppressed the people of Shang. Mighty Shang Di has seen all these evidences." Prostrating twice, hands to face and head to the ground, King Wu said, "I have carried out the command change the Mandate to overturn Yin, to receive the glorious Mandate of Heaven."[38]

In his relatively short reign — he was to die just six years after securing power — King Wu was overwhelmed with the responsibility of ruling the nation. As he expressed to his brother and trusted aide, the Duke of Zhou 周公 (Zhou Gong), in a conversation that remains part of the historical records, " ... now that I have received the clear Mandate of Heaven, I must aim to make the favor of Heaven secure, to build up a fitting seat for Heaven .... I want to make virtue shine in every corner of the world like a brilliant daybreak."[39]

The death of King Wu, so soon after the traumatic fall of the Shang Dynasty, threw the land into renewed turmoil. King Wu's heir was but 13 years old, clearly too young to take on the responsibility of ruling such a vast country. King Wu had made it clear while he was still alive that he wished his trusted younger brother, the Duke of Zhou, to keep the empire secure for his son. And indeed, upon installation as King Cheng 成王, the young emperor appointed his uncle, the Duke, as prime

37. 《尚書-周書-泰誓上》 *Classic of History*, Book of Zhou, The Great Declaration, Part 1.
38. "'《殷之末孫季对，殄廢先王明德，侮蔑神只不祀，昏暴商邑百姓，其章顯聞于天皇上帝。' 于是武王再拜稽首，曰：'膺更大命，革殷，受天明命，'" in 《史記-傳四-周本記》 *Historical Records*, Volume 4, History of Zhou.
39. Wu, *Chinese Heritage*, p. 315. Translation of 《史記-傳四-周本記》 *Historical Records*, Volume 4, History of Zhou.

minister. Shortly after, the Duke proclaimed himself regent, a move interpreted by some restive vassal princes as a power grab. In reality, nothing could have been farther from the truth, for when the Chinese refer to their ancient sages, in addition to Confucius, they mention seven names, six of which we have already considered: Yao, Shun, Yu, Tang, King Wen, and King Wu. The seventh and final one is the Duke of Zhou.

So exemplary was the Duke's life that K. C. Wu seems unable to contain his effusive praise of the regent's conduct during the seven years following King Wu's death and preceding the young emperor's assumption of power.

> Out of the entire panorama of tangled events, we perceive the giant of a man towering above all his contemporaries both in ability and virtue, who despite the fact that he had been thrust into circumstances over which he had no control, blackened and tormented by calumnies he had every reason not to expect, and suspected and distrusted by the very ones he loved and was exerting his utmost to serve and protect, managed eventually to emerge out of this all but impossible situation completely vindicated and triumphant.[40]

In all his decisions in the seven years of his regency, the Duke of Zhou put the welfare of the empire and the security of the young ruler ahead of all other considerations, including his own reputation. He was buffeted by one crisis after another, including the specter of fraternal warfare when two of his brothers allied themselves with the vanquished house of Shang in a move to rebel, the sudden life-threatening illness of the young sovereign while the Duke was away on an inspection tour (had the emperor died under such circumstances, the suspicion of foul play and of the Duke's alleged grab for power would seem to be grounded in reality), and the unexpected retirement of one of his most trusted advisers. Through it all, though, the Duke of Zhou labored tirelessly to keep the kingdom intact. For more than two years, he traveled throughout the most agitated parts of the empire, in the east, on a two-fold mission: to win for his emperor the hearts and minds of those living where the reins of power were weakest, and to prove by absenting himself from the capital that he had no designs on the throne.

The Duke himself explained the motivation for all his labors: "The Mandate of Heaven is not easy to gain .... The Mandate is lost when men fail to live up to the

40. Wu, *Chinese Heritage*, p. 322.

reverence and illustrious virtues of their forefathers."[41] When he returned from his two years of travel, he took up the task of preparing his nephew to rule alone.

At the age of 20, the young sovereign received the full authority of his throne in an elaborate ceremony, thus ending the regency of the Duke of Zhou. The Duke and an aging general, a trusted aide of the young emperor's grandfather, led the procession of 1,800 princes and royals doing honor and paying respect to young Cheng Wang. Interestingly, no special document honoring the Duke was composed on this momentous occasion. A scribe simply noted, "Thus the Duke of Zhou greatly protected the Mandate, as received by King Wen and King Wu, for seven years."[42] This was not an oversight. The Duke of Zhou exhibited to the very end a heart motivated by service. He had never had designs on the throne, and when the time came to hand over the reins of power entirely to his nephew, he did so without drawing any attention to himself or his sacrifices, labors, or achievements. He was indeed a servant-leader.

The Duke of Zhou is revered in Chinese history for yet another reason. On two separate occasions, the Duke offered his own life in exchange for the life of his emperor—first on behalf of his brother, King Wu, and later, for his young nephew. His prayers show striking parallels to Jesus' substitionary death for the sake of all mankind. When King Wu lay on his sickbed with all signs indicating his imminent demise, the Duke of Zhou pleaded for his own life to be taken rather than that of the emperor, whose death would throw the empire into turmoil. The Duke implored their ancestors, saying, "Whereas your principal descendant ... is suffering from a severe and dangerous sickness, and whereas you three emperors in heaven have the responsibility of looking after him, I pray to you to beseech the Lord above to let me ... substitute for his person .... [He] is the one who has received the Mandate from the Lord to extend protection and blessings to the four corners of the empire .... Oh, do not let the precious Heaven-conferred Mandate fall to the ground .... "[43] Later, when his young nephew fell ill while the Duke was away from the capital, the Duke's prayer was much simpler, "The emperor is young and without knowledge; if there is any offense against God, it is I who have given the offense, so take my life."[44] The young emperor wept upon hearing of the Duke's prayer. In both cases, the prayers of the Duke of Zhou were answered and the emperors recovered.

41. "天命不易。……乃其墜命，弗克經歷，嗣前人，恭明德" in 《尚書-周書-君奭》 *Classic of History*, Book of Zhou, Jun Shi.

42. "惟周公誕保文武受命，惟七年" in 《尚書-周書-洛誥》 *Classic of History*, Book of Zhou, The Announcement Concerning Luo, last paragraph.

43. "惟爾元孫某，遘厲虐疾，若爾三王，是有丕子之責于天，以旦代某之身……乃命于帝庭……無墜天之降寶命" in 《尚書-周書-金縢》 *Classic of History*, Book of Zhou, Jin Teng.

44. "王少未有識，奸神命者乃旦也" in 《史記-卷三十三-魯周公世家》 *Historical Records*, Volume 33, Genealogy of Duke Zhou of Lu.

Finding God in Ancient China

These seven men—Yao, Shun, Yu, Tang, King Wen, King Wu, and the Duke of Zhou—all wielded unprecedented power over the largest empire of their time, but each checked his authority by accepting the absolute and ultimate authority of the One True God. Thus, the Chinese nation was not established as a democracy; neither did its people attempt to set up a democracy over the intervening thousands of years. Nonetheless, China did flourish in its early existence, and its genius carried it through several millennia. The key was not the goodness of men, but rather the restraining power of an Almighty God.

Little Emperor

The term "little emperor" is frequently used today to refer to the children growing up in single-child families as a result of China's one-child policy, which went into effect in the late 1970s. These children have earned this moniker because they have been thoroughly spoiled by the six adults in the family—their parents plus two sets of grandparents—who cater to their every whim. With no siblings, these only-children grow up being the center of the family universe.

Young Emperor Kang Xi

In China's history, there were a few real-life little emperors, boys who ascended the throne upon the early demise of their fathers. The most famous of them all was Emperor Kang Xi 康熙 (A.D. 1654–1722), of China's last dynasty, the Qing. As recounted in the previous chapter, Kang Xi became emperor at the age of six, when his father, Emperor Shun Zhi 顺治, died suddenly of smallpox in 1661. Because of the emperor's tender age, four regents were appointed to administer the government on his behalf. Kang Xi started to attend to affairs of state at age 13 and took on full power at age 15. He ruled for 61 years, making him China's longest-reigning emperor since Qin Shi Huang Di unified the whole of China in 221 B.C. Kang Xi is regarded by the Chinese as one of their best emperors, who reunited Taiwan with the mainland, squelched a rebellion of three generals in the south, kept the Mongolians at bay, and negotiated a peace

treaty with Russia. He also made many literary contributions, including the *Kang Xi Comprehensive Dictionary*, which we consulted in Chapter 1.

Imagine a teenager becoming the master of a vast empire at age 15. For the next six decades, his every word is the law of the land. Recall that dynastic rule in the preceding centuries had been characterized by the abuse of unrestrained power and endemic corruption. The inevitable question then is: What kept Kang Xi a person of integrity and high morals? After all, the oft-quoted saying goes, "Power corrupts, and absolute power corrupts absolutely." Even Kang Xi himself was aware of the historical legacy that he inherited, writing in his valedictory: "Among the Ancients, only those who were not boastful and knew not to go too far could attain a good end. Since the Three Dynasties,[45] those who ruled long did not leave a good name to posterity."[46] Why was Kang Xi the exception?

The key certainly was not anything intrinsic in the Chinese imperial system, which provided no real or long-term safeguards against the corrupting influence of power. Kang Xi had to have been influenced by internal convictions. It is quite likely that those convictions were the fruit of the work of the Magi introduced in the preceding chapter. Recall that the Jesuit priest Ferdinand Verbiest was Kang Xi's personal tutor and friend. He, along with the other Jesuit missionaries, evidently left an indelible mark on Kang Xi's life. Their influence on the emperor can be seen in these two poems attributed to him:

The Treasure of Life

Heaven's treasures are the sun, moon and stars;
Earth's treasures are grain, gold and silver.
A kingdom's treasures are righteous officials;
A family's treasures are filial offspring.

Gold and jade are not real treasures,
Only a life of tranquility [is].
To live to be one-hundred is but [the passage of] thirty-six thousand days,
Without purpose, life is abject misery.
We come confused and we leave dying,
An empty life is as meaningless as a dream.

45. The Three Dynasties referred to are the Xia, the Shang (Yin), and the Zhou.
46. Jonathan D. Spence, *Emperor of China, Self-Portrait of Kang Hsi* (New York: Random House, Vintage Books, October 1988), p. 145.

FINDING GOD IN ANCIENT CHINA

My mouth has tasted only the best of a hundred flavors;
I have worn only the finest court clothes;
My guests are the most esteemed the world over;
How is it that it is I who is emperor?
The greatest event in the world is life and death,
Gold and jade are futile then.
Even plain rice and unseasoned porridge can satisfy,
Even brocade clothes cannot last a thousand years.

Long has Heaven's gate been shut because of the First Man,
The blessed way is opened by the Sacred Son.
I am willing to receive the Sacred Son of God,
To have the birthright of a son to eternal life.

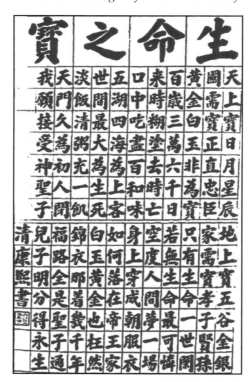

The Death of Christ[47]

When the work on the Cross was finished, blood formed a creek;
Grace from the west flowed a thousand yards deep.
He stepped onto the midnight road, to subject Himself to the four trials;
Before the rooster had crowed twice, thrice by His disciple was he betrayed.
Five hundred lashes tore every inch of skin;
Two thieves hung on his either side, six feet high.
Sadness greater than any had ever known;
Seven utterings, one completed task, ten-thousand spirits weep.

基 督 死
功成十字血成溪，
千丈恩流分自西。
身列四衙半夜路，
徒方三背兩番雞。
五S鞭撻寸厲裂，
六尺凝垂二盜齊。
i瞎慟八瑰驚九品，
七言一畢萬靈啼。

47. The beauty and full meaning of this poem, which has also been titled "The Cross," cannot be adequately captured in translation. Although there is an English version that has been widely circulated on the Internet, we have made our own attempt here, in part to correct some inaccuracies in that translation. The writer of this poem employed a number of difficult literary techniques and masterfully combined them in a single poem. To start, each line is seven characters. This requires as much skill and discipline to compose as does a Shakespearean sonnet or a haiku. Furthermore, this poem can be classified as a 七言絶句 (qi yan jue ju) because every stanza is so tight that it cannot be improved upon. Such poems had to adhere to a strict pattern of four lines per stanza, seven characters per line, all with a strict tonal pattern and rhyme scheme. The poem has only eight lines, which means the writer had a total of only 56 characters to work with. The writer also cleverly included all the numbers from 1 to 10, as well as references to "hundred," "thousand," and "ten-thousand" and to the measurements "inch," "feet," and "yard." The inclusion of these numerical references further reduces the available number of characters, from 56 to only 40. Despite this, the writer is able to tell the entire story of the Crucifixion.

The references to the numbers 1 to 7 are: 1 completed task, 2 thieves, 3 betrayals, 4 trials, 5 hundred lashes, 6 feet high, and 7 utterings. The numbers 8 and 9 are found in "eight graves and nine rankings," which means "everyone" or "all peoples" and which we have translated as "any" in the sense of "anyone" in the line, "Sadness greater than any had ever known." The number 10 is the most significant for several reasons: in Chinese, it denotes completeness; even more profoundly, the word for "cross" in Chinese is 十字, which literally means "the character 10"; finally, by opening the poem with this number, the writer immediately focuses on the Cross and Christ's accomplishing of his life's purpose there.

After describing the scene at the Cross, the writer recounts the Passion: "the midnight road" refers to the walk in the middle of the night from the Garden of Gethsemane; "the four trials" refer to Jesus being questioned by the Jewish Sanhedrin, by Pilate, by Herod, and then again by Pilate; the betrayal refers to the apostle Peter's denial of Christ three times before the cock crowed twice; the 500 lashes refers to Jesus being scourged on Pilate's orders. The "seven utterings" refer to the seven times Jesus spoke while nailed to the Cross.

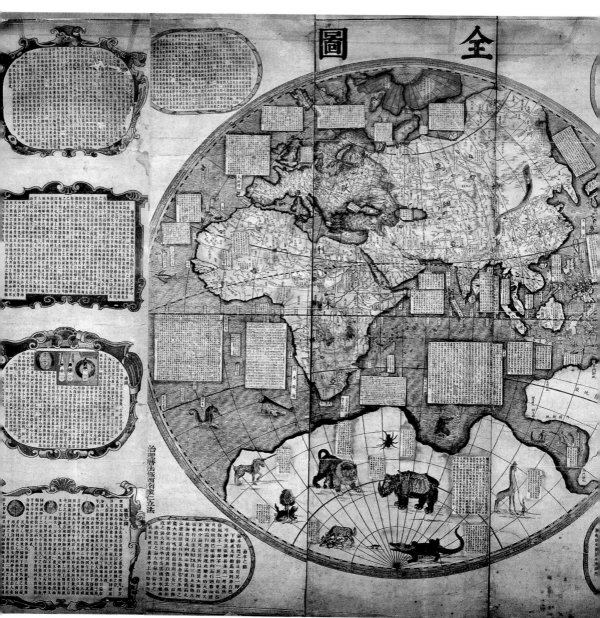

Chapter Seven 　 God's Country

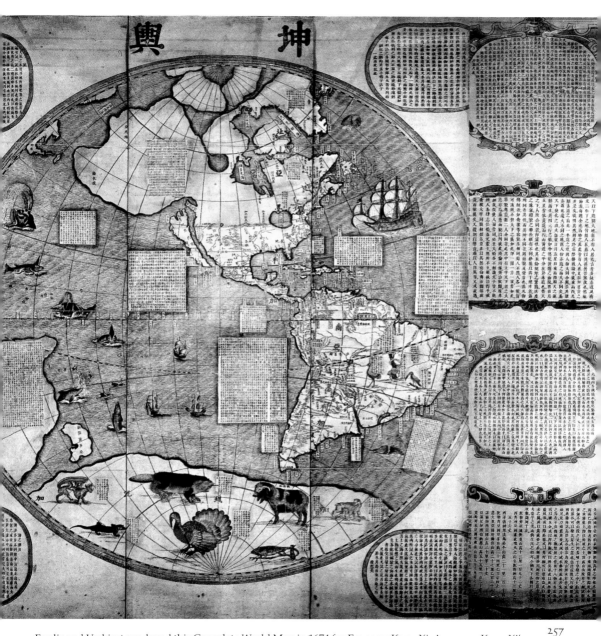

Ferdinand Verbiest produced this Complete World Map in 1674 for Emperor Kang Xi. As young Kang Xi's personal teacher, Verbiest likely played a decisive role in the character formation of his student, who went on to become one of China's most effective rulers. This world map, which measures 1.72 x 4 meters (5.64 x 13.12 feet) is comprised of eight scrolls pieced together.

Credit: Cultural Relics Publishing House

FINDING GOD IN ANCIENT CHINA

Although these poems have not been authoritatively confirmed to be Kang Xi's, they clearly show the writer's knowledge of the Christian faith and his understanding of eternal life. What is without dispute is that Kang Xi studied for many years under the tutorship of the Jesuits, had defended to the Vatican the authenticity of the faith of Chinese Catholic converts, and had protected and supported the Jesuits' mission in China. Although he had declined baptism on many occasions, Kang Xi said that in his heart he believed in the same God as the Jesuits. It could be that he knew the Jesuits were uncompromising in their stand against polygamy, of which he, as an emperor with his requisite concubines, certainly was guilty. There is no way for us to know if he had a genuine conversion. Nonetheless, whatever he had absorbed from the Jesuits was sufficient to make him one of the most virtuous of all the Chinese emperors. Like the seven righteous emperors of so long ago, the secret of Kang Xi's virtuous government was founded not on competency alone, but on his submission to God as the ultimate authority.

REFLECT and RESPOND

The Mandate of Heaven guided the Chinese nation for several thousand years because it expressed the will of God. The will of God led them to peace and prosperity. Are you walking in the will of God? Though it is narrow, it is still the better way. What drives you; what pulls at your heart? What commands your mind and consumes your life? Are you in the center of God's will?

Founding fathers of the Chinese race, Huang Di and Yan Di as depicted in the "Tribute to Chinese History" mural at the Millennium Monument in Beijing. Huang Di and Yan Di unified the tribes living in the Yellow River valley in the 27th Century B.C. For this reason, Chinese call themselves descendants of Yan Di and Huang Di.

捌

8 Enter the Dragon

It is the last hour; and even now many antichrists have appeared.

~ John the Apostle

8

Enter the Dragon

The Chinese dragon. Only the Great Wall rivals the mythical dragon as a symbol of China to the rest of the world. This association is not without basis: the Chinese themselves proudly claim it and promote it. They call themselves the "Descendants of the Dragon 龍的港人" and refer to their culture as "Dragon Culture 龍文化." To the Chinese, the mighty dragon is a symbol of power and mystique because of its exclusive association with the emperor. In dynastic times, only the emperor could use the dragon symbol; anyone who appropriated that right was subject to the death penalty. In the Forbidden City, dragons marked the exclusive path of the emperor: where they coiled, only the emperor could trod. Dragons adorn the throne rooms and embellish the eaves and ridges of the roofs of old imperial halls. Even using the character for dragon 龍 in a name was permitted of the emperor alone. That has all changed, and today "dragon" is found in the names of everything from mountains and rivers to restaurants and businesses. Indeed, the dragon has proven to be more enduring than the long line of Chinese emperors. Although nearly a century has passed since the end of the last dynasty, the dragon is still invoked today throughout China and in Chinese communities all over the world in the dragon dances that are a requisite part of the festivities for the major Chinese holidays and on important occasions such as the opening of a new business. How did the dragon come to be almost universally revered and even worshipped by the Chinese?

In our journey of discovery, we have looked at historical records that clearly

Photo at left shows a jade medallion with a dragon carved on it.

show that the Chinese once revered and worshipped Shang Di, not the dragon. The memory of Shang Di, however, is distant, and He has been forgotten by most Chinese. This was vividly brought home to me on one of my visits to the Altar of Heaven when I encountered an old man standing before the Imperial Vault of Heaven. He was having difficulty reading the tablet bearing the name of the Most High God, and when I read it to him, he expressed surprise. "I did not know that our ancestors used to worship Shang Di," he said. His response is typical of most Chinese today, who think of the dragon as part of their culture while knowing nothing of Shang Di.

The Dragons 龍

At the signpost for the Blood Covenant, we saw that some of the most significant elements of the all-important imperial sacrifices to Shang Di were abandoned in the early Zhou Dynasty out of a desire to preserve the dignity of the emperor. This breakdown in the observation and preservation of these ancient rites to Shang Di ushered in a two-millennium period in which many new religions gained ascendancy. At some point, the dragon too gained ascendancy. Although there is no historical record indicating precisely when or how this happened, at this signpost for "Enter the Dragon," we find some compelling clues about how the dragon usurped Shang Di's role in the hearts of the Chinese people.

The Chinese Dragon

The dragon in Chinese mythology is a majestic creature that roams the skies and dwells in rivers, lakes, and oceans.[1] This mythical animal is depicted as a four-legged creature with horns, claws, large demonic eyes, and a scaly, snakelike body. The Chinese consider it the king of all animals. Unlike its vicious Western counterpart, the Chinese dragon is regarded as an auspicious animal, capable of bringing good fortune.[2] Because the ancient Chinese described lightning as having the shape of the dragon—the jagged strokes of a bolt of lightning were seen as the dragon's body and claws—thunder and rain also became associated with this creature. By extension, since rain is of utmost importance in an agrarian society, the sea-dragon god 海龍神 (hai long shen) became an object of worship. When rain

1. A frequent question about the Chinese dragon is whether it was a real creature or just a mythical one. The Chinese dragon is probably the mythological version of the Chinese alligators of the Yangtze River, which nowadays are among the most endangered species in the world. In ancient times, alligators populated a much larger area of China. It is not difficult to see how the alligator became the dragon because of its shape, its habitat, and its cunning and power. From fear of its power, the Chinese developed a reverence for the dragon, and even worshipped it.

2. The Chinese consider three other animals auspicious: the phoenix, unicorn, and tortoise.

was needed for crops, farmers would plead for the appearance of the dragon—that is, for the lightning and thunder that often precede rain. Rain rituals often began with a dance by a lively and colorful dragonhead trailed by a procession of dancers forming the dragon's body and tail.[3]

As we saw in the previous chapters, the pure worship of Shang Di was corrupted over time, and the understanding of the emperor's relationship to the One True God became distorted. As virtue replaced power as the key to government, a parallel development also occurred: China's emperors appropriated the image of the dragon as the sacred symbol of imperial authority. They were no longer simply "Son of Heaven 天子" (Tian Zi), or "Son of Heaven with a True Mandate 真命天子" (Zhen Ming Tian Zi). Instead, they were now "Son of Heaven from the True Dragon 真龍天子" (Zhen Long Tian Zi). The earlier title, "Son of Heaven with a True Mandate," emphasizes the Mandate of Heaven, which is conferred by a virtuous Shang Di, and reminds the emperor and the people that he must "rule with virtue 政" (Ren Zheng). The new title, "Son of Heaven from the True Dragon," emphasized the emperor's autocratic power. Instead of relying on the delegated authority of a gracious Creator God, China's rulers allied themselves with the power of a fearsome creature.

There is no documentation to indicate when this switch happened, but the *Historical Records* refer to Qin Shi Huang Di 秦始皇帝 (259–209 B.C.) as the "Ancestral Dragon 祖龍" (Zu Long).[4] We will see from his life's story later in this chapter why this designation was so appropriate. The Qin Dynasty was short-lived, lasting a mere 15 years, but the subsequent Han Dynasty reinforced the idea that the emperor was the personification of the dragon. A Han emperor was the first to use the dragon as his reign title: Yellow Dragon 黃龍 in 49 B.C. The circumstances surrounding this switch from the worship of Shang Di to worship of the dragon are even more difficult to explain when we realize that the Chinese did not always regard the dragon as an auspicious animal. Ancient Chinese records indicate that the dragon originally was not honored but feared, and that it was hunted and was bred for its meat.[5] Etymology provides strong supporting evidence for this negative view of the dragon.

龙 (pronounced "long"), complex form 龍, ancient form 龍.

---

3. These dragon dances are still performed in traditional Chinese communities throughout the world on auspicious occasions such as Chinese New Year. Nowadays, the purpose is not to bring rain, but good fortune. The dragon continues to be viewed as a symbol of awesome power that brings material well-being to the people.

4. 《史記-卷六-秦始皇本紀》 *Historical Records*, Volume 6, Chronicle of Qin Shi Huang.

5. See 《左傳-昭公二十九年》 *Zuo Zhuan*, Duke Zhao, Year 29 (513 BC). Oracle bone inscriptions (dating to 1700 B.C.) also confirm that dragons were hunted and eaten.

Finding God in Ancient China

In the ancient form of this character, the top left part is 辛 (xin), which is simplified in the complex form as 立 (li). 辛 means "bitter" or "a cruel instrument of torture." All other Chinese words that contain 辛 are negative terms, such as 辜 (gu), which means "sin" or "to fail"; 宰 (zai), which means "to kill"; 辣 (la), which in usages such as 辛很手辣 (xin hen shou la) means "cruel and violent"; and 辥 (nie), which means "sin." This suggests that at the time the character for "dragon" was formed, the Chinese did not regard the dragon as an auspicious animal; if they had, the character would not contain 辛. The dragon, therefore, was associated with sin, bitterness, cruelty, violence, and suffering. This shows that the ancient Chinese must have regarded the dragon the same way the Hebrews did: as a creature that was hostile towards humanity, especially the common people.[6]

The Dragon in the Bible

In the Bible, "serpent," "dragon," and "sea-monster" are images associated with Satan, the chief enemy of God. These images represent the negative power of fear and chaos, which has been at odds with God from the beginning and will continue to be so until the end of time.

Satan, like man and the angels, was created by God; in fact, he was the foremost of the angels, perfect in form, beautiful, and full of wisdom.[7] He was given a glorious name, "Lucifer," which means "Day Star,"[8] and was entrusted with the job of guarding a holy mountain of God.[9] Despite his perfection and wisdom, he sinned by exerting his will against God's will.[10] His sin was pride: his rightful place was second-in-command in heaven, but he wanted God's position, and he wanted to control all the other angels and all of God's children. Even more, he desired the glory that belonged to God alone as well as the power and authority of the Most High. In short, he desired to be sovereign of heaven and earth. Satan led a rebellion against God, and one-third of the angels joined him. Because God is omnipotent, the outcome was a foregone conclusion: He defeated Satan and then cast him out of heaven. According to the Bible, God is awaiting the end times to mete out Satan's final punishment.

For the present, however, God allows Satan to wield power in this world. Satan's

6. See Deuteronomy 32:33; Isaiah 27:1; Isaiah 51:9; and Revelation chapters 12, 13, 16, and 20.
7. He is called the anointed cherub of God in Ezekiel 28:14. For more details, see also Isaiah 14 and Ezekiel 26–28.
8. Isaiah 14:12.
9. This information about Satan is found in Ezekiel 27, which is a lament against Tyre. On closer examination, we can conclude that the object of this lament was more than Tyre and that it extends to Satan.
10. In Isaiah 14:13–14, Satan exerted his will over God's will five times.

tactic, ever since his rebellion, has been to try to get every human being to do his will instead of God's. He is an adversary of the person and the purposes of God and seeks to usurp God's position. His schemes are carefully planned and executed; he does not work haphazardly. His ways are subtle. To deceive mankind, he often appears attractive. His aim, however, is to hold us captive to sin and to destroy us. Recall that when man sinned, he allowed Satan to occupy his heart, resulting in guilt 槐 (kui), or "evil in the heart." The central characteristic of Satan's *modus operandi* is fear, not love. He uses counterfeits, such as lust instead of love. While God draws people to Himself with His unfailing love, Satan uses deception coupled with fear to gain control over mankind. I have experienced this personally. When I was a staunch atheist, I was afraid of the dark and the devil. Once, after standing before a large audience and arguing vehemently that there is no God, I was filled with fear walking alone across the campus as an eerie feeling filled me that I was surrounded by unseen spirits. What I experienced was the reality that when we separate ourselves from the love of God, we fall into Satan's realm of fear. Just as the Bible explains, the opposite of love is not hatred, but fear,

> There is no fear in love; but perfect love casts out fear, because fear involves punishment, and the one who fears is not perfected in love.
> 1 John 4:18

It is this same cruel fear that is present in the original Chinese character for dragon—the fear associated with sin, bitterness, cruelty, violence, and suffering. When the Chinese people lost sight of the all-powerful goodness and holiness of Shang Di, they fell under the counterfeit power of the dragon; they were led astray by their emperors who usurped the worship of Shang Di and set themselves up as the personification of the dragon.

The Ancestral Dragon

One of the first emperors, if not the first, to do this is the one referred to as the "Ancestral Dragon" by the grand historian Sima Qian in the *Historical Records*. Just as China's ancient history provides vividly instructive examples of men who ruled in accordance with the character of the Most High God, it also offers equally dramatic accounts of rulers who aligned themselves against God's purposes. One such vividly instructive drama is the intertwined lives of two of the most powerful

men in China's history: the man who created this ancestral dragon and the one who became the ancestral dragon.

This early dragon emperor is in fact probably the most famous of all the Chinese emperors: Zhao Zheng 趙政 (259–209 B.C.), better known as Qin Shi Huang Di 秦始皇帝, which literally means First August Emperor of Qin. His name is commonly shortened in Chinese to Qin Shi Huang. Throughout more than two millennia of Chinese history, he has been renowned as the ruler who reunified the nation after 400 years of civil war, orchestrated the building of the Great Wall, and standardized the written language and the system of measurements. In recent decades, he has achieved worldwide fame because of the army of terra-cotta soldiers unearthed from his partially excavated tomb complex in Xi'an, now a major tourist draw. The man behind Qin Shi Huang, the one who essentially "created" this most powerful of emperors, was the infamous Lü Bu Wei 吕不韋, a merchant who turned to politics and literally became a kingmaker.

Lü was a successful merchant from the small state of Wei 魏, part of present-day Henan province. Despite his financial success, Lü was not happy with his social status because the merchant class in those days had little influence and was poorly regarded. Merchants were not considered intelligent like the scholars or government officials, productive like the farmers, or useful like the soldiers. Merchants were stereotyped as deceptive people who benefited unfairly from transactions that had no added value; in essence, they were viewed as freeloaders.

While trading in Han Dan, capital of the state of Zhao, Lü met Prince Yi Ren 异人, one of the 20 grandsons of the king of the state of Qin. Yi Ren's mother was out of favor with the crown prince, which meant that Yi Ren was dispensable. The 400-year civil war had divided China into seven major competing states, and to maintain the appearance of peace between states, members of royal households were exchanged. In fact, however, these royal representatives were little better off than hostages. Prince Yi Ren was one of these ambassador-hostages, held in the state of Zhao to ensure peace between the states of Zhao and Qin.

After meeting with Yi Ren, Lü consulted his father, asking, "What is the expected profit for farming?" His father replied, "Ten-fold returns." He asked again, "What about trading in gems?" His father said, "One-hundredfold."

Then he asked, "What if we invest in making someone a king?" His father paused and then said, "This is immeasurable." So Lü concluded that investing in politics, specifically in Yi Ren, would bring wealth, status, and power for him and his future generations, and he considered Yi Ren to be an exceptional investment.[11]

Lü set about cultivating his relationship with Yi Ren. Since the states of Qin and Zhao were often at war, Yi Ren was in a highly precarious position and very much needed Lü's friendship and support. Lü proposed using his wealth to make Yi Ren king of the state of Qin. Although Yi Ren did not think that was possible, he agreed to appoint Lü the prime minister of Qin if Lü could accomplish this. Their relationship was further cemented when Yi Ren met Lü's favorite concubine, Zhao Ji 趙姬, at a banquet and immediately took a liking to her. Pretending to be drunk, he asked Lü for her. Though at first angry with Yi Ren, Lü gave in after weighing the costs and benefits of such an arrangement. He handed Zhao Ji over to marry the prince. Within a year, in 259 B.C. in the Zhao capital of Han Dan, she bore Zhao Zheng, who would later be known as Qin Shi Huang. With the birth of the child, Prince Yi Ren made Zhao Ji his official wife.

The Qin crown prince's favorite wife was Lady Hua Yang 華陽, and Yi Ren was her step-son. Through Lü's scheming and financial influence, the childless Lady Hua Yang adopted Yi Ren as her own son. It was a win-win situation: it immediately improved Yi Ren's position, and it secured for Lady Hua Yang her position as the future empress. When the state of Qin attacked the state of Zhao in 257 B.C., Lü found a way through bribery for him and Prince Yi Ren to return to Qin, leaving Zhao Ji and the child Zhao Zheng in hiding in the state of Zhao for the next seven years. In 251 B.C., the Qin king died and Yi Ren's father, the crown prince, became the new king. Thus, Yi Ren became the new crown prince because he had been adopted by Lady Hua Yang. Within a year, the new king had died and Yi Ren ascended the throne, just as Lü had proposed to him years before. Lü became the Chief Minister, and Zhao Ji and Zhao Zheng were brought back to Qin.[12]

Yi Ren reigned as King Zi Chu for only three years before dying under mysterious circumstances. So it was that in 247 B.C., Zhao Zheng, son of one of 20 grandsons of

11. The Chinese proverb that stems from this story is 奇货可居 (qi huo ke ju), literally, "exceptional goods worthy of investment."
12. Zhao Zheng had used his mother's family name while in exile, but in order to claim his royal heritage, he changed his name to Ying Zheng 贏政, as Ying was the family name of the house of Qin.

the king of Qin and grandson of an out-of-favor wife of the crown prince, became king himself at the age of 13 — entirely due to the machinations of merchant Lü. Because of Zhao Zheng's youth, Lü and Zhao Ji, Lü's former concubine and now the empress dowager, reigned as regents. Lü held on to power for nine years though it would have been appropriate to relinquish power to Zhao Zheng when he turned 20 years old. While serving as co-regents, Lü and Zhao Ji resumed intimate relations, but when Lü realized that these secret liaisons were putting at risk their own positions as well as that of the young emperor, he made alternate arrangements for Zhao Ji. Though she was empress dowager, Zhao Ji was only in her early 30s, so Lü installed a fake eunuch in the inner palace to serve her sexual needs. In setting up this peculiar and unnatural arrangement, Lü sowed the seeds for his own eventual demise. As time passed, the power of the fake eunuch, Lao Ai 嫪毐, grew, especially after he fathered a son with Zhao Ji, the empress dowager.

In 238 B.C., the 22-year-old Zhao Zheng decided he had been sidelined long enough. Without Lü's consent, he arranged his own "coming-of-age" ceremony so that he could gain full control of the state. The fake eunuch Lao Ai saw this as an opportunity to revolt, planning to assassinate the emperor during the ceremony and place his own illegitimate son with Zhao Ji on the throne. Lao's rebellion, however, was quashed and Lü was implicated because he was the one who had placed the fake eunuch in the inner chambers of the palace. Lü was first stripped of all his titles and exiled to his home. Later, when other states sought him out for service in their courts, Zhao Zheng offered Lü, whom he officially called "uncle 仲父" (Zhong Fu), the dignity of taking his own life by drinking poisoned wine. After all, this merchant had proven to be one of the craftiest statesmen in all of Chinese history and could not be trusted if he were allowed to live.

Sima Qian in his authoritative history wrote that Zhao Ji was pregnant before she married Yi Ren but stopped short of saying that Zhao Zheng was Lü's own son. Chinese tradition, however, holds this to be the case. Even if Lü were not Zhao Zheng's biological father, he certainly was responsible for the political fortunes of this monster of a tyrant. Lü craved power and his protégé took this craving to its extreme. Zhao Zheng reunified China by ruthlessly conquering the other six states: then he proclaimed himself Qin Shi Huang, the "first August Emperor of Qin."

Chapter Eight　Enter the Dragon

The Great Wall of China at Ji County, 80 miles East of Beijing.

Though he is considered one of the greatest rulers in history, Qin Shi Huang's reign was laced with intrigue and darkness. He seemed driven by a huge ego: every initiative had to be the greatest and had to be accomplished in record time. In just ten years, he conquered the other six states and reunified a country that had been divided for four centuries. He built the Great Wall, in Chinese known simply as the "10,000 Li-Long Wall,"[13] parts of which are still standing today. His network of highways totaling 4,700 miles (7,500 kilometers) is some 500 miles longer than the acclaimed Roman road system two centuries later. His E-Fang Palace was so huge that it burned for four months when his capital was sacked a few years after his death. Even in death, he was grandiose. He constructed a mammoth underground tomb-city guarded by an army of life-size warriors. According to historian Sima Qian, the tomb, still mostly unexcavated to this day, had a ceiling depicting the cosmos and grounds filled with life-size hills and mercury-filled rivers.

Psychiatrists would have little trouble coming up with theories to explain Qin Shi Huang's cruelty and anger, his ego, and his lust for glory. He was plagued with an illegitimate birth, a tumultuous childhood, a dysfunctional family, a promiscuous mother, and a doubtful claim to the throne. When he conquered the Zhao capital of Han Dan, where he was born and grew up, he slaughtered the people who were once his neighbors and burned the city to the ground, as if to erase his childhood nightmares. Driven by this dark side, Qin Shi Huang, much like his mentor Lü, sought power and used it wantonly. What these two men exercised was

13. "萬里長城" (wan li chang cheng). A "li" is a Chinese measure word for distance. Today, it is equivalent to a half-kilometer, but there was no set standard during imperial times.

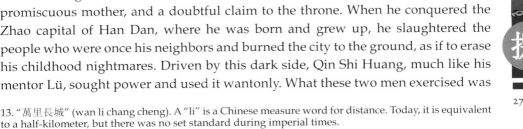

an unrestrained, intimidating, and destructive power that can be called "dragon power." Though they used this power to change the course of history and to build colossal monuments, they callously and cold-bloodedly destroyed hundreds of thousands of lives in the process.

A block print of Qin Shi Huang Di's mammoth E-Fang Palace.

Qin Shi Huang was certain that his Qin Dynasty would last for thousands of years; in fact, it lasted only 15. Sadly, however, the autocratic dynastic system that he instituted survived for more than 2,000 years. The dark shadow of the dragon power of merchant Lü and Emperor Qin reaches through the intervening millennia and still haunts the nation of China today.

Dragon Worship

When the Chinese stopped worshipping Shang Di and started to revere and worship the dragon, they fell into the practice of idolatry and became worshippers of a totem. As we will see, both of these practices lead to a life lived in fear and can result in moral corruption.

Idolatry occurs whenever a person denies the existence of the true God or relegates Him to anything less than the object of his most intimate desire. On a personal level, our relationship with God is like that of a marriage: He is our groom and we are His bride. When we choose to put something else in His place, we have committed spiritual adultery, which is idolatry. On a national level, when a country does not choose God as its King, it has committed spiritual adultery or idolatry on a national scale. The consequences of both personal and national idolatry are the same; the only difference is the magnitude of the transgression.

When a Chinese person refers to himself as a "Descendant of the Dragon," he is in effect subscribing to totemism, a term used for a cluster of traits that is common in the religious practices and the social organization of many primitive peoples.[14] Totemism is a system of belief in which humans are regarded as having a mystical relationship or kinship with a totem. The totem is an object, such as an animal or plant, which serves as the emblem or symbol of a people and is usually an object to be feared.

Idolatry

We have already seen through the prayers made during the Border Sacrifice ceremonies that the ancient Chinese not only knew the Creator God, but also worshipped Him for the same attributes that are ascribed to the God of the Hebrew patriarchs. Like the nation of Israel, the ancient Chinese knew this One True God who is without form, yet known through His attributes. Also like the nation of Israel, the ancient Chinese were greatly tempted to fall into idolatry.

The worship of created things as opposed to worship of the Creator is idolatry. Idolatry can also be the worship of a deity in visible form or iconic worship. One of the problems with iconic worship is that God's glory cannot be adequately captured in any tangible form or image. It makes no sense for a person who has carved an idol with his own hands then to either be afraid of what he has made or expect this created object to protect him or bless him. Jesus said, "God is spirit, and those who worship Him must worship in spirit and truth."[15] That means we can only know God when our spirit communicates with His Spirit and through His attributes (truth).

Let us look again at the "Zhong He 中和之曲," Song of Central Peace, from the Border Sacrifice ceremony:

> Of old in the beginning, there was the great chaos, without form and dark. The five planets had not begun to revolve, nor the two lights to shine. In the midst

14. See *Encyclopædia Britannica* for a more complete explanation of totemism.
15. John 4:24.

of it there existed neither form nor sound. You, O spiritual Sovereign, came forth in Your sovereignty, and first did separate the impure from the pure. You made heaven; You made earth; You made man. All things became alive with reproducing power.[16]

This song from China's most important religious ceremony clearly shows that the ancient Chinese worshipped the One who brought order out of chaos and created all things. Idolatry, by contrast, does not bring order to a society; in fact, it often results in chaos and moral corruption. This prayer song also shows that the Creator God brought light to the world. When men worship other gods, they do so out of fear and to gain favors and protection, but they do not receive light.

The worship of the sun and the moon often is the beginning of idolatry. The second song of the Border Sacrifice ceremony clearly shows that the ancient Chinese regarded these heavenly bodies as created to provide light, not to be objects of worship:

You did produce, O Spirit, the seven elements [the sun and the moon and the five planets]. Their beautiful and brilliant lights lit up the circular sky and square earth.[17]

Most people will pray when they are in trouble, as if calling for the police. Indeed, everyone, almost to a person, will pray when in dire need even if he has no assurance that his prayers are ever heard. The confidence expressed in this third song of the Border Sacrifice, however, reflects a far more intimate kind of relationship between God and man, one that is not found in worship offered to lesser deities:

You have promised, O Di, to hear us, for You are our Father. I, Your child, dull and unenlightened, am unable to show forth my dutiful feelings. I thank You, that You have accepted our pronouncement. Honorable is Your great name. With reverence we spread out these gems and silks, and, as swallows rejoicing in the spring, praise Your abundant love.[18]

Chinese who practice idolatry do not view their idols as their father; rather, they regard the idol as a source of protection or the giver of fortune. True worship is based on this intimate father-child relationship described in both the Bible and the Border Sacrifice ceremony, and meaningful prayers are those offered with the assurance of an attentive and loving God.

16. 《大明會典》 *Ming Statutes,* Volume 82, p. 28.
17. Ibid.
18. Ibid., p. 29.

These prayers from the Border Sacrifice, the marked absence of idols or icons at the Altar of Heaven, and the presence at the Altar of only a tablet inscribed with nothing but the name of Shang Di to indicate the object of worship all constitute substantive evidence that the ancient Chinese, like the Hebrews, were solidly aniconic[19] and monotheistic—until the dragon crept in. By the time of Confucius in the 5th century B.C., the state of affairs had so degenerated that the sage longed for a return to the days of the virtuous rulers. He regretfully said:

> *The practice of the Great Way, the illustrious men of the Three Dynasties—these I shall never know in person. And yet they inspire my ambition! When the Great Way was practiced, the world was shared by all alike .... Now the Great Way is hidden, and the world is the possession of private families.*

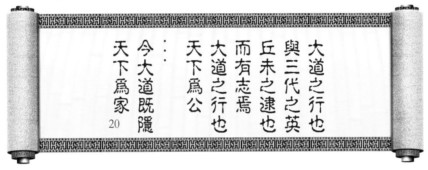

We have gained some insight into "how" and "when" the dragon assumed the throne in the hearts of the Chinese people, but the "why" question still remains. Why has the dragon reigned supreme in China for so long?

Totemism and Fear

Worship of the dragon in China is associated with a national trait that one modern Chinese philosopher has called "submissive individualism."[21] Although Chinese culture appears to promote conformity, in fact, Chinese people are no less highly individualistic than Americans, but with at least one significant difference. That difference is found in their response to fearful or dangerous situations. The Chinese response is one of almost instinctive submission to authority for the sake of self-preservation. This trait is the product of more than two millennia of conditioning

19. Worship without idols or images.
20. 《禮記 – 禮運》 *Record of Rites*, Li Yun, Chapter 9, Paragraph 2.
21. See Liang Yan Chen (梁燕城), *Prospects of an Ancient Kingdom* 《古國蒼茫》 (Hong Kong: Wah Hon Publishing Co., 1995), p. 44 (in Chinese).

FINDING GOD IN ANCIENT CHINA

Dragon dance performance Singapore's National Day celebration in 1988. These dragon dances are still a requisite part of festivities at special events in Chinese communities all over the world.

under the dictatorial, authoritarian rule set in place by Qin Shi Huang, the Ancestral Dragon. This conditioning has resulted in hundreds of generations of submissive individuals who care only for their own personal welfare and who tend to ignore spiritual, civic, social, and political responsibilities.

An individual may respond with fear to a particular situation, but that same situation need not always trigger in other people the same or even a similar fear response. For instance, one person may be deathly afraid of dogs, but to many other people dogs are man's best friend. Even situations widely acknowledged to be dangerous — jumping out of a plane, for example — are attractive to some people for the sheer excitement of that rush of adrenaline brought on by fear. In China, however, as a result of generations of autocratic rule, this fear-response has become a collective behavior, with a number of observable characteristics that have been noted by psychologists.

First, the typical Chinese response is to take flight physically, psychologically, or emotionally. A good example of this was the collective panic response to the

SARS epidemic in the spring of 2003. Flight, in the form of avoidance, was the only conceivable course of action. For weeks, the entire country ground to a near-standstill because people locked themselves in their homes. This flight response is also seen in the exodus of talented individuals who are dissatisfied with the conditions in China. Rather than working to effect change from within, they have simply left. This fear-response on an individual basis gets reinforced because of the collective response: fear-signals are sent back and forth, compounding the individual fear-response and intensifying and reinforcing each individual's reaction. The end result of this instinctive response is that people work against each other. Rather than working together to bring about a solution, their actions have a mutually nullifying effect so that the appropriate measures needed to resolve the threatening or problematic situation are never taken.

This entire sequence can be seen every day thousands of times over at major traffic intersections all over China. It takes no time at all for gridlock to occur on Chinese roads once a traffic light malfunctions. Within minutes, every driver has "taken flight"—abandoning all the conventions and rules of the road, creating extra lanes, jumping curbs, and generally ignoring common courtesy of any kind. Anyone who tries to continue to obey traffic regulations quickly becomes frustrated and soon joins in the confusion, resulting in a situation where everyone works against everyone else.

This kind of collective behavior is driven by fear and selfishness. Its root can be traced to the Chinese cultural totem—the dragon. The dragon represents power, greedy and selfish power that controls through fear. It is this fear and the resulting conditioned, collective fear-response that have kept the Chinese people in the grips of the power of the dragon for more than 2,000 years.

THE POWER OF THE DRAGON

Qin Shi Huang has been called the Ancestral Dragon and may have been the one who introduced dragon worship into Chinese culture. Even if he was not, this emperor was indisputably the first to wield dragon power on a grand scale. He certainly is the archetype for the power of the dragon, and his life story, as we will see, offers many a cautionary tale of the destructive power of the dragon.

FINDING GOD IN ANCIENT CHINA

Qin Shi Huang reunified China and consolidated his power in 221 B.C., about the time of the Second Punic War when the Carthaginian general Hannibal crossed the Alps. The vast empire under his rule was greater in size than Western Europe with a population larger than that of the Roman Empire at the time. With his lust for power and his inflated ego, this new emperor clearly was not content with taking up the role of his predecessors: as a mere regent for Shang Di, a humble servant-leader beholden to a Higher Power and required to act for the good of the people in order to retain the authority to rule. Rather than modeling himself after the righteous leadership of Yao, Shun, and Yu, he followed in the path of the angel Lucifer who became Satan. Qin Shi Huang wanted for himself the veneration that the Chinese people until then had accorded only to Shang Di. The problem, though, was that he could not portray himself as the personification of Shang Di because the people were well-acquainted with the One whom they had worshipped for so long. So instead, Qin Shi Huang appropriated the power of the dragon, which is rooted in fear. Without some kind of an external source of power, Qin Shi Huang would have found it extremely difficult to hold together the vast and diverse nation he had brought under his control. Unwilling to submit to the loving and compassionate power of Shang Di, he turned to the terrible power of the dragon and used fear to exercise iron-fisted control over his realm.

Subsequent emperors followed suit and used dragon power over more than two millennia to keep millions of people subservient to their autocratic rule. This dragon power, though expedient, inevitably results in an assortment of personal and societal troubles and even disasters over time. It promotes selfish motivations and leads to disharmony and violence, a marked contrast to the wisdom taught in the Bible—the same wisdom that was exhibited in the lives and reigns of China's early righteous emperors.

Dragon Power and Conflict

What is the source of quarrels and conflicts among you? Is not the source your pleasures that wage war in your members? You lust and do not have; so you commit murder. You are envious and cannot obtain; so you fight and quarrel. You do not have because you do not ask. You ask and do not receive, because you ask with wrong motives, so that you may spend it on your pleasures.
James 4:1 – 3

The rest of the world may hold Qin Shi Huang in high regard for his grand accomplishments, but the Chinese do not accord him similar honor. Instead, he is remembered not for just "quarrels and conflicts" but for causing untold suffering, great destruction, and the senseless deaths of hundreds of thousands of people.

The Great Wall has never been called "great" by the Chinese themselves; too many lives were tragically and pointlessly sacrificed to build this structure. Tradition has it that each meter of the wall cost a life. Numerous stories and dramas have survived over these many centuries to keep alive the memory of the immense suffering and great loss of life caused by the building of the wall. Chinese also remember Qin Shi Huang for ordering the great book burning and massacre in 213 B.C., called 焚害, 坑攞 (Fen Shu, Keng Ru). Not only did Qin Shi Huang reduce to ashes all of the Chinese *Classics*, but more morally reprehensible was that he buried alive 460 scholars who disagreed with his heartless, legalistic policies. Qin Shi Huang's selection of books consigned to the huge bonfires is noteworthy. All the books on philosophy, religion, and literature were destroyed, but not those on technical subjects such as medicine and carpentry. This bias of favoring science and technology while scorning other branches of knowledge continues in China to this day. Recall that the Millennium Hall in Beijing celebrates Matteo Ricci and the Jesuits, but only for their technical and scientific contributions. The Chinese as a nation have yet to accept the most precious gift the Jesuits came to offer: their faith in God. The Chinese are still missing the point of Ricci's mission!

Qin Shi Huang showed no hesitation in resorting to murder to get his way, but like other megalomaniacal autocrats in history, he regarded his own life as of utmost value and wanted to live on forever. He became obsessed with his quest for immortality. He traveled all the way across his empire, from his capital, Xian Yang 咸陽, in present day Shaanxi province, to the coast of Shandong province, seeking a herb that would give him everlasting life. He also went to sacred Tai Shan 泰山 to seek God's favor. It was while on his fifth such trip that he suddenly became ill and died on the road. He was only 50 years old. Qin Shi Huang received no favor from God because he was driven his whole life by wrong motives.

Dragon Power and Covetousness

> *Adulterers and adulteresses! Do you not know that friendship with the world is enmity with God? Whoever therefore wants to be a friend of the world makes himself an enemy of God. Or do you think that the Scripture says in vain, "The Spirit who dwells in us yearns jealously"? But He gives more grace. Therefore He says: "God resists the proud, but gives grace to the humble."*
>
> James 4:4–6 (NKJV)

God loves us with the passionate and jealous love of a husband for his wife and wants to regain the position in our hearts that was usurped by Satan in the Garden. His Spirit yearns to commune with our human spirit. In other words, God wants us entirely for Himself. Just as no husband is willing to share his wife with another man, God does not want to share us, His bride, with the world or Satan. There are those, however, who become so evil that they will compromise even a wife for their own selfish ends. Lü Bu Wei was such a person! Most men have not gone that far, but once we start down the slippery slope of sin, it is not long before we will compromise every good thing for some momentary pleasure or for some possession that will not last. Lü and Qin Shi Huang thought they could secure good fortune for many generations, but what they created did not last. They were unable to leave behind even a good name!

God's warning is very clear for those who lust for the rewards of this world. Such people are no better than adulterers because they have spurned the love of God and are pursuing worldly power, position, and pleasures. Adultery is covetousness, which is the desire for what does not rightfully belong to us; therefore the love of the world—its pleasures and its power—is a form of spiritual adultery. When we seek anyone or anything other than God, we are committing adultery!

God has set a very high standard, but in His goodness He has also given us sufficient grace to meet His rigorous demands. A humble man does not seek power or to fulfill his own pleasure, rather he submits himself to God and others. The Bible is full of stories and advice about the benefits of humility. Such exhortations seem to go against the way the world works, but as we will see later in this chapter, the wisdom of this approach is evident even in the cut-throat world of big business.

Dragon Power and Conceit

Therefore submit to God. Resist the devil and he will flee from you. Draw near to God and He will draw near to you. Cleanse your hands, you sinners; and purify your hearts, you double-minded. Lament and mourn and weep! Let your laughter be turned to mourning and your joy to gloom. Humble yourselves in the sight of the Lord, and He will lift you up.
James 4:7–10 (NKJV)

A conceited person has an exaggerated opinion of his worth and abilities; he is proud, not humble. Satan fell from grace because of his pride, and those who follow him share this prideful nature. Lü was one such person. He compiled a hodgepodge literary collection that he pompously called "Lü's Chronicles 呂氏春秋," literally "Lü's Spring and Autumn."[22] Although none of the material was his own, he used his surname in the title and then hung the completed manuscript at the city-gate, challenging anyone to edit the text and offering 1,000 pieces of gold for each word altered.[23] Of course, no one dared to suggest any changes, not because his manuscript was flawless but because no one dared criticize the Regent and Chief Minister!

Qin Shi Huang was equal to Lü in egomania. After he conquered the six other states and reunified China, his ministers suggested that he should adopt a new title to show that he ranked higher than the rulers of the vanquished states, who were called "kings 王."[24] They suggested a few names, including "Supreme Emperor 泰帝" (Tai Di), but he felt this title was not lofty enough. Instead, he decided to call himself "August Emperor 叟帝" (Huang Di), with "Huang" meaning "supreme greatness" and "Di" meaning "Lord or Emperor."[25]

Some commentators have said that he was comparing himself to the ancient sovereigns of China, who were called the "Three Huangs and Five Dis 三皇五帝," but these rulers never used 叟 (huang) and 帝 (di) together to form the title "Supreme Emperor" or "August Emperor," as Qin Shi Huang did. I believe that by doing this Qin Shi Huang was usurping the role of God. The supreme name for God in ancient China was 昊天上帝 (Hao Tian Shang Di) or 叟天上帝 (Huang Tian Shang Di). Both these names mean the same thing: Supreme Lord of the Great

22. In Chinese literary language, seasons refer to the passing of events.
23. This story resulted in a Chinese saying, "One thousand pieces of gold for every word," 一字千金 (yi zi qian jin), which is used to stress the importance — the great value — of every single word.
24. 帝 (Di) or Lord was the title used by Chinese emperors before the Zhou Dynasty. Wu Wang switched it to 王 (Wang) or King to disassociate his reign from the corruption of the previous emperors.
25. Although 秦 (Tai) and 皇 (Huang) can both be translated as supreme, the scale of difference in the meaning of these two words in Chinese is vast. This difference can be seen in the fact that while one of China's tallest mountain is called 泰山 (Tai Shan), the sky is described as 皇天 (huang tian).

Heaven. By choosing to call himself Huang Di, Qin Shi Huang elevated himself to a position that no other ruler before him had dared. With this new title, he became known as Qin Shi Huang Di, which means the First August Emperor of Qin. He boasted that his descendants would rule as the Second Emperor, the Third Emperor, and so on for thousands of generations.

Though the Qin Dynasty lasted only into a second generation and for a mere three years after Qin Shi Huang's death, subsequent dynasties continued to use this title for the sovereign. More significantly, they also adopted his autocratic dragon power, whereby every word spoken by the emperor was law. The emperor of China sat on the Dragon Throne and was accountable to no one. No longer was the ruler of the Middle Kingdom the Son of Heaven who served as a regent of Shang Di; now the emperor wielded dragon power and was a law unto himself.

It has been wisely said that "power corrupts and absolute power corrupts absolutely." Therefore, it is for our good that the Bible advises us to be submissive to God and to resist the devil. Submission is not exactly the same as obedience. Submission is the surrender of our own will to another's will, which leads to obedience. Submission to God is possible as we become increasingly aware of God's divine attributes. When we are assured of His love, His power, and His faithfulness, we can peacefully fall into His arms. On the other hand, we are to resist the temptation to think more highly of ourselves than we ought. This is the devil, Satan, at work, and although his methods may seem enticing at first, to fall into his ways inevitably leads to a violent and destructive end. The great empire that Lü and Qin Shi Huang built lasted only three years after the emperor's death; Lü himself was forced by Qin Shi Huang, his protégé and most likely his own son, to commit suicide. Lü did not make a good lasting investment!

Dragon Power and Contempt

> *Do not speak evil of one another, brethren. He who speaks evil of a brother and judges his brother, speaks evil of the law and judges the law. But if you judge the law, you are not a doer of the law but a judge. There is one Lawgiver, who is able to save and to destroy. Who are you to judge another?*
> James 4:11 – 12 (NKJV)

Chapter Eight  Enter the Dragon

When a person is consumed by the pursuit of worldly power and pleasures, he will start to despise people and use them. Such a person believes the universe exists only for him; other people become nothing more than mere objects to be used and exploited to attain his personal, selfish goals. This kind of thinking was at the heart of the way Qin Shi Huang ruled. At the core of his form of government was a set of stifling laws that was based on the idea that the people existed to serve the emperor. Qin Shi Huang's way of governing fit neatly into a school of thought called Legalism 法家 (fa jia) that was then gaining ground in China. Although the origins of Legalism are unclear, one of its earliest proponents was Shang Yang 商鞅 (361–338 B.C), prime minister of the state of Qin under the Zhou Dynasty. It was this espousal of Legalism that made the state of Qin powerful enough to conquer its rivals and gain control of the whole of China.

Legalism is based on the view—the judgment—that man is by nature selfish and ignorant. Therefore the best way to control human behavior is through strict laws, harsh punishments, and fear. Obedience was paramount, and this was assured through draconian measures of punishment. It is easy to see how such a philosophy would appeal to Qin Shi Huang, and it was during his reign that Legalism reached its apogee. All the people were organized into "productive occupations" such as agriculture and military services, whereas merchants and intellectuals were considered nonproductive. The emperor was regarded as the source of all knowledge. Therefore books were no longer necessary; imperial edicts alone determined the conduct for all people.

This view runs counter to the roots of Chinese culture. Classical Chinese values regard the government as the servant of the people; we saw this in the reigns of Yao, Shun, Yu, and the Duke of Zhou. Legalism and dragon power turned the ancient Chinese value system on its head. They also run contrary to the Bible, which teaches that there is only one source of the Law.

Qin Shi Huang, however, saw himself as the ultimate judge of all people, and his decrees were the only law of the land. This kind of elevated self-view can only have as its corollary a low view of other people, which is contempt. Other people

are regarded as of lesser importance and value, and hence expendable. When the learned men of the land opposed him, Qin Shi Huang simply got rid of them, by burying 460 of them alive. When he died, the 700,000 workmen who had labored to construct his massive tomb were buried with him, on his orders; keeping the tomb's location secret was more important than the lives of hundreds of thousands of men. This kind of attitude and behavior clearly runs counter to God's supreme law of love, and those who think and act this way are putting themselves above God's law and divine principles. When we show contempt for other human beings, we are actually showing contempt for His law and ultimately for the Creator Himself!

The ruins of the Great Wall of China at Gu Bei Kou, 80 miles (128 kilometers) north of Beijing.

forced the Second Emperor to commit suicide and attempted to claim the throne for himself. When none of the ministers was willing to follow him, because he was a eunuch, Zhao Gao appointed Hu Hai's nephew, Zi Ying 子嬰, as the new emperor. Zi Ying reigned for a mere 46 days before his capital was captured by Liu Bang 劉邦, founder of the Han Dynasty.

Qin Shi Huang, however, did not die without a legacy. Sadly, what he left to the great nation of China was a heritage of violence, hatred, immorality, and instability. Of the 611 emperors who reigned after him, only 339 died of natural causes. Most of the others suffered violent deaths: by the sword (137), poisoning (33), strangulation (17), suicide (16), drowning (14), starvation (4), and other violent ends (28). The transfer of power reflects even more starkly the destructive forces of "dragon power." Less than five percent of the emperors, only 29, peacefully abdicated the throne. Of the remaining 582 emperors, 299 ruled until their deaths and the 283 other imperial successions were violent and full of intrigue.[26]

The Apostle John wrote in about A.D. 70, "Children, it is the last hour; and just as you heard that antichrist is coming, even now many antichrists have appeared; from this we know that it is the last hour."[27] Qin Shi Huang was a type of antichrist in that he was an enemy of God and God's standards. His approach to leadership conditioned a massive nation to fear for more than 2,000 years. Even his choice of color and number—black and 6—hinted at his relationship with Satan.[28] When he standardized measurements, six was the unit he chose. Carriages were six Chinese feet wide, pulled by six horses. Even hats were six Chinese inches in diameter!

A More Excellent Way

In this journey of discovery, we have already encountered Emperor Kang Xi 康熙 (A.D. 1654–1722) several times. We meet him once again, this time atop the wall that Qin Shi Huang built. Kang Xi was on an inspection tour of the Great Wall when he saw this inscription:

萬里長城萬里空，百世英雄百世夢

which means, "The wall of ten thousand 'li' is but ten thousand 'li' of vanity; a

26. See Yuan Zhiming (遠志明), *China's Confession* 《神州懺悔錄》 (Petaluma, Calif.: China Soul, 2001), p. 313 (in Chinese).

27. First John 2:18.

28. In Revelation 13:18, the archenemy of God, the man who is an agent of Satan, is identified as having the number 666.

hundred generations of heroes are but a hundred generations of dreams." Kang Xi was astonished and immediately wanted to know who had written these words. It was Zhang Tingyu 張廷玉, a learned scholar of the time. The ministers in attendance assumed that Zhang was in trouble for pointing out the futility of building the wall. In fact, however, Kang Xi recognized the wisdom of Zhang's assessment and immediately gave him a ministerial position. Kang Xi also decreed that the wall should never be rebuilt; he understood all too well that the celebrated wall built to keep out "barbarian" invaders was useless. After all, it was his very own Manchurian grandfather who had successfully "breached" the wall simply by bribing a gatekeeper.

Zhang Tingyu subsequently rose to become one of the greatest civil servants in the Qing Dynasty, serving three emperors. This wise imperial aide recognized that power alone could not build a kingdom. Nations rise and fall on their internal strength or weakness, not because of external forces. Because the Roman Empire fell to barbarian invaders, many have wrongly concluded that external forces are the greater threat. In fact, Rome first decayed from within, and in its weakened state, invaders were able to finish it off. In the same way, earthly dragon power carries within it its own inevitable demise; its power ultimately poisons and destroys. Only the One True God creates and sustains the life of nations and individuals; only those who humbly walk before Him will make a lasting difference.

Humility Works

Does humility really work? The answer is a resounding Yes. This is not just the gentle advice of the Christian Bible. It is also now the conclusion of the world of international business and is being acknowledged by the secular media. Jim Collins, a highly influential business management consultant, comes to this startling conclusion in his *New York Times* bestseller, *Good to Great: Why Some Companies Make the Leap ... And Others Don't*. He and his team of researchers set out looking for companies that had progressed from "good to great." Five years and US$13 million later, they identified six principles that make a company "great."

Defining "great" as "performance that is at least three times better than the market over a fifteen-year period," they identified 11 companies that met this criterion:[29]

29. Jim Collins, *Good to Great: Why Some Companies Make the Leap ... And Others Don't* (New York: Harper Collins, 2001).

Good-to-Great Companies	Result from Transition Point to 15 Years Beyond Transition Point	Period	Direct Comparison
Abbott	3.98 times the market	1974–1989	Upjohn
Circuit City	18.5 times the market	1982–1997	Silo
Fannie Mae	7.56 times the market	1984–1999	Great Western
Gillette	7.39 times the market	1980–1995	Warner Lambert
Kimberly Clark	3.42 times the market	1972–1987	Scott Paper
Kroger	4.17 times the market	1973–1988	A & P
Nucor	5.16 times the market	1975–1990	Bethlehem Steel
Philip Morris	7.06 times the market	1964–1979	R J Reynolds
Pitney Bowes	7.16 times the market	1973–1988	Addressograph
Walgreens	7.34 times the market	1975–1990	Eckerd
Wells Fargo	3.99 times the market	1983–1998	Bank of America

After studying these 11 companies, Collins and his team distilled their corporate keys to success into these operating principles:

1. Level 5 Leadership (Personal humility and professional will)
2. First Who Then What
3. Confront the Brutal Fact (Yet Never Lose Faith)
4. Hedgehog Concept (Simplicity)
5. Culture of Discipline
6. Technology Accelerators (Pioneers in select technologies)

At the outset, Collins was determined not to include leadership in his study because he felt that too many books had already been written on the importance of leadership. When the results were in, however, they overwhelmingly showed that leadership played a highly pivotal role in turning these companies from good to great. Collins and his team gave a very creative name to this operating principle: Level 5 Leadership.

What is this "Level 5 Leadership" that is the key to creating a great organization? Based on their extensive research, the Collins team discovered that those who were Level 5 leaders exhibited two prevailing characteristics: personal humility and professional will. By contrast, Level 3 and Level 4 leaders might be described as operating according to "dragon principles." Looking out for No. 1 and using fear as a motivator, these leaders might fool many with their arrogance and self-assurance, but their results are temporary. They cannot even fool the market long enough to rank among the companies that perform three times better than their peers for 15 years.

How interesting that even Wall Street is talking about humility! God's Word never fails: He said that when we humble ourselves, He will lift us up—and this principle applies even in the competitive, cut-throat, capitalist world of big business! The leaders who are making a lasting difference in the world are the ones who are humble. That's God's way, not Satan's way; that's the power of humility, not dragon power.

REFLECT and RESPOND

Power, pleasure, and position are very enticing. But they do not last. Like the dragon, they do not serve us; we end up serving them when we pursue them. Have you slain the "dragon" within? If not, give your life to Jesus of Nazareth, who has slayed the dragon. He will free you, and you will enjoy His peace and freedom.

玖

All Truth Is God's Truth

9

From antiquity till now, the name of Dao has never disappeared, in order that through Dao we may know the genesis of all things. How do I know the genesis of all things? Through Dao.

~Lao Zi, Chinese philosopher, *Dao De Jing*

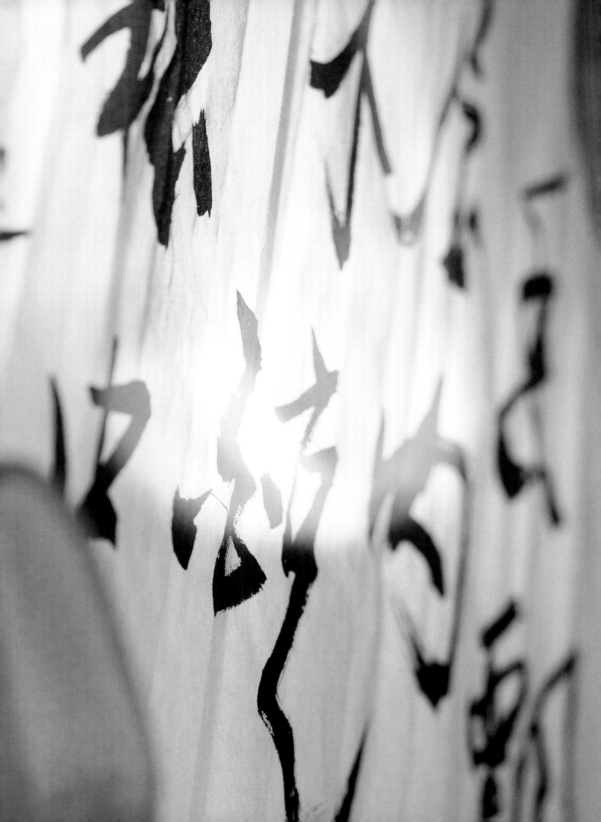

9

All Truth Is God's Truth

Sir Francis Bacon (A.D. 1561–1626) was one of the larger-than-life figures of Elizabethan England, serving both Elizabeth I and her successor, James I. Bacon's political career flourished in King James's court, and in 1618 he was appointed Lord Chancellor, the most powerful position in England. Bacon's lasting contribution to history, however, was not his three years as Lord Chancellor, nor his skills as lawyer, statesman, and master of the English language. Bacon's life passion was the search for scientific truth,[1] and he is best remembered as the "father of modern science" for promoting inductive reasoning and pushing for its use in scientific pursuits. In contrast to the scientific approach of his time, Bacon argued that truth required evidence from the real world. He promoted empirical and inductive principles, pushed for the scientific method of testing a theory by controlled experiment, and stressed the value of careful observation of nature to reach logical conclusions. In so doing, Bacon played a key role in bringing scientific methodology from Renaissance thinking into the early modern era.

Therefore, as an advocate of inductive reasoning in science, Bacon's views on God and nature are perhaps even more worthy of consideration than the predictable sermons of Christian clergy. Today, the generally accepted view is that science and God do not and should not have anything to do with each other, but Bacon thought differently:

> *Let no man ... think or maintain that a man can search too far or be too well studied in the book of God's Word or in the book of God's Works, divinity or*

1. Bacon was, literally, a scientist to his dying breath. He died of a cold or pneumonia or bronchitis (the accounts vary), caught when he went out into the cold of winter to test whether a rabbit or a chicken (again, the accounts vary) could be preserved fresh by stuffing it with snow.

philosophy; but rather let men endeavor an endless progress or proficiency in both.[2]

There are two books laid before us to study, to prevent our falling into error; first, the volume of Scriptures, which reveal the will of God; then the volume of the Creatures, which express His power.

There never was found, in any age of the world, either philosophy, or sect, or religion, or law, or discipline, which did so highly exalt the good of the community, and increase private and particular good as the holy Christian faith. Hence, it clearly appears that it was one and the same God that gave the Christian law to men, who gave the laws of nature to the creatures.[3]

Bacon believed that all knowledge points to God, and his words urge us to be engaged in a never-ending pursuit of the knowledge and experience of God through nature and through His Word, the Bible. When we respond positively to the little we understand of God, He guides us further into His truth. On the other hand, if we reject what we already know of Him, we will gain no further knowledge and experience of Him and we will have no opportunity to know the Truth that is in Him. As Bacon also observed, "A little philosophy inclineth man's mind to atheism, but depth in philosophy bringeth men's minds about to religion."[4]

On this journey of discovery, we have looked at some of the important ways that God has revealed Himself to the Chinese people. We have also considered the similarities between the God—Shang Di—that the ancient Chinese knew and worshipped and the God–Yahweh–that the Hebrew people followed. At this signpost called "All Truth Is God's Truth," let us use Bacon's method of inductive reasoning to observe how the ancient Chinese and the Hebrews viewed truth and what they understood about truth, and see what logical conclusion that leads us to.

Bacon's life passion was the pursuit of scientific truth, that is, what can be learned from the natural world that God created. Earlier in our journey, we saw that God has left His creative "fingerprints" in nature to reveal Himself through nature. If, however, we stop at this general revelation, we will miss the mark altogether. The Bible teaches that the purpose of this general revelation is to point us to God's specific revelation, His ultimate revelation and the ultimate Truth.

2. Francis Bacon, *Of the Proficience and Advancement of Learning, Divine and Humane* (1605), Book 1, *Great Books of the Western World*, Volume 28: *Bacon, Descartes, Spinoza* (Chicago: Encyclopedia Britannica Inc., 1990), p. 4.
3. Francis Bacon as quoted by Federer, W. J., *Great Quotations: A Collection of Passages, Phrases, and Quotations Influencing Early and Modern World History* (St. Louis, Mo.: AmeriSearch, 2001), electronic edition.
4. Francis Bacon as quoted by R. J. Morgan, *Nelson's Complete Book of Stories, Illustrations, and Quotes* (Nashville, Tenn.: Thomas Nelson Publishers, 2000), electronic edition.

WHAT IS TRUTH ?

Pontius Pilate, the fifth Roman governor of Judea and the one who signed the death warrant to crucify Jesus, asked, "What is truth?" He directed this question to Jesus, but he asked it rhetorically; he was not really interested in the truth. In fact, his question was actually a lame attempt to avoid the truth. To the person who seeks with sincerity, however, the knowledge and experience of truth is readily attainable.

It is readily attainable because it is found in God. God, the Creator of the Universe, is the source of all truths. If anything is true, it must issue from Him because all things originated from Him. This is how the Hebrews described the God of truth:

> *He is the Rock, His work is perfect; For all His ways are justice,*
> *A God of truth and without injustice; Righteous and upright is He.*
> Deuteronomy 32:4 (NKJV)

> *Because he who is blessed in the earth*
> *Will be blessed by the God of truth;*
> *And he who swears in the earth*
> *Will swear by the God of truth.*
> Isaiah 65:16

Put another way, God is the fountainhead of truth. Just as following a stream will eventually lead to its source, so will the pursuit of what is true lead to the source of truth, which is God Himself.

The Hebrew psalmist also said:

> *Righteousness and justice are the foundation of Your throne;*
> *Lovingkindness and truth go before You.*
> *How blessed are the people who know the joyful sound!*
> *O LORD, they walk in the light of Your countenance.*
> Psalm 89:14 – 15

Righteousness and justice guide us to Him; lovingkindness and truth accompany us as we seek Him. Those who know the joyful sound of truth will be blessed, and, they will walk in the light of God's truth. And at the end of this journey, they will come

face to face with the loving Creator. That is why the psalmist says that they will walk in the light of His countenance, because His loving gaze will be upon them.

Not only is God the source and creator of truth, but He is also the guardian of truth and preserves it forever, as the psalmist says:

> *Happy is he ...*
> *Whose hope is in the Lord his God,*
> *Who made heaven and earth,*
> *The sea, and all that is in them;*
> *Who keeps truth forever.*
> Psalm 146:5–6 (NKJV)

The Two Dimensions of Truth

Truth has two dimensions: intellectual, and existential and moral. In the common modern usage, truth is intellectual. In this sense, truth consists of facts that may be ascertained to be true or false. Chinese express this concept as 真理 (zhen li). "Zhen" means real. Truth in this sense is the full or actual state of affairs. It is the standard by which conflicting or incorrect ideas or statements are evaluated. For example, historians use truth to denote real events as distinct from myths, and philosophers describe truth as what is real. The other dimension of truth, which is espoused in both the Hebrew and Chinese cultures, is existential and moral. Chinese express this sense as 道理 (dao li). "Dao" means "the way." Truth in this sense refers to an attribute; that is, whether a person is dependable, consistent, and of reliable character. The emphasis is upon reliability: something or someone true will stand up under testing. In this sense, truth is moral and relational, not merely intellectual.

A term related to truth is knowledge, which also is not merely intellectual. True knowledge is experiential and dynamic. That is why, in Chinese, the verb "to know" is 知道 (zhi dao), which means "to understand the way." To know, particularly in a relationship, is not merely to understand a set of abstract facts; rather, it is a knowledge that leads to intimacy or clarity of direction and movement. For instance, a man may be known as a loving father because he has been observed performing loving acts, but only his wife and children truly know his loving

heart because of their intimate interactions with him. This truth about him will be common knowledge, but the knowledge is of differing degrees based on proximity and intimacy.

The 道理 (dao li) meaning of truth—that of a person's reliability—is one of the attributes of the One True God. As we saw in the earlier chapters, the ancient Chinese and the Hebrews both described their God as One who is personal and fundamentally different from fickle pagan gods; He was true—that is, consistent. God is true in His loving care for His creation. He is also true in His relentless hostility to sin, because sin is the antithesis of His nature, the antithesis of Truth. He governs the universe with principles that are true in the sense that they are permanently valid. His unchanging truth is the standard by which He judges; it is by this standard that He has judged throughout history and will judge in the final days.[5] The Chinese understand this truth about God, which is reflected in the saying "天網恢恢, 疏而不漏," meaning, "The net of Heaven is vast but loose, yet nothing can escape from it."

Truth as a moral attribute of God has many distinctive and recognizable characteristics. When we encounter God's truth, we will recognize that it is from Him by these characteristics. As in earlier chapters, we will see striking similarities in the Hebrew and Chinese cultures: both recognized these fundamental characteristics in their understanding of truth.

Truth Is Universal

Since God is One and truth issues from Him, there are no geographical, historical, cultural, or economic distinctions when it comes to truth. Most people will have no difficulty accepting the unity of truth as it relates to the physical world. For example, there is no dispute that the law of gravity works in China just as it does in Europe, that it worked 2,000 years ago the same way it does today. This crucial characteristic of truth applies to all other areas as well, including our relationship to the Creator and with other human beings.

This being the case, it is not surprising that another ancient culture even more renowned for its scholarship than the Chinese and the Hebrew had a term for truth that is almost identical to the Chinese word 道 (dao). This is the Greek

5. See Psalms 54:5; 96:13; 57:3.

term "logos." According to one Bible dictionary, "Logos is the transliteration of a common Greek word that generally means 'word,' 'speech,' 'account,' 'story' or 'message.'" Dao is similarly broadly used and just as rich in connotation as its Greek counterpart. It can mean "road," "path," "way," "method," "to say" or "to speak."

The same Bible dictionary in the entry on "logos" goes on to say, "Around 500 B.C. Greek philosophers began to adopt the word and use it to signify that which gives shape, form or life to the material universe."[6] The Apostle John went one step further by using "logos" to refer to Jesus as the "expression" of God:

> *In the beginning was the Word [Logos], and the Word was with God, and the Word was God. He was in the beginning with God. All things came into being through Him, and apart from Him nothing came into being that has come into being.*
> John 1:1–3

> *What was from the beginning, what we have heard, what we have seen with our eyes, what we have looked at and touched with our hands, concerning the Word of Life — and the life was manifested, and we have seen and testify and proclaim to you the eternal life, which was with the Father and was manifested to us — what we have seen and heard we proclaim to you also, so that you too may have fellowship with us; and indeed our fellowship is with the Father, and with His Son Jesus Christ.*
> 1 John 1:1–3

"Logos" in these verses is translated as 道 (dao) in the Chinese Bible. As noted in an earlier chapter, translating God's name into Chinese has sometimes been controversial, but about "logos" there has never been any dispute. There is no better translation in Chinese than *Dao*. In fact, *Dao* is so full of profound meaning that the impact on a Chinese reader upon reading the opening words of the Gospel of John "太初有道" (tai chu you dao) is far greater than an English reader reading, "In the beginning was the Word," which can seem almost nonsensical. A Chinese reader immediately and almost intuitively grasps the deep and profound meaning captured by and contained in *Dao*, which the English word "Word" lacks.

Like the ancient Greeks, the ancient Chinese also personified this term. We find

6. J. B. Green, S. McKnight, and I. H. Marshall, *Dictionary of Jesus and the Gospels* (Downers Grove, Ill.: InterVarsity Press, 1992), electronic edition.

7. The *Dao De Jing* is most commonly associated with Taoism (Daoism), which is considered one of the major religions of China. In fact, Taoism is more a philosophy than a religion. While Taoism as a philosophical system stems from the *Dao De Jing*, Taoist religious beliefs are an amalgamation of interest in alchemy and the search for the elixir of life, both of which predate the *Dao De Jing*, of Mahayana

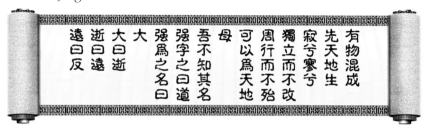

this in a short document of just 5,000 characters that is the definitive text on *Dao*. It is called the *Dao De Jing* 道琉經,[7] better known in Chinese simply by the name of the 6th-century philosopher who wrote it, *Lao Zi* 老子.[8] Just as John uses Logos as the name for Jesus, whom he described as being with God from the beginning of creation, so Lao Zi uses *Dao* to refer to the Creator of heaven and earth:

> *There is something formless yet complete, existing before heaven and earth; without sound, without substance, yet independent and unchanging; ever existing, never failing. We may think of it as mother of heaven and earth. I do not know the name. If I must give a name, I will say Dao. And if I must give a description, I will say Great. Great in that He is unending, unending in that He is expansive, and expansive in that He is ever-recurring.*

Dao De Jing 25:1 – 5

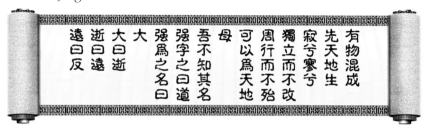

Buddhist teachings, and of the worship of a pantheon of local folk gods. (See "Taoism," *The Columbia Encyclopedia*, 6th ed., New York: Columbia University Press, 2001–04. Available online at www.bartleby.com/65/ta/Taoism.html.) Therefore, to understand, interpret, or explain the *Dao De Jing* from or in the context of Taoist religious belief is a wrong-headed and backwards approach. In this chapter, we examine the *Dao De Jing* removed from any Taoist teachings or interpretations.

The *Dao De Jing* has become popular in the West among some students of philosophy, religion, and Chinese culture, some of whom consider it a mystical text containing deeply profound and nearly incomprehensible meaning. This has given rise to the view that the *Dao De Jing* is impossible to fully grasp, that it can be interpreted in myriad ways, and even that Lao Zi deliberately wrote ambiguously so as to preserve the mystery of the Dao from all but the most astute students. Such a view has resulted in a staggering array of translations (see www.bopsecrets.org/gateway/passages/tao-de-ching.htm, which provides more than 100 different translations of the *Dao De Jing*), as well as some interpretations ranging from the amusing to the far-fetched.

I have taken an entirely different approach. My view is that Lao Zi wanted us to know about *Dao* and wrote the *Dao De Jing* to teach and enlighten, not to confuse. The very fact that he uses 道 (dao) in the sense of 道白 (dao bai), which means to expound, and 道明 (dao ming), which means to elucidate, reflects the idea that *Dao* wants to communicate unambiguously with us. This is also the essence of Logos, as used by the Apostle John to refer to Jesus. Therefore, the most obvious and simplest interpretation is probably Lao Zi's intended meaning. I am also of the view that there can be only one meaning, not myriad, and that one meaning is Lao Zi's intended meaning. The translations of the *Dao De Jing* that are presented in this chapter are our own, based on reading of the original text and consultation of other translations. In every case, we have striven to hew as closely as possible to Lao Zi's original language in word choice, definition, style, rhythm, and, most significantly, in its succinctness and sparseness.

Finally, I wish to acknowledge that my interpretation of the *Dao De Jing* is broadly influenced by Yuan Zhi Ming's works, such as 《老子原文與譯文》 *Lao Zi Original Text and Interpretation* and 《老子 vs. 聖經》 *Lao Zi versus The Bible*.

8. Though Lao Zi's impact on ancient Chinese culture was equal to that of Confucius, very little was known about him. Lao Zi, which literally means Old Master, probably lived in China in the 6th century B.C. around the time of Confucius.

The Apostle John was Jesus' bosom friend; they walked, talked, worked, and ate together for three years. He was intimately acquainted with the One he called Logos. Lao Zi did not know Jesus, yet he describes *Dao* as having the same awe-inspiring transcendence and eternal nature as John's Logos.

Truth Is Great

For Your lovingkindness is great to the heavens/And Your truth to the clouds.
Psalm 57:10

God's lovingkindness and truth are beyond the ability of words to concretely define, and so the psalmist uses figurative language to describe their extent and vastness. The greatness of God's truth is in its size, measure, extensiveness, and expansiveness. It is also great in its excellence and superiority in character and quality. In contrast to the useless answers given in the story below, God's truth does not contain empty knowledge that is irrelevant.

> *Two friends went on a hot-air balloon ride. As they were novices, they lost control of their balloon and were soon lost. Lowering their balloon, they noticed a farmer working in the field below. One shouted to the farmer, "Hello sir, do you know where we are?" Startled, the old farmer looked up and mumbled, "Oh, you are in the air." The other friend thought he could phrase the question better and asked, "But sir, where are you?" Incredulous, the old farmer said, "Well, I am on the ground."*

The farmer's answers were "right," but they were of no help whatsoever to the lost balloonists. By contrast, God's truth is great because it is neither useless nor irrelevant to our lives. Lao Zi writes with awe of the greatness and superiority of *Dao*. Although his writing can seem puzzling to modern readers, it is clear that this esteemed philosopher of ancient China believed *Dao* to be real, though transcendent.

> *Dao, when expressed, is no ordinary Dao; when given a name, it is no ordinary name.*
> Dao De Jing 1:1
>
> 道可道，非常道。名可名，非常名。

All say my Dao [i.e. the Dao I teach] is great, that nothing resembles [Dao]. It is because [Dao] is great that nothing resembles [Dao]. Were [Dao]to resemble something, [Dao] would long ago have become trivial!
Dao De Jing 67:1

天下皆謂我道大，似不尚。夫睢大，故似不尚。老尚，久矣其細也夫！

Truth Is Inviolable

God is not a man, that He should lie, Nor a son of man, that He should repent; Has He said, and will He not do it? Or has He spoken, and will He not make it good?
Numbers 23:19

As truth derives from the very being of God, God will not allow interference with or violation of the truth; that is the meaning of "inviolable" — to be secure from violation. Although we sometimes say that someone is "bending the truth," in reality, no one can do that. "Bending the truth" or "twisting the truth" are figurative expressions only, and they simply mean "telling a lie." To twist or bend the truth actually has no impact on truth itself; man's actions cannot change the truth in any way. God's truth can withstand any assault, and when man attempts to redefine, reinterpret, or negate God's truth, he is actually usurping God's authority. The Chinese have a saying that "once a word is spoken, a carriage drawn by four horses is not able to retrieve it 言既出，四馬難道." If that is true of the words spoken by mere men, how much more true is that of words that emanate from God!

Lao Zi expresses this aspect of truth in a different way, using the analogy of a novice trying to challenge the master craftsman and the inevitable price he pays for his failure:

Since antiquity there has always been a Judge who determines life and death. When a man usurps this right to determine life and death, he is like a novice imitating a master craftsman; how can he expect not to hurt his hands?
Dao De Jing 74:3

常有司殺者殺。夫代司殺者殺，是謂代大匠，夫代大匠
者，希有不蕩其手矣。

Truth Is Abundant and Transcendent

But You, O LORD, are a God merciful and gracious,
Slow to anger and abundant in lovingkindness and truth.
Psalm 86:15

God's truth is abundant and transcendent in that it is everywhere to be seen and experienced. If we want to experience God's truth, all we need to do is to pay attention and we can encounter Him in all the spheres of our lives. His truth is not restricted to the spiritual realm. We can experience the truth of God in our work, in our play, in all our human relationships, in science, in music, in art, in finance … in every aspect and in every experience of our lives.

Lao Zi expressed the availability and transcendence of Dao this way:

Seen, though it is not visible — it is above form; heard, though it is not audible —
it is above sound; felt, though it cannot be held — it is beyond touch. These three
[aspects of Dao] are too deep to be understood; obviously, they are blended
into one …. Following ancient Dao, one is able to manage what is now. To
understand the beginning of creation is to discover the mystery of Dao.
Dao De Jing 14:1, 2, 7

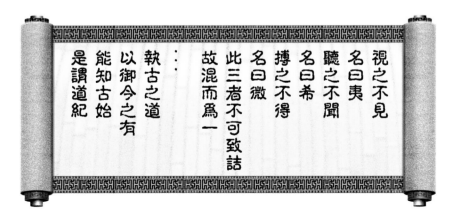

Truth Endures Forever

> *For the* LORD *is good;*
> *His mercy is everlasting,*
> *And His truth endures to all generations.*
> Psalm 100:5 (NKJV)

Truth withstands the tests of time. Once it has issued from God, He will not and cannot retrieve it. Truth is timeless, and it transcends cultural and spatial differences. As the wise Hebrew ruler, King Solomon, observed, "There is nothing new under the sun" (Ecclesiastes 1:9). We need to be on the alert when someone claims to have some new truths. Truth is as old as God Himself. We may gain new insights into truth, that is, into God's character, but it is not new in the sense of being a new development or an improvement. Truth cannot be improved upon or developed; that is so because not only is truth timeless, it is also perfectly good because its source,"God Himself," is perfectly good.

Lao Zi understood the eternal nature of *Dao*, saying:

> *From antiquity till now, the name [of Dao] has never disappeared, in order that through [Dao] we may know the genesis of all things. How do I know the genesis of all things? Through Dao.*
> Dao De Jing 21:4 – 5

> 自今及古，其名不去，以閱衆肅。吾何以知衆肅之狀哉？以此。

Truth Is Righteous

> *O* LORD, *who may abide in Your tent?*
> *Who may dwell on Your holy hill?*
> *He who walks with integrity, and works righteousness,*
> *And speaks truth in his heart.*
> Psalm 15:1 – 2

Truth is characterized by righteousness. The one who knows the truth will act with integrity and will live out his or her life in a right way. Truth cannot lead us to falsehood. Many people, such as those who lost the best years of their lives during

China's disastrous 1966–1976 Cultural Revolution, have been hurt by false beliefs and have become skeptics. They are cynical about believing in anything because they fear being misled again. Following the truth, however, can only lead to goodness and right living. A good tree will bear good fruit. If what I embrace does not guide me to live rightly and does not cleanse my heart, then it is not the truth. On the other hand, when we live in truth, our hearts will tell us that we are living with integrity, and that results in a peace that surpasses human understanding.

Lao Zi too recognized that the heavenly *Dao* leads mankind to righteousness, and he uses the analogy of light and darkness to describe *Dao*, just as the Bible does to describe truth:

> *Dao is from Heaven, to do good not harm. Dao is from the Holy One, for man,*
> *not against man.*
> Dao De Jing 81:5

天之道，利而不害；聖人之道，爲而不争。

> *Above [Dao], there is no light; below [Dao] there is no darkness.*
> Dao De Jing 14:3

其上不敏，其下不昧。

Truth Is Full of Grace

> *Lovingkindness and truth have met together;*
> *Righteousness and peace have kissed each other.*
> Psalm 85:10

Truth, because it is relational and moral, is always tempered with grace. Though we may think that when the truth is known, pain and harsh judgment will result, truth that comes from God is always loving and gentle because these are His attributes, just as truth is one of His attributes.

Lao Zi likened such grace and gentleness to that found in an infant:

> *The one who is full of virtue is like an infant. Poisonous bugs do not sting him,*
> *nor fierce beasts seize him, nor clawed birds maul him.*
> Dao De Jing 55:1–2

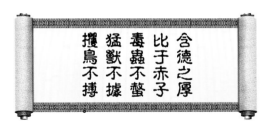

Truth Is Objective and Absolute

In our modern world today in which cultural diversity is promoted, it is often said that truth is relative, that it can vary from person to person and from culture to culture. We also hear remarks such as, "This may be true for you, but not for me." If we understand truth in a moral and personal way, however, we know that this cannot be so. Truth is not the creation of an individual's mind; it exists independently of us and is out there to be discovered. That is, it is objective and absolute. Truth is truth for all peoples, in the same way that gravity acts on all people and at all times, as we saw earlier. If this were not so, if truth were relative depending on individuals and communities, then truth would not be just and fair.

Although Lao Zi uses almost mystical language to describe *Dao*, he leaves no doubt that *Dao* is also absolute and real:

> *Dao as an object is intangible and incomparable. Incomparable and intangible, yet it has form. Intangible and incomparable, yet it has substance. Incomprehensible and mysterious, yet it has essence; its essence is real and it is believable.*
>
> Dao De Jing 21:2–3

FINDING GOD IN ANCIENT CHINA

Truth Brings Freedom

> *... and you will know the truth, and the truth will make you free.*
> John 8:32

A common misconception about truth is that living in truth can be constraining and stifling, that one becomes subject to a strict list of "dos and don'ts." The reality is just the opposite. Knowing and living the truth sets us free. One of the best examples of this inherent relationship between truth and freedom is the U.S. Declaration of Independence, which proclaims, "We hold these truths to be self-evident .... " It is these very truths embodied in this historic document that form the basis for the unprecedented freedom in American life, freedom greater than any society in all of human history has ever enjoyed. In the verse above, Jesus makes an even greater promise to all mankind: equal access for all to truth and freedom that no one and nothing but truth can provide. Jesus followed up this first promise of freedom with another:

> *Truly, truly, I say to you, everyone who commits sin is the slave of sin.... So if the Son makes you free, you will be free indeed.*
> John 8:34, 36

Jesus is saying quite plainly in the two passages quoted here that He is truth personified; He is the truth that can set us truly free. Truth is more than just a set of ideals and principles; it is a Person; therefore, it can free us because only a person can release us from bondage. If He sets us free, we will be free indeed because not only does He have the power to accomplish this, but He also has already paid the penalty so that we can be set free.

Lao Zi too believed that *Dao* can set men free from sin, which was why the ancient Chinese valued *Dao* so highly:

> *Dao is the Cornerstone of all things; the good man's treasure, the evil man's hoard. Why did the ancients prize Dao highly? Is it not because they said that those who seek shall find, those who have sinned shall be forgiven? Therefore everyone considered [Dao] most precious.*
> Dao De Jing 62:1, 4

道渚萬物之奧。善人之簧，不善人之所保。 . . . 古之所
以貴此道港何？ 不曰：求以得，有罪以免邪？ 故爲天
下貴。

Truth Is Revealed

For nothing is hidden, except to be revealed; nor has anything been secret, but
that it would come to light. If anyone has ears to hear, let him hear.
Mark 4:22–23

God planted truth in the world for us to discover, but whether we see the light
or hear the truth is determined by our will. Pride can stop us from accepting the
Truth.

If we think soberly and carefully about it, we can see why truth is not determined
by humans. That is, we do not formulate truths; all we can do is discover truth.
Our success in discovering the truth is dependent upon the One who has hidden
the truth removing the veil. (The word "reveal" literally comes from "removing the
veil.") This process is like watching a magic show. Try as we might, we cannot figure
out how the tricks are done. When the veil is removed, however, and the tricks are
explained, we will have no problem understanding the "truth."

Lao Zi knew that as we encounter truth, we might find it unappealing, but he
advised us not to underestimate it:

When Dao is spoken, it may be bland almost to the point of being flavorless,
seen but not worth looking at, heard but not worth listening to; but its uses
are inexhaustible.
Dao De Jing 35:3

道之幽口，淡手其無味，視之不足見，聽之

不足聞，用之不足既。

Truth is revealed to us so that we can, step by step, make our way back to
God, until we are restored into a full and perfect relationship with Him. Jesus, the
Ultimate Truth, came to live and die for us so that we can enjoy God forever. Since it

is God's intention that we come to know the Ultimate Truth, He has provided ample evidence for us. Dozens of biblical prophecies and signs foretold and accompanied the birth, the life, the death, and the resurrection of Jesus. God, however, did not restrict Himself to the Bible. He prepared other signs for those in ages past who did not have the Bible, to lead them to the Bible and to Jesus.

TRUTH REVEALED BY THE STARS

In this final stage of our journey to discover what the ancient Chinese knew of God, we will examine some remarkable Chinese historical records from around the time of Jesus' birth and death that clearly show that there were unmistakable signs pointing to Him. Even more astonishing is the near-perfect interpretation given by the Chinese astronomers of the heavenly phenomena they observed that coincided with the Advent and the Crucifixion of Jesus Christ, the Son of God, the Ultimate Truth that God sought to reveal to all mankind.

The material we are going to look at is not about astrology, which Webster's dictionary defines as "the divination of the supposed influences of the stars and planets on human affairs and terrestrial events by their positions and aspects."[9] The stars and planets, as created objects of God, do not and cannot exert any influence on human affairs; they can, however, be tools that God uses, as He uses all His creation, to reveal Himself and His glory:

> *The heavens are telling of the glory of God;*
> *And their expanse is declaring the work of His hands.*
> *Day to day pours forth speech,*
> *And night to night reveals knowledge.*
> *There is no speech, nor are there words;*
> *Their voice is not heard.*
> *Their line has gone out through all the earth,*
> *And their utterances to the end of the world.*
> *In them He has placed a tent for the sun.*
> Psalm 19:1 – 4

Astrology claims that the stars and their movements are the *causes* of earthly events. As we have seen, however, the ancient Chinese and the Hebrews believed

9. "Astrology," *Merriam-Webster's Collegiate Dictionary* (10th ed.), includes index (Springfield, Mass.: Merriam-Webster, 1996, c1993).

that the heavenly bodies were created by the One True God; therefore, as created objects themselves, the stars cannot be the causes of events on earth, although they can certainly impact aspects of human life on earth. Hebrew history as recorded in the Bible tells us that God *used* the stars to send messages about His interventions in human history, several of which we will look at shortly. In the passage above, the Hebrew psalmist uses many words to describe a highly communicative God, words such as "tell," "declare," "speech," "reveals," "words," "voice," and "utterances." Since God is the One who placed the stars in the sky and set them on their ordered paths, and if He wants to communicate with us, then the idea that He arranges the heavenly bodies to give us important messages should not be difficult to accept.

The ancient Chinese had no problem believing that heavenly events were divine signs. Recall that they viewed cosmic irregularities as a sign of a change in the Mandate of Heaven. They clearly understood the importance of watching the skies, as noted in the *Classic of Changes* 易經 (Yi Jing):

> *Observe the heavenly bodies, to discern the changes of the ages. Observe humanity, to teach people and govern the world.*
> 觀乎天文以察時變，觀乎入文以化成天下.[10]

The Star in the East

The most important message of all time was the incarnation of the Truth. The heavenly signs that God gave concerning the birth of Jesus were the Star in the East and the Star of Bethlehem, as described in the Bible.

> *Now after Jesus was born in Bethlehem of Judea in the days of Herod the king, magi from the east arrived in Jerusalem, saying, "Where is He who has been born King of the Jews? For we saw His star in the east and have come to worship Him."*
> Matthew 2:1–2

Herod (73–4 B.C.) was an Arab appointed by Rome to rule as king over the region of Judea, geographically covering most of modern Israel and the west bank of modern Jordan. During Herod's reign, wise men followed an unusual star to Jerusalem, seeking

10. 《易經-傳文-象辭-賁卦》 *Classic of Changes*, Commentary, Tuan Notes, Bi Hexagram.

FINDING GOD IN ANCIENT CHINA

Drawing of a Chinese astronomer studying the stars

the "King of the Jews." They came from the East by way of the Silk Road, which was the only major land link between the East and the West. These wise men were also called "magi," a word that is associated with the word "magic." A magus ("magi" is the plural form) was a "magician" or a learned man skillful in a variety of disciplines, particularly astronomy. It is not surprising, then, that magi were the ones who noticed this unusual star. It must truly have been an extraordinary astronomic occurrence to have caused them to embark on a long journey all the way to Jerusalem to seek the source and the reason for it. In effect, they embarked on a journey to seek the truth. Since this was an astral event, it must also have been seen by other astronomers of that time. The magi said that they saw the star in the east, that is, the star they saw rose from the east. Is there corroborating evidence for this?

Indeed there is. The astronomers in far-off China saw the same star! Like their counterparts in the Near East, Chinese emperors were served by imperial astronomers who kept careful watch of the skies for signs from heaven. This imperial office consisted of 14 night observers and three day observers who were on duty in shifts.[11] In addition, a few dozen other astronomers formulated and permutated their observations to gain insights into the signs of the time. And so it happened that Chinese astronomers observed and recorded several unusual astronomic phenomena around the time of the birth of Jesus.[12]

The entry below is found in the *Astronomy Records of the Book of the Han Dynasty* (206 B.C – A.D. 220) from the second year of Jian Ping 建平 of Emperor Xiao Ai 孝哀 (reigned 7 – 1 B.C.) :[13]

312

11. "Chinese Ought to Have the Right of Free Speech" (Zhong Guo Ren Yingyou Fayan Quan), *Unlocking the Secret of the Star of Bethlehem* (Jiekai Boliheng zhi Xing de Mimi), Teen's website, in Chinese. Available online at: http://vw.nthu.edu.tw/science/shows/xmas/shows/xmas5a.html#top (Cited September 2006).

12. See the appendix to Dr. W. C. Tan's "*Same God in the Bible and Chinese Classics*" 《共同的上帝》陳慰中博士著 (Victoria, B.C.: Canadian College for Chinese Studies, 1994, in Chinese).

13. Jian Ping is the name given by the emperor to this period of his reign. Xiao Ai is his official title.

In the second month of the second year, the comet was out of Altair for more than 70 days. It is said, "Comets appear to signify the old being replaced by the new." Altair,[14] the sun, the moon and the five stars are in movement to signify the beginning of a new epoch; the beginning of a new year, a new month and a new day. The appearance of this comet undoubtedly symbolizes change. The extended appearance of this comet indicates that this is of great importance.

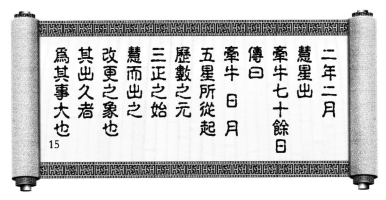

The second month of the second year of Jian Ping correlates to March 9 to April 6, 5 B.C. This timeframe is highly significant because most experts place the birth of Jesus at 5 to 4 B.C.

Although the Chinese did not know about the birth of Jesus, they were so convinced of the "great importance" surrounding the comet's appearance and its association with a new beginning that, according to the same historical record, some imperial ministers proposed changing the name of that year from the "Second Year of Jian Ping" to the "First Year of Tai Chu 太初," which literally means "Genesis" or "the Grand Beginning." This change was adopted and lasted until the eighth month when the original reign title of Jian Ping was restored.

There is at least one other Chinese historical record that documents this same heavenly occurrence:

> *In the second year of Jian Ping of Emperor Xiao Ai, in the spring, the first month, a Bei comet was found at Altair.*
>
> 建平二年，春，正月，有星孛汙牽牛。[16]

14. Altair is one of the 15 brightest stars, the brightest star in the constellation Aquila, which means "the eagle." Its Chinese name is 牽牛 (Qian Niu), literally a cowherd, or to lead or walk a bull.

15. 《漢書-天文志》 *History of the Former Han Dynasty*, Volume 26, Record of Astronomy.

16. 《資治通鑒-漢紀二十六》 *Zi Zhi Tong Jian*, Volume 34, Chronicles of Han Dynasty No. 26. A bei comet, 星孛, has no tail; a regular comet, which does have a tail, is called a hui comet, 彗星.

These Chinese records also help us to understand why, when the magi arrived in Jerusalem, King Herod questioned them closely about why they had set off on their journey. According to the Chinese record, the star was seen in the east and was observed for a period of more than 70 days. Since traveling from the East to Jerusalem could have taken up to a year, the star was no longer visible by the time the magi arrived in Jerusalem. That is why Herod had to question them closely to determine the exact time of the star's appearance.

These records show that ancient Chinese astronomers observed a highly unusual astral event and concluded that something of monumental significance was happening that involved heaven, earth, and mankind and that it pertained to the beginning of a new epoch. Interpreting the events with their limited knowledge, they responded by instituting a new reign title. They did not know that this new epoch was far more significant and that the extent of its significance was for the entire world! This new epoch was actually the full and direct revelation of God, when God stepped down into time and space to lead us to the Truth:

> God, after He spoke long ago to the fathers in the prophets in many portions
> and in many ways, in these last days has spoken to us in His Son, whom He
> appointed heir of all things, through whom also He made the world.
> Hebrews 1:1 – 2

Even more significant than the response of changing the reign title was the association the Chinese astronomers made between Altair and the Border Sacrifice. The Chinese historical records show that the Chinese interpreted all phenomena associated with Altair as having to do with sacrifice, that is, the Border Sacrifice described in Chapter 4.[17]

> The primary meaning of Altair, the key supporting pillar of the heavens, is the
> Perfect Sacrifice.

正義牽牛爲犧牲，亦爲關梁。[18]

They made this connection because Altair's Chinese name is "Bull 牛" (niu). As we have already seen in Chapter 4, an unblemished calf was the sacrifice of choice to Shang Di, so the Chinese linked the appearance of this star to the

17. References are found in the *Historical Records*, the *History of the Latter Han Dynasty*, and the *Zi Zhi Tong Jian*.
18. 《史記–卷二十七–天官書》 *Historical Records*, Volume 27, Book of Astronomy.

Border Sacrifice. In the case of the event recorded in the second year of Jian Ping, or 5 B.C., however, this was no ordinary sacrifice. The Chinese at that time, of course, had no way of fully understanding that it was to be the ultimate sacrifice: God had become man so that He could fulfill a mission of death to bring eternal life to all mankind.

> *... Christ Jesus, who, although He existed in the form of God, did not regard equality with God a thing to be grasped, but emptied Himself, taking the form of a bond-servant, and being made in the likeness of men. Being found in appearance as a man, He humbled Himself by becoming obedient to the point of death, even death on a cross.*
> Philippians 2:5–8

The magi probably knew to go to Jerusalem to look for the "King of the Jews" because of knowledge gleaned from centuries of interactions with Jewish exiles in Babylon and Persia. In fact, many Jews in exile in these regions rose to prominence because of their expertise and their contributions to their host nations; Daniel, Nehemiah, and Mordecai were just several of the best-known of them. The most notable of all was Daniel, himself a magus and an expert at interpreting dreams and astral phenomena. His knowledge, including knowledge of the star in the East, was probably passed on to later generations of magi.[19] Therefore, when they saw this strange heavenly sign, they knew that the Hebrew Scriptures long ago foretold the Baby who would be King, and they knew to head toward Jerusalem. Some of the Scripture references that they might have known include:

> *I see him, but not now; I behold him, but not near; A star shall come forth from Jacob, A scepter shall rise from Israel.*
> Numbers 24:17

> *Therefore the Lord Himself will give you a sign: Behold, a virgin will be with child and bear a son, and she will call His name Immanuel.*
> Isaiah 7:14

The Star of Bethlehem

> *After hearing the king, they went their way; and the star, which they had seen*

19. See Daniel 2:10; 4:7–9.

FINDING GOD IN ANCIENT CHINA

in the east, went on before them until it came and stood over the place where the Child was. When they saw the star, they rejoiced exceedingly with great joy.
Matthew 2:9–10

The biblical account says that after the magi left Herod, a star appeared that led them to Jesus. Once again, the Chinese records provide historical corroboration. They show a Bei star appearing at Altair on the day of Ji You 己酉, the third month of the third year of Jian Ping.[20] This would be April 24, 4 B.C., according to one calculation. The more significant fact that this historical record reveals is that the time elapsed between the appearance of the first star and the second star was approximately 13 months. This suggests that the magi were on the road for about a year, which is roughly how long a journey of that distance would have taken at the time. More significantly, it explains why Herod ordered all male infants in Bethlehem under the age of two killed: he wanted to be absolutely certain of killing the one who would be King of the Jews, who he thought would take his throne!

Then when Herod saw that he had been tricked by the magi, he became very enraged, and sent and slew all the male children who were in Bethlehem and all its vicinity, from two years old and under, according to the time which he had determined from the magi.
Matthew 2:16

The story of the magi, the stars, and Herod is instructive, showing the three different attitudes that we can maintain towards the truth. The first was exemplified by the magi, who were seekers of the truth. They were motivated by such a strong desire to find the truth that they willingly undertook a long and arduous journey in pursuit of it, and they stayed the course — traveling across much of the then-known world — until they found Him and met Him face to face.[21] Then there are those who respond like Herod, who did not want to know the truth because of his self-centeredness. The truth was a threat to all that Herod considered most important: his power and his position. Those who respond in this way are enemies of the truth and will resort to anything to suppress truth in their own hearts and in others. Finally, there are those who, like the people of Jerusalem and Bethlehem, are indifferent to the truth because they have no idea what is going on. Their ignorance and indifference, however, does not mean they are off the hook. The truth will be

20. "三月己百，⋯⋯。有星孛于河鼓" in 《漢書‐哀帝紀》 *History of Former Han Dynasty*, Chronicles of Emperor Ai, 3rd year.
21. See Matthew 2:11.

revealed to them at some point, and they will have to face the consequences of accepting or rejecting the truth!

The Day of the Cross

Not much is known of Jesus' childhood and adult life until he reached the age of 30 and started His public ministry. For more than three years, He taught a small band of disciples and went about preaching to large crowds. His itinerant preaching ended with His crucifixion when, based on biblical accounts, He would have been 33 or 34 years old. The Bible recounts a dramatic astronomic phenomenon occurring at the crucifixion:

> *It was now about the sixth hour, and darkness fell over the whole land until the ninth hour, because the sun was obscured; and the veil of the temple was torn in two. And Jesus, crying out with a loud voice, said, "Father, into Your hands I commit My spirit." Having said this, He breathed His last.*
> Luke 23:44 – 46

Note that this solar eclipse lasted for three hours—from the sixth to the ninth hour, which is roughly noon to 3 p.m. in modern timekeeping—before Jesus breathed His last. At that moment, the veil of the Jewish temple was supernaturally torn in two: a dramatic symbolization that the barrier between God and man was removed once and for all.

Once again, this event is corroborated in the Chinese historical documents, which record a highly significant solar eclipse occurring around the time indicated in the biblical account:

> *In the day of Gui Hai, the last day of the month, there was a solar eclipse. [The emperor] avoided the Throne Room, suspended all military activities, and did not handle official business for five days. And he proclaimed, "My poor character has caused this calamity, that the sun and the moon were veiled. I am fearful and trembling. What can I say? ... Anyone who presents a memorial is not allowed to mention the word 'holy'."*
>
> 癸攻晦，曰有食之，避正殿，寢兵，不聽事五日。詔曰：吾婕薄致灾，譴見日月，戰栗愁糰，夫坷言哉！其上書者，不得言聖。[22]

22. 《後漢書-光武帝第七年》 *History of Latter Han Dynasty*, Volume 1, Chronicles of Emperor Guang Wu, 7th year.

Another entry made a short time later, referring to the same eclipse, said:

> *Summer, fourth month [of the year], on the day of Ren Wu, the imperial edict reads, "Yin and Yang have mistakenly switched, and the sun and moon were eclipsed. The sins of all the people are now on one man. [The emperor] proclaims pardon to all under heaven."*

夏四月壬午，詔曰：比陰陽錯謬，日月薄食。百姓有過，
在予一人，大赦天下。[23]

This solar eclipse was recorded in the *Record of Latter Han Dynasty*. Gui Hai was the last day of the third month in the spring, during the 7th year of Han Emperor Guang Wu 光武 (reigned A.D. 25–57). That corresponds to A.D. 31, which means that this major eclipse happened 34 years after the astral events involving the magi! China's imperial capital at the time was in Luo Yang 洛陽, about five hours east of Jerusalem. If the eclipse appeared from noon to 3 p.m. in Jerusalem, then in Luo Yang it would have been from around 5 to 8 p.m. This may explain why the Chinese refered to both the sun and the moon in their record.

In comparing the Chinese astronomy records with the biblical accounts, we are not trying to pinpoint the exact date of Jesus' crucifixion or trying to prove that this particular eclipse observed by the Chinese was definitely the same one recorded in the Bible. There are just too many variables involved in trying to arrive at an exact date by matching Chinese, Gregorian, and Hebrew calendars. The more important point that we want to draw attention to is the remarkable interpretations the Chinese astronomers arrived at to explain this astral event. These interpretations are astonishingly consistent with the Bible's teaching about the birth and death of Jesus Christ.

The emperor's reaction to this solar eclipse is both highly significant and astonishing. Eclipses were not uncommon events, but this was a prolonged eclipse that fell on a special day, and the Chinese understood that it signified something of extraordinary import. The emperor was convicted of his sins and expressed deep remorse. He even proclaimed his sinfulness and took responsibility for it. This act alone was virtually unheard of in all of Chinese history. Even more significantly, he knew that the sins of all the people were laid on One Person! This might suggest some acquaintance with the ancient Chinese understanding of the concept of

23. Ibid.

propitiation that was behind the Border Sacrifice ceremony and blood covenants; that is, the requirement that sin must be borne by a pure, unblemished, perfect sacrifice whose blood must be shed to cover sin. Although the emperor did not articulate this idea in his proclamation, the fact that he further proclaimed that his ministers should avoid talking about holiness during that time and that he also proclaimed pardon for all suggests some awareness that holiness and forgiveness were somehow involved in this dramatic event in the heavens.

Even more incredibly, a commentary in the *Record of the Latter Han Dynasty*, said simply,

> *Eclipse on the day of Gui Hai, Man from heaven died.*

癸亥日蝕，天人崩。[24]

The Man from heaven died! Could there be a more apt description or a more accurate understanding of the Crucifixion? We do not know how the ancient Chinese arrived at this interpretation, but it is an interpretation that certainly fits the monumental event of that day: the ultimate sacrifice made by a God of both justice and love for the sake of all mankind.

God's love extends to all the nations of the world, and in some unique and unknown way, He gave special insight to Chinese astronomers to understand what He was doing. We are all sinners, even the emperor, but God laid all our sins on His only Son, Jesus Christ. When Jesus took on our sins at the cross, He paid the penalty that God demanded for sin, the penalty of death for all mankind, and pardon was proclaimed to all, including the Chinese. Jesus, the Man from heaven, came to die for us on the cross!

But that's not the end of the story.

> *For I delivered to you as of first importance what I also received, that Christ died for our sins according to the Scriptures, and that He was buried, and that He was raised on the third day according to the Scriptures, and that He appeared to Cephas, then to the twelve.*
> 1 Corinthians 15:3–5

Jesus did not just die; He rose again on the third day. Once again, the *Record of Latter Han Dynasty* has a special entry:

---

24. 《後漢書-志第十八、》 *History of the Latter Han,* Annals No. 18. Gui Hai, 癸亥, is the last number in the ancient Chinese system of numbering in cycles of 60s, and it was on a Gui Hai day that the solar eclipse occurred.

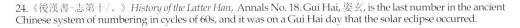

FINDING GOD IN ANCIENT CHINA

During the reign of Emperor Guang Wu, on the day of Bing Yin of the fourth month of Jian Wu, a halo – a rainbow – encircled the sun.

光武建武七年四月丙寅，曰有肇抱，白虹霄肇。[25]

This rainbow-halo effect occurred three days after the earlier heavenly manifestation, coinciding with the day of the resurrection of Jesus Christ. The Chinese astronomers, of course, could not have made the connection to Christ's resurrection, but they read the skies and recorded this heavenly sign.

The significance of the resurrection is that if Jesus had only died for us, we would not know that our sins had been forgiven. But Jesus rose from the dead! And He lives forever, which gives us the chance to have eternal life:

> *Jesus said . . . , "I am the resurrection and the life; he who believes in Me will live even if he dies, and everyone who lives and believes in Me will never die. Do you believe this?"*
> John 11:25 – 26

Jesus asks each of us the same question as well. Do we believe in this Truth? If we do not, we remain lost in our sins. If we believe in Him, His promise becomes a reality in our lives!

TRUTH DEMANDS A RESPONSE

Jesus said, "I am the way, and the truth, and the life; no one comes to the Father but through Me" (John 14:6). In other words, Jesus is Truth personified; He is the revealed reality of God. Recall from early in this chapter that the Chinese word 道 (Dao) refers to a person's attribute. Now consider Jesus' words here: I am the way, the truth, and the life. In this single statement, Jesus has captured the essence of the concept of *Dao*, which is that truth leads the way to life. Jesus is the Truth that opens the way to eternal life.

If Truth is a Person, then the process of revealing and accepting the truth is not simply the unveiling of knowledge or facts and the acknowledgment of them. Rather, it is the unveiling and the acceptance of a Person: Jesus, who is both the messenger and the message, both the Way to the Truth and the incarnation of Truth.

25. Ibid.

Consequently, since truth is personal, accepting truth must be a personal decision. Embracing truth goes beyond simply accepting a set of principles or formulae intellectually. Truth is much more than mere words; it is a quality of action, and it is powerfully dynamic. Our lives are transformed when we know the truth internally. Of course, not everyone is ready and willing to accept truth. Though the truth of God is real, it is always possible for people to reject it. Whichever it is, though — whether to accept it or reject it — truth always demands a response.

After I spoke to a group of Chinese students in Houston, in the United States, in the spring of 2002, a doctoral student in material sciences responded to my presentation with this objection, "The Chinese Shang Di cannot be the same as God in the Bible because the latter is a Western deity." In response, I picked up two porcelain teacups and asked him, "If I tell you that both cups are of the same material and you object to my assertion, how can we resolve that difference?" The answer was obvious, especially to an expert in the material sciences: we break down the composition of each cup, and if they prove similar or identical, then the two cups are the same. This process is simply applying the same inductive reasoning that Sir Francis Bacon championed and that is foundational to all modern scientific pursuits. It is arriving at a logical conclusion based on careful observation and a critical examination of the facts.

That is what we have sought to do in this chapter and indeed throughout this book. We have presented facts from China's ancient historical records, records that secular scholars and experts agree are reliable and true, and we have arrived at our conclusions, which we have presented in this book. These facts are now before you, for you to draw your own conclusions.

Reflect and Respond

If you do not have personal knowledge of the Truth, know that Truth demands an affirmative response from you. Ultimately, relationship with God is not an intellectual exercise; it is a choice. The Truth has been revealed to you. How are you going to respond? We urge you to accept Him right now with this prayer:

Dear Jesus,

I need You. I acknowledge that I have not known You in a personal way and that I have sinned against You. I turn away now from my old ways and accept You as my personal Lord and Savior. Thank You for dying on the Cross and for pardoning my sins. Please help me become the kind of person You created me to be.

I pray this in the name of Jesus, the Son of God. Amen.

If you are already a believer in Jesus, you can pray this prayer:

Dear Jesus,

Thank You that I know You and that I am known by You. I thank You that You have placed enough evidences in this world to guide us to Yourself. I pray that I will continue to see You in all things. I pray that my walk with You will become ever more intimate and that I will reflect Your Truth in my life.

In the name of Jesus, Amen.

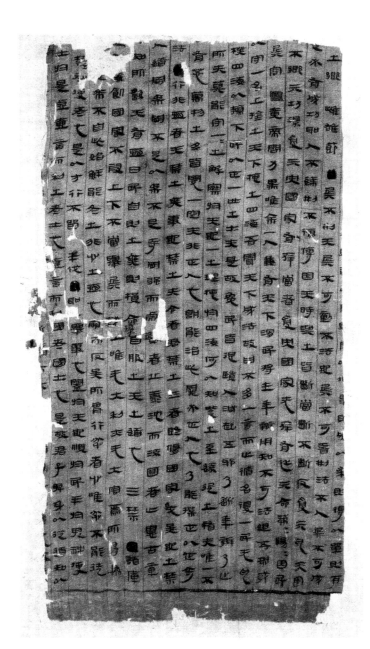

A page from the silk book of Lao Zi (Dao De Jing) from the 2nd Century B.C. Western Han Dynasty. Actual height is 48 cm. Two copies of Lao Zi were unearthed in Mawangdui, Changsha, Hunan Province. Copy A is written in archaic official script, while this Copy B is written in the official script of the Han Dynasty.

Credit:
Hunan Provincial Museum

Afterword

Some people go on a journey intent on racing to the end. These travelers miss the joy of discovery all along the way. We have come to the end of a long and at times arduous journey, but along the way I have learned and experienced so much about my Creator. It is as if He planned a treasure hunt for me. Each discovery brought great joy and, as the discoveries mounted, so too did the anticipation of the next signpost.

God, who is Spirit, can only be worshipped in spirit and in truth, and what we have set forth in this book are facts found in China's earliest historical documents that show that the ancient Chinese knew the truth about God. We are not saying that all ancient Chinese had a personal relationship with God or that they were "saved," in the Christian sense of that word. Based on the historical facts, the conclusion we have drawn is that the ancient Chinese worshipped a monotheistic God whom they called Shang Di and that this Shang Di is the same God the Hebrews of the Bible worshipped as Yahweh.

When I became a Christian in 1974, I had no idea that such a journey of discovery was ahead of me. My first visit to the Temple of Heaven was in 1988, but because I abhorred going to Chinese temples after my conversion, I went only as a casual tourist. It was not until almost a decade later, in 1996, that I started to notice that the Temple of Heaven had no idols, unlike every other Chinese temple I had ever visited. Then I started to see the incredible similarities between the ancient sacrifices performed there and the one described in the Bible. This

Photo at left shows the entrance to the Imperial Vault at the Altar of Heaven Complex.

discovery led to the other discoveries described in this book. Each discovery was accompanied by the joyful realization that God is loving and faithful, and each new discovery reinforced and reconfirmed God's love and faithfulness.

My joy climaxed in 2002 with the discovery that two thousand years ago, when God the Creator of Heaven and Earth came to live among us and to die for us, He used the stars to signal to the Chinese people what He was doing. A few days ago, a woman from Beijing who had read the already published Chinese edition of this book told me that she broke into heavy sobs of joy when she read about the "Truth Revealed by the Stars." She said that she was overwhelmed by the immense love of God; the thought that He had gone to the trouble of leaving signs for her even in the sky touched her deeply. This joy is joy unspeakable, and it is a joy I must share with others. This is the reason for this book, to bring others along on this journey, so that they might also experience the joy of discovering the loving and faithful God, who long ago planted signposts for those who want to know Him more.

We realize that some who hold the view that the Bible is the only revelation of God might question our conclusions. What we have attempted to do here is to strike a balance between the final authority of the Bible and the general revelations that exist in Chinese history and culture. We do not promote syncretism, which is the view that we can come to know God through many means and belief systems. Such a view is dangerous, because God has prescribed one single, specific way for us to know Him. We believe that God has spoken through the Hebrew prophets and through the Word and the Word made flesh, which is Jesus Christ. To compromise on this important point is to relegate Jesus to being a mere mortal, a common man. Those who hold the view, however, that apart from the Bible everything is error and falsehood have neither sympathy with nor understanding for those who do not embrace the Bible as the only source of truth.

Fortunately, there is a happy balance. The position that biblical revelation is the final authority does not preclude the possibility of glimmers of truth to be found outside of the Bible. The will plays a vital role in the act of faith: no one will believe what he does not want to believe, and many will not believe the Bible if they think that doing so will rob them of their cultural heritage. To those who want to know the truth, however, the Bible can actually be very attractive, if they are guided step-by-step to an understanding that there is no conflict between their cultural heritage and the Bible and if they accept the sprinkling of evidence God has left in an ancient culture.

Our journey through this book has shown that God has been, and is, reaching out to us in many ways. He has designated Jesus Christ as the only Way, but the Omnipotent God can employ myriad ways to bring each of His beloved sons and daughters to the foot of the cross on which Jesus the Savior died. For the Chinese people, He has left clues throughout their long, colorful, and unique 4,000-year history — in their language, in their cultural values, in the example of their righteous emperors, in their most ancient religious practices, and even in their night sky — to show that He has been their ever-present Shang Di and loving Father, And to lead them to the saving knowledge of His own Son of Heaven, Jesus Christ.

To order copies of this book as well as its Chinese, German, Korean or French edition and PowerPoint presentation, please write to orderfoof@yahoo.com.

Bibliography

Chinese Sources

1. 《道德乡 亜，老子》 *Lao Zi*, or *Dao De Jing*.
2. 《尚書》 *Classic of History*.
3. 《易敏》 *Classic of Changes* or *I-Ching*.
4. 《会經》 *Classic of Poetry*.
5. 《禮記-禮運》 *Record of Rites*, Li Yun (Ritual Usages).
6. 《禮記-郊特牲》 *Record of Rites*, Jiao Te Sheng (Border Sacrifice Animal).
7. 《禮記-祭统》 *Record of Rites*, Ji Tong (Summary of Sacrifices).
8. 〈禮記-禮器》 *Record of Rites*, Li Qi (Ritual Articles).
9. 《春秋左傳》 *Spring and Autumn Annals with Zuo Commentary*.
10. 《論語》 *The Analects*.
11. 《吕氏春秋-第九卷》 *Lü's Chronicles*, Volume 9.
12. 《孟子-卷十三》 *Mencius*, Volume 13.
13. 《大學》 *Great Learning*.
14. 《中恭歷史文庫》 北京银冠电子出版有限公司. *Library of Chinese Histories*. Beijing: Beijing Yin Guan Electronic Publishing Company Limited, 2001,
15. 《中庸》 *Zhong Yong, The Doctrine of Mean*.
16. 《史言己-夏本纪》 *Historical Records*, History of Xia.
17. 《史言己-书五-天官书》 *Historical Records*, Book 5, Book of Astronomy.
18. 《史記-书六-封禅书》 *Historical Records*, Book 6, Book of Feng Shan Sacrifices.
19. 《史言己-世家八-宋微子世家》 *Historical Records*, Genealogy 8, Genealogy of Song Wei Zi.
20. 《史言己-本纪六-秦始皇本纪》 *Historical Records*, Chronicle 6, Chronicle of Qin Shi Huang.
21. 《史記-本纪十-如文本纪》 *Historical Records*, Chronicle 10, Chronicle of Xiao Wen.
22. 《漢書-卷二十五下-郊祀志第五下》 *History of Former Han Dynasty*, Volume 25, History of the Border Sacrifice, Volume 5.
23. 《漢書-卷二十六-天文志》 *History of Former Han Dynasty*, Volume 26, Record of Astronomy.
24. 《漢書-卷六十二 -司马迁传》 *History of Former Han Dynasty*, Volume 62, Sima Qian.
25. 《漢書-哀帝纪》 *History of Former Han Dynasty*, Chronicle of Emperor Ai.
26. 《後漢書-光武帝》 *History of Latter Han*, Emperor Guang Wu.
27. 《後漢書志第十八》 *History of Latter Han*, Annals No. 18.
28. 《资治通鉴-汉纪》 *Zi Zhi Tong Jian*, Chronicles of Han Dynasty.
29. 《韩非子-说林上》 *Han Fei Zi*, Shuo Lin Parti.
30. 《大明会典》 第82卷 *The Collected Statutes of the Ming Dynasty*, Volume 82.
31. 《神付1忏'瞎录》 Yuan Zhiming, *China's Confession*. Petaluma, CA: China Soul, 2001.
32. 《老子原文与译文》 Yuan Zhiming, *Lao Zi, Original Text and Interpretation*. Taipei: Cosmo, 1997.
33. 《共同的上帝》 Tan, Dr. W. C. *Same God in the Bible and Chinese Classics*. Victoria, British Columbia: Canadian College for Chinese Studies, 1994.
34. 《龙：神化与真相》 He Xin, Dragon: *Myths and Truths*. Shanghai: ReninJn Publisher, 1989.
35. 《字里乾坤》 华语教学出版社 Wang Hong Yuan, *The Origins of Chinese Characters Zi Li Qian Qun*. Beijing: Sinolingua, 2000.

English Sources

36. Barthel, Manfred. *The Jesuits, History and Legend of the Society of Jesus.* Translated by M. Howson, New York: William Morrow, 1984.

37. Billington, Michael. "Matteo Ricci, the Grand Design, and the Disaster of the Rites Controversy." *Executive Intelligence Review*, Volume 28, Issue 43, (2001), http://www.larouchepub.com/other/2001/2843m_ricci.html.

38. Bilsky, Lester James. *The State Religion of Ancient China.* Asian Folklore and Social Life Monographs, Volumes 70–71. Taipei: Oriental Cultural Service for the Chinese Association for Folklore, 1975.

39. Byfield, Ted, Ed. *The Christians, Their First Two Thousand Years.* Edmonton, Canada: Friesens Corp., 2003,

40. Chen, Heyi, ed. *Tiantan.* Beijing: Pictorial Publishing House, 1992.

41. Collins, Jim. *Good to Great: Why Some Companies Make the Leap ... and Others Don't.* New York: HarperCollins Publishers, Inc., 2001.

42. Cronin, Vincent. *The Wise Man from the* West. New York: Dutton, 1955.

43. De Bary, William Theodore, et al. *Sources of Chinese Tradition, Volumes 1* and 2. New York: Columbia University Press, 1960.

44. Dunne, George. *Generation of Giants.* Notre Dame, Ind.: University of Notre Dame Press, 1962.

45. Edkins, Joseph. *Religion in China.* London, 1905; Elibron Classics, 2001.

46. Fales, R. M. "Archaeology and History Attest to the Reliability of the Bible" *The Evidence Bible.* Compiled by Ray Comfort. Gainesville, Fla. Bridge-Logos Publishers, 2001.

47. Federer, W. J. *Great Quotations: A Collection of Passages, Phrases ....* St. Louis: AmeriSearch, 2001.

48. Fraser, Gordon Holmes. "The Gentile Names of God," *A Symposium of Creation (Volume V).* Donald W. Patten, ed. Grand Rapids, Mich.: Baker Book House, 1975.

49. Giles, Herbert Allen. *Chinese-English Dictionary.* London: A. H. de Carvalho, 1912.

50. Lang, Andrew. *The Making of a Religion.* London and New York: Longmans, Green and Co., 1898.

51. Legge, James. *The Chinese Classics*, Volumes 1–5, Hong Kong: Hong Kong University Press, 1960.

52. Legge, James. *The Notions of the Chinese Concerning God and Spirits.* Hong Kong: Hong Kong Register Office, 1852; reprint, Taipei: Ch'eng Wen Publishing Company, 1971.

53. Legge, James. *The Religions of China.* New York: Charles Scribner's Sons, 1881.

54. Li, Dan J., trans. *China in Transition.* New York: Van Nostrand Reinhold Company, 1969,

55. Lindsay, D. G. *The Canopied Earth: World That Was.* Dallas: Christ for the Nations, 1999.

56. Lu, Matthias. "Dialogue of Christianity with Cultures in China:" Address to The Second World Congress of Christian Philosophy, Monterrey, Nuevo Leon, Mexico, October 1986.

57. Medhurst, W. H. *A Dissertation on the Theology of the Chinese with a View to the Elucidation of the Most Appropriate Term for Expressing the Deity, in the Chinese Language.* Shanghai: The Mission Press, 1847.

58. Morgan, R. J. *Nelson's Complete Book of Stories, Illustrations, and Quotes*, electronic edition. Nashville, Tenn.: Thomas Nelson Publishers, 2000.

59. Nelson, Ethel Richard Broadberry, and Ginger Tong Chock. *God's Promise to the Chinese*. Dunlap, Tenn.: Read Books Publisher, 1997.

60. *The New Encyclopaedia Britannica*, Volumes 6 and 7. Chicago: Encyclopaedia Britannica, Inc., 1994.

61. "Peking: the City of the Unexpected," *National Geographic Magazine* (1920): Volume XXXVIII, No. 5.

62. Ricci, Matteo S. *The True Meaning of the Lord of Heaven*. St. Louis, Mo.: Institute of Jesuit Studies, 1986.

63. Ross, John. *The Original Religion of China*. London: Oliphant Anderson & Ferrier, 1909.

64. Spence, Jonathan D. *Emperor of China, Self-Portrait of K'ang-Hsi*. New York: Random House, 1988.

65. Spence, Jonathan D. *The Memory Palace of Matteo Ricci*. New York: Penguin Books, 1984.

66. Spence, Jonathan D. *To Change China: Western Advisors in China*, 1620–1960. Boston: Little, Brown & Co., 1969.

67. Trumbull, Clay. *The Blood Covenant*. Minneapolis, Minn.: James Family Christian Publishers, n.d. Original: Philadelphia, 1893.

68. *Unger's Handbook of the Bible*. Chicago: Moody Press, 1984.

69. Wang, Samuel, and Ethel R. Nelson. Dunlap, Tenn.: Sinim Bible Institute, 1998.

70. Wiener, Philip P., ed. *The Dictionary of the History of Ideas: Studies of Selected Pivotal Ideas*, Volume 4. New York: Charles Scribner's Sons, 1973–74.

71. Wu, K. C. *The Chinese Heritage*. New York: Crown Publishers, 1981.

72. "Xia-Shang-Zhou Chronology Projects." *The Journal of East Asian Archaeology* (2002): Volume 4, No. 14.

Share Your Thoughts

With the Author: Your comments will be forwarded to the author when you send them to *zauthor@zondervan.com*.

With Zondervan: Submit your review of this book by writing to *zreview@zondervan.com*.

Free Online Resources at
www.zondervan.com

Zondervan AuthorTracker: Be notified whenever your favorite authors publish new books, go on tour, or post an update about what's happening in their lives.

Daily Bible Verses and Devotions: Enrich your life with daily Bible verses or devotions that help you start every morning focused on God.

Free Email Publications: Sign up for newsletters on fiction, Christian living, church ministry, parenting, and more.

Zondervan Bible Search: Find and compare Bible passages in a variety of translations at www.zondervanbiblesearch.com.

Other Benefits: Register yourself to receive online benefits like coupons and special offers, or to participate in research.